FAMINE DIARY

Wie viel ist aufzuleiden

(how much suffering there is to endure)
– Rilke

A cabin was seen closed one day a little out of the town, when a man had the curiosity to open it, and in a dark corner he found a family of the father, mother and two children lying in close compact. The father was considerably decomposed; the mother, it appeared, had died last and probably fastened the door, which was always the custom when all hope was extinguished, to get into the darkest corner and die, where passers-by could not see them. Such family scenes were quite common, and the cabin was generally pulled down upon them for a grave.

(Asenath Nicholson during her 1847 travels in Connacht, quoted in *The Feminization of Famine* by Margaret Kelleher, Cork University Press)

FamineDiary

BRENDAN Ó CATHAOIR

IRISH ACADEMIC PRESS
DUBLIN • PORTLAND, OR

First published in 1999 by
IRISH ACADEMIC PRESS
44, Northumberland Road, Dublin 4, Ireland
and in the United States of America by
IRISH ACADEMIC PRESS
c/o ISBS, 5824 NE Hassalo Street,
Portland, OR 97213–3644

Website: http://www.iap.ie

British Library Cataloguing in Publication Data
O'Cathaoir, Brendan
 Famine diary
 1. Ireland – History – Famine, 1845–1852   2. Ireland – Social conditions –
 19th century
 I. Title
 941.7'081

 ISBN 0–7165–2655–7 (cloth)
 ISBN 0–7165–2731–6 (paper)

Library of Congress Cataloging-in-Publication Data
Ó Cathaoir, Brendan, 1941 –
 Famine diary / Brendan Ó Cathaoir.
    p.   cm.
 "Contains the text of the Famine dairy column, published in The Irish Times,
during 1995–7"—Pref.
 Includes bibliographical references and index.
 ISBN 0–7165–2655–7 (hc.)
 1. Ireland—History—Famine, 1845–1852. 2. Famines—Ireland—History—19th
century. 3. Ireland—History—Famine, 1845–1852—Sources. 4. Famines—Ireland—
History—19th century—Sources.
 I. Title.
 DA950.7.O33   1998   98–46747
 941.5081—dc21   CIP

Typeset in 11pt on 13 pt Goudy
by Carrigboy Typesetting Services, County Cork
Printed by
Creative Print and Design (Wales), Ebbw Vale

*In memory of my parents, Michael Cahir (1902–94)
and Nancy Burke (1907–2000), and
Joe Cahir (1978–2001)*

Contents

Foreword

The Great Famine in Ireland between 1845 and 1850 was the most appalling calamity to affect any Western European country in peacetime since the Black Death of the fourteenth century. Or was it? Might not those London officials who warned against the tendency towards exaggeration in the reports of the stereotypically and axiomatically excitable Celt, constantly clamouring for English assistance, while displaying singular ingratitude for it, have been right? Just how great was the Great Irish Famine in comparative perspective?

Cormac Ó Gráda, a leading authority on comparative famine mortality, has estimated that the death rate in Ireland was in fact possibly ten times, or more, higher than the death rate in the post-war famines in Malawi, Bangladesh, the Sahel, Ethiopia and the Sudan. And we have seen images of the horror of these famines. Indeed, to grasp something of the Famine in Ireland we should imagine a country widely populated by Irish versions of those gaunt and traumatised skeletal figures, young and old, men and women, gazing helplessly from out of our television screens.

The memory of those horrors would linger long in the Irish mind, and indeed in the minds of many outside witnesses, like the intrepid and perceptive American lady, Asenath Nicholson, and relief workers like the Quakers. Many among the roughly two million emigrants, who fled the country during the Famine itself and in its immediate aftermath, would retain memories that would haunt them to their dying day. Some, like many Holocaust survivors in our own terrible century, could never bring themselves to speak about it. Others would pass the memory down to their children and grandchildren, fuelling their hatred for a British government which, in one telling, allowed these things to happen, and in a more extreme version, caused them to happen.

This charge of genocide, indelibly expressed in the searing prose of John Mitchel, most elaborately in *The last conquest of Ireland (perhaps)* which interpreted the Famine as a deliberate, cold blooded attempt by the British government to seize the opportunity offered by the failure of the potato, on which millions of Irish lives depended, to pursue policies that would inevitably result in the elimination of so many refractory subjects, remains highly controversial. It would not be accepted by the majority of specialist opinion today.

Yet Mitchel's pungent formulation that the Almighty indeed sent the blight, but the English created the Famine, has remained vivid in popular imagination as the only rational explanation of how so many could die in a country that came within the jurisdiction of the greatest power on earth, and was so close to both the political and economic centre of the world of the time. Mr Ó Cathaoir himself prefers a more sophisticated version of the culpability of the British government, exonerating it from a charge of deliberate genocide, but still holding it responsible for much wanton death and suffering.

Death would continue to stalk the land after 1847, as the author reminds us in the valuable Epilogue he especially added for this book. 'Black '47' has indeed become the emotional epicentre of the Famine in popular memory. It is from 1847 that many of the most graphic and detailed contemporary accounts date. But we should not overlook the fact that the scenes and attitudes recorded here persisted well beyond the end date of the actual diary. Readers will be able to imagine for themselves what death from famine, and the fear of that death, continued to be like.

No famine in history had received as much coverage by contemporaries. Apart from the reports from travellers and relief workers, many Irish newspapers of the time, to say nothing of the greatest newspaper in the world, the London *Times*, devoted extensive coverage to the Famine. Relatively little of this contemporary reporting, much of it highly graphic, has hitherto been republished. The Diary draws on a wide range of reports from all around the country. The focus is naturally on what is happening in the areas most decimated, particularly in the west. But it is equally interesting to read reports on other areas, not least from Ulster. By any normal standards virtually the whole country suffered. It is only in comparison with the horrors in the west that the east can be said to have escaped relatively lightly. The reporting on a week-by-week basis gives an immediacy to these accounts, conveys the sense of hoping against hope, and then of hope withering, that can only come from the pens of those looking forward, fearing but not yet knowing what lies in store, and that cannot be ever fully captured in any purely retrospective reconstruction.

It is one of the many merits of Brendan Ó Cathaoir's indefatigable researches that he makes available to us the observations of these contemporaries at the moment of observation. The horror, the uncertainty, the fear, the hope, as reporters struggled to grapple with an experience beyond their imagination, are all vividly conveyed in the extracts that Mr Ó Cathaoir has compiled so assiduously and so judiciously. The horror was graphically captured by contemporaries, who often wrote with a type of fascinated incredulity about the scenes happening before their eyes, as if they belonged to a different sphere of existence from anything that could be captured in words.

Here one can sense, indeed feel, at first hand, the anguish, the consternation, the incredulity, the despair, of the victims, and of many of the observers themselves. One can also note the detachment, even the disdain, of those who took refuge in the serene conviction that it was all a matter of God's will, or who believed that their socio-economic doctrines decreed that countless numbers must die in fulfilment of their fundamentalist faith in the laws of political economy. What is more, many of these same policymakers succeeded in persuading themselves that the laws of political economy were also the laws of God.

For myself, whenever I hear pundits or professors (not necessarily mutually exclusive creatures) pronouncing on the laws of economics, or on any alleged laws to which human behaviour should be axiomatically subject, irrespective of the suffering they cause, in the name of some greater abstract good, the picture that always leaps before my eye is that of the frontispiece to this volume, Bridget O'Donnell and her children, as sketched in the *Illustrated London News* in 1849. *Famine Diary* allows us understand more fully what lay behind the condition to which Bridget O'Donnell and her children were reduced in the name of a determinist doctrine which was prepared to endure, or rather inflict, any amount of hardship and humiliation on the weak and defenceless as a sacrifice on the blessed altar of economic growth.

The Famine Diary attracted enormous attention when it first appeared in *The Irish Times* on a weekly basis. In the midst of so much famine commemoration between 1995 and 1997, it served as a weekly reminder of what the grizzly reality on the ground had been like. It was a pioneering venture in Irish journalism, for which *The Irish Times* as well as Mr Ó Cathaoir deserve immense credit. In reprinting the column in accessible book form, supplemented with a penetrating introduction and epilogue, and most usefully annotated, Mr Ó Cathaoir, already the author of an admirable life of *John Blake Dillon: Young Irelander*, who co-founded with Thomas Davis and Charles Gavan Duffy the most famous newspaper in Irish history, *The Nation*, which itself serves as a main source of contemporary famine comment, has put the historical profession and the general public even further in his debt. *Famine Diary* opens rich seams to be mined for insight and instruction for as long as the Irish care about their country, and as long as human beings care about wanton suffering.

JOE LEE
27 October 1998

Preface

This book contains the text of the Famine Diary column published in *The Irish Times* during 1995–7. Additional source material has been incorporated into the introduction and concluding chapter.

Famine Diary concentrates on the areas of highest excess mortality: the then densely-populated western seaboard, most of Connacht, parts of Munster, the midlands and south Ulster. It seeks to give an impression of conditions throughout the country, however, as few areas escaped the Famine completely.

Many have helped with this project. I am grateful to my colleagues for their encouragement – particularly the Editor, Conor Brady – and to the Irish Times Ltd for sabbatical leave which enabled me to complete this task. Linda Longmore of the Irish Academic Press was always supportive.

The staff and archivists of the following institutes were unfailingly courteous: the National Archives, the Royal Irish Academy, the National Library, the Gilbert Library, the Dublin Diocesan Archives; and Bray Public Library.

I wish to thank Professor Joe Lee for his gracious foreword, and Dr Thomas McGrath for reading the introduction and 1848–50 chapter.

Most importantly, I wish to acknowledge my gratitude to those who have lived with me during the research and writing of this book: my wife Eva Ó Cathaoir, who was on hand to explain the tortuous ramifications of the Poor Law, and our dear children, Emer, Pat and Katie.

Luke Gibbons concluded (in his essay in *Irish Hunger: Personal Reflections on the Legacy of the Famine* edited by Tom Hayden) that the cultural experience of catastrophe demonstrates the past is not over until its story has been told. Recording the accumulated horrors of the Famine induced a reverence for our forebears – which is, hopefully, translated into compassion for the hungry in today's world. The most satisfying personal discovery was the name of my great-great-grandfather, Patrick Cahir, among the subscribers to a north Clare relief fund in 1846.

Introduction

One overriding impression of the Famine is the truth of R. Dudley Edwards's dictum: 'Nothing is inevitable in history.' The Famine of 1845–50, during which one million people died, was not inevitable – just as world hunger today is avoidable. The political will of the powerful was lacking. Britain, the leading world power in the mid-19th century, was unwilling to take the steps necessary to avert an Irish cataclysm. Ireland was looked on as an inferior relation, who must be dominated but left ultimately to fend for herself.

Failures of the potato crop, attendant famines and outbreaks of disease were endemic in Ireland's subsistence economy. The Great Famine was merely the worst.

Moreover, it formed part of the general European agricultural and industrial crisis of the late 1840s. But Ireland had the highest degree of potato dependency in Europe. While famine conditions also threatened the Scottish Highlands, the worst consequences were largely averted. The Netherlands, with a population of three million, recorded 60,000 excess deaths during 1846–7; the Belgian figure was 48,000 in a population of 4.3 million.[1]

Ireland differed from other famine-stricken European countries in being interpreted through the lens of colonialism. Ultimately, what made the Irish experience unique in terms of state response was Britain's perception of the potato blight as an opportunity to remould its backward dependency.

The Whig government which replaced Sir Robert Peel's administration in 1846 confronted the Irish poor with a particularly harsh ideological climate. Lord John Russell, a weak Prime Minister, allowed Irish relief policy to be dictated by a few ideologues, notably the Chancellor of the Exchequer, Sir Charles Wood, the Home Secretary, Sir George Grey, and Charles Edward Trevelyan, Permanent Secretary at the Treasury. Racial and sectarian prejudices confirmed economic dogma.

A rigid adherence to *laissez-faire* doctrines replaced limited state intervention. Archbishop John MacHale of Tuam warned the new prime minister in prophetic language: 'You might as well at once issue an edict of general starvation.'[2]

The British authorities were overwhelmed by the scale of the disaster in Ireland and initially public sympathy was widespread. None the less, the begrudging tone of the Treasury response, the obsession with preventing a dependency mentality emerging, the constant injunction to self-help to the starving, and the abdication of responsibility after 1847 left a bitter legacy.

Despite the expenditure of £5.5 million (mostly in the form of loans), the public works system failed to prevent mass starvation during the terrible winter of 1846–7 in the face of uncontrolled food prices. People were forced to undertake hard labour as a 'test' of destitution. Wages were insufficient and each week families fasted for up to thirty-six hours until next pay day. Under this system labourers gradually became weaker. 'If only', an English engineer in charge of public works remarked, 'the people had been treated with a little kindness.'[3]

The poor were left at the mercy of a small number of speculators in Indian corn. Lord Bessborough informed the prime minister: 'I cannot make my mind up entirely about the merchants. I know all the difficulties that arise when you begin to interfere with trade, but it is difficult to persuade a starving population that one class should be permitted to make 50 per cent profit by the sale of provisions whilst they are dying in want of these.'[4]

Controlled directly by the Treasury, government food depots were permitted to sell only at market rates to local relief committees. The depots, seen as inhibiting the growth of a retail grain trade in the west, were phased out in 1848.

As the public works system collapsed, the government was forced to distribute food directly for a few months. By pioneering soup-kitchen relief, the Quakers galvanized the state into feeding three million people during the summer of 1847. The record of the Society of Friends is one of the few bright pages in the Famine story. Although considered ideologically incorrect, the soup-kitchen operation was Britain's most effective response to the Famine. It showed the administrative capabilities of the Victorian state.

Bewilderment had already been succeeded by panic, however, as the Irish poor began their headlong flight to the New World. Neither reports of adverse conditions abroad, nor the lack of provisions aboard unsafe vessels could check the lemming-like march to the ports. Departures under such conditions were bound to produce disasters at sea or on landing.

Famine refugees generally walked from western counties to Dublin and crossed to Liverpool on the decks of cattle boats. Thousands who had escaped typhus in Ireland picked up infection in that city's notorious lodging houses. The holds of the 'coffin ships' in turn provided a congenial breeding ground for lice-borne bacilli, and fever ravaged the emigrants during and after the voyage to North America.

An eyewitness wrote from Grosse Île quarantine station, Quebec:

> I cannot describe the horrors and misery . . . at least 1,300 terrible cases of typhus, in addition to smallpox and measles. People died right before our eyes at all hours of the day . . . People perished in much greater numbers on the vessels than in the hospitals. Over 50 sailing ships with more than 15,000 passengers aboard were moored off the island.

Fr Elzéar-Alexandre Taschereau – later Archbishop of Montreal – observing how numbed to horrors the victims had become, saw 'this as a new mark of degradation caused by an excess of suffering'.[5]

The shipping of the destitute and diseased to Canada continued until perilously late in the 1847 navigation season. The *Superior* arrived at Grosse Île in October. Of the 366 passengers who sailed from Derry, the medical officer found that not more than twelve were free of disease, while twenty had died during the voyage. The *Quebec Mercury* asked what 'will be the fate of those poor souls arriving here at a time when employment of every description is about to end? For winter seals up almost every channel of industry . . . Begging alone is open to them.'[6]

Approximately one million emigrated during the Famine. Some fifty ships foundered in the course of 5,000 Atlantic crossings. Although most vessels reached Canada and the United States safely, others, like those carrying the tenants of the Mahon and Palmerston estates, buried a third of their steerage passengers at sea and disgorged near-corpses at the quarantine stations.[7]

In 1994 Mary Robinson, then President of Ireland, recalled on Grosse Île: 'There is no single reason to explain the disaster of the Great Hunger and the Diaspora to which it contributed greatly. The potato failure was a natural disaster which affected other countries in Europe at the time. But in Ireland it took place in a political, economic and social framework that was oppressive and unjust.'

From the autumn of 1847 to the end of the Famine as a national, if not regional, event in 1850, British ministers largely washed their hands of financial responsibility for Irish relief. Opinion hardened as hordes of disease-carrying paupers descended upon British cities. The 1847 Poor Law Amendment Act reflected a determination by the House of Commons to make Irish property pay for Irish poverty. The viceroy Lord Clarendon warned the prime minister in October that 'Ireland *cannot be left to her own resources*, they are manifestly insufficient'. Russell replied: 'The state of Ireland for the next few months must be one of great suffering. Unhappily, the agitation for Repeal has contrived to destroy nearly all sympathy in this country.'[8]

The moralist policy-makers were, A.J.P. Taylor commented, 'highly conscientious men and their consciences never reproached them'. Cormac Ó Gráda observed: 'History suggests that "good" government can help avert famines.' Peter Gray believes the charge of culpable neglect is 'indisputable'; government policy amounted to a 'death sentence on many thousands'.[9]

Dr Gray sums up in his new book that, while making allowance for factors beyond government control such as the scale of the Irish ecological disaster and a commercial recession in Britain:[10]

> the inescapable conclusion remains that the state failed to make optimum use of its resources to contain the number of deaths, especially in the later stages of the Famine from the autumn of 1847. This policy failure was due in large measure to the success of the dominant faction in the government of prioritising another, ideologically-driven, agenda – that of grasping the heaven-sent opportunity of famine to deconstruct Irish society and rebuild it anew. Liberal moralists were prepared to play a deadly game of brinkmanship in their campaign to impose a capitalist cultural revolution on the Irish. Their intention was not genocidal, nor was it grounded in any Malthusian assumption of the necessity of Irish depopulation; rather it was the fruit of a powerful social ideology that combined a providentialist theodicy of natural laws with a radicalised and optimistic version of liberal political economy. God and nature had combined to force Ireland from diseased backwardness into healthy progressive modernity; any unnecessary suffering incurred in the transition was the result of human folly and obstruction . . .

Furthermore, identifying and eradicating the 'abuse' of relief mechanisms acquired a higher priority than saving lives.

This moralist fixation was attacked by some contemporary observers, who attributed the cataclysm to delusive social theory and landlord avarice. A correspondent of the *Illustrated London News* – probably the Cork artist, James Mahony – writing from amid the ruined villages of west Clare, attributed the condition of the Irish mainly to 'ignorant and vicious legislation' (15 December 1849):

When more food, more cultivation, more employment, were the requisites for maintenance of the Irish in existence, the legislature and the landlords set about introducing a species of cultivation that could only be successful by requiring fewer hands, and turning potato gardens, that nourished the maximum number of human beings, into pasture grounds for bullocks . . . The Poor Law, said to be for the relief of the people and the means of their salvation, was the instrument of their destruction. In their terrible distress, from that temporary calamity with which they were visited, they were to have no relief unless they gave up their holdings. That law, too, laid down a form for evicting the people, and gave the sanction and encouragement of legislation to exterminating them.

The English philanthropist Sidney Godolphin Osborne found, during a visit to Ireland in 1849, 'a sort of tacit determination to let things take their course, at any cost'. Defending the government's record, Anthony Trollope, then a postal official in Munster, wrote that the 'severity of circumstances ordained by Providence' had been necessary to promote the anglicisation of Irish morals and society.

Lord George Bentinck indicted the Russell administration: 'The time will come when we shall know what the amount of mortality has been, and though you may groan and try to keep the truth down it shall be known, and the time will come when the public and the world will be able to estimate, at its proper value, your management of the affairs of Ireland.'[11]

Ireland's prolonged colonial experience reached a climax during the Great Famine. The cumulative effect of misperception, mistake and mischance was the greatest peacetime tragedy of 19th-century western Europe. The Whigs considered Ireland a diseased body in need of the uncaring medicine of political economy. Trevelyan, an evangelical Protestant, viewed the disaster as 'the judgment of God on an indolent and unself-reliant people'; as God had 'sent the calamity to teach the Irish a lesson, that calamity must not be too much mitigated'.

In vain Bishop John Hughes of New York urged British policy-makers 'not to blaspheme Providence by calling this God's famine'. They persisted in seeing it as an opportunity to modernise Ireland. This providentialism, combined with minimum state intervention and reliance on market forces, turned a natural disaster – the repeated failure of the potato crop on which up to four million people depended – into the greatest social catastrophe in Irish history.

Famine Diary
1845–1847

Arrival of blight

16 SEPTEMBER 1845

With tragic irony, the issue of the *Nation* which reports the potato crop failure asserts in a leading article that the Irish peasant 'now moves about, a man full of life, energy and hope, where he but lately was a trembling and ignorant slave'.

The arrival of the blight in Wexford and Waterford from the Continent is recorded by the *Dublin Evening Post* on 9 September. David Moore, curator of the Botanic Gardens, Glasnevin, says the specimens of potatoes sent to him 'afford only too convincing proofs of the rapid progress this alarming disease is making'.

The effects are obvious but the cause is a mystery. Moore continues: 'From the frequent examinations I have made personally, one thing appears certain – that the disease originates at the root of the plant, and that the blacking of the leaves and decay of the haulm are occasioned from the root and, further, that the fungi found on the stems and diseased potatoes are only the effects not the cause of the evil.'

Initially, he blames the weather: 'Owing to the universal coldness of the months of July and August and want of sunshine, the plant could not probably rid itself of the watery vapour it imbibed from the earth and, consequently, the tissue became surcharged by moisture and deranged.'

This may have led members of a commission appointed by the Lord Lieutenant to mistake dampness rather than a fungus for the decay. Moore, whose work is hampered by influential people, predicts recurring blight.

The constabulary is instructed to report weekly on local crops and estimate the extent of the loss.

In a stop-press, Professor John Lindley of the University of London announces: '. . . the potato Murrain has unequivocally declared itself in Ireland. The crops about Dublin are suddenly perishing. Where will Ireland be in the event of a universal potato rot?' Nearly half the population depends on the potato for food.

The poor need employment not workhouses, the *Nation* contends: 'It is said that English capital would flow in, of its own accord, if we were only quiet. When we were quiet, there was no appearance of English capital. It was when we were quiet that the Poor Law was enacted.'

A 'revolting sample of English legislation' is the separation of husband and wife, parents and children (over two years), when they enter the poorhouse.

In a grim portent, Thomas Davis, the chief hope of effective leadership from the *Nation*/Young Ireland group, dies suddenly aged thirty.[1]

'Intolerable stench'

23 SEPTEMBER 1845

While the blight has struck in Ireland, the full extent of the potato failure will not be known until the general digging of the crop in the second half of October.

Two disquieting features are beginning to emerge, however: although the potato stem seems luxuriant, when dug the root is rotten; and potatoes which appear sound upon digging, decompose into a putrid mass when stored.

Already a correspondent predicts in the *Freeman's Journal*: 'The potato crop is a failure, so much as to render it very doubtful where untainted seed can be had for planting in spring.' A famine will ensue unless the government directs oats and wheat from distillation to food. 'Not an hour should be lost, that is if the lives of the poor are (in the eyes of any government) worth preserving.'

Potatoes are inedible in Wexford, while an 'intolerable stench' is encountered during digging in Mayo.

The *Freeman* comments: 'Should this fearful malady spread among the crops of the rural population dreadful indeed must be the consequence to the poor, whose sole dependence in this country is the potato crop.'

During a brief Indian summer, the *Longford Leader* reports that potatoes are selling at 2d a stone, 'and there never was such a breadth of them planted in this county. If this fine weather continues for another fortnight, there is every prospect of a plenty for the next twelve months.'

But the *Cork Examiner* contrasts the reaction to the blight in the Netherlands – where the king has issued a decree reducing import duties on food – with the British attitude summed up by the prime minister, Sir Robert Peel: 'There is such a tendency to exaggeration and inaccuracy in Irish reports that delay in acting upon them is always desirable.'

John Gray, the Protestant nationalist editor of the *Freeman*, asserts that until the 'accursed' Union is repealed, 'our fine country must remain the trampled and insulted province of a people whose hatred and jealousy of us have furnished to history the blackest pages of cruelty and outrage at which posterity will revolt.'

Eighteen Catholic bishops renew their condemnation of the proposed undenominational colleges as 'dangerous to faith and morals'. Significantly, nearly a third of the hierarchy, including Archbishop Daniel Murray of Dublin, do not join this protest as the Colleges Bill is passed.[2]

'Ourselves alone'

30 SEPTEMBER 1845

A bank manager, who is not dependent on the potato, claims the 'alleged failure was very greatly exaggerated'.

Daniel O'Connell – 'The real potato blight in Ireland', according to *Punch* – is still trying to revive his repeal agitation. Although the bubble was burst when Peel called his bluff in 1843, the Liberator estimates the crowd at a demonstration in Thurles at 300,000–400,000.

The *Annual Register* notes the presence of 'an immense mass of stout small farmers', with a sprinkling of squireens on horseback, and considers it more respectable – if less formidable – than the monster meetings of two years ago.

The *Nation* devotes four pages to O'Connell's procession through County Tipperary. Michael Doheny, still a constitutional nationalist, presents him with an address on behalf of the Cashel repeal reading-room.

The London *Times* has commissioned Thomas Campbell Foster to report on Irish social conditions. Ireland does not need yet another inquiry, O'Connell tells the vast crowd in Thurles: 'For did not Lord Devon's Commission prove that nearly half the people are in great distress; that they had bad houses; that the rain poured into their habitations; that they had neither bed nor blanket – and were, in fine, worse off than the peasantry of any part of Europe.'

At a repeal dinner, toasts are drunk to Queen Victoria and other members of the British royal family. This does not inhibit a priest, responding to a toast to the bishops, declaring: 'We must depend upon ourselves alone – *shin fane*.'

On returning to Dublin O'Connell renews his attack on the *Times* commissioner, who is not only guilty of racist but ungallant remarks as well (claiming Irish women are ugly).

The 'gutter commissioner' retaliates by visiting the Liberator's Kerry estate and publishing a description of the squalor in which his tenants are living.

The Dublin coroner finds that a mendicant, Patrick Walsh, has died of fluid on the chest brought on by cold, hunger and other privations.[3]

'A Loathsome Lazarus'

7 OCTOBER 1845

Everyone agrees something should be done about the condition of the Irish poor – without upsetting the constitutional or land settlements.

Denouncing the Ulster tenant-right system, Commissioner Campbell predicts: 'The energetic population of the north and east will thrive, be English partisans and triumphant Orangemen, while the patient and much enduring, but unenterprising and unenergetic, population of the west will be steeped in poverty and discontent and be violent Repealers.'

He is, the *Nation* comments, the latest in a long list of commissioners 'that have sat upon us, and inquired and reported on us, lecturing us with a more or less insolent compassion, suggesting this or the other method of quackery for us . . . Is Ireland, indeed, a loathsome Lazarus, laid at England's gate full of sores – faintly craving such crumbs as may fall from her well-spread table – crying out to have his offensive wounds and endless grievances probed and salved and experimented on, soliciting every cur to come and lick his sores?'

There are well-spread tables in County Galway, too. After a cattle show in Ballinasloe, 300 members of the Royal Agricultural Improvement

Society sit down to a banquet 'comprising all the choicest viands and the rarest delicacies of the sea . . . The wines, including champagne and claret, were of the richest vintage and the choicest aroma.'

Among the speakers is the Earl of Devon, who has reported on the land question. He asserts confidently that, whatever disturbing influences may for a time retard progress, 'the condition of the people of Ireland is steadily and certainly improving'; the interest shown by all classes in the development of agriculture is laying the surest foundation for prosperity and peace.

The ubiquitous *Times* commissioner tells the assembled landowners that the Irish press 'should endeavour to advocate the interests of the empire rather than the interests of Ireland (hear, hear)'. His agenda is to make Ireland imitate England, 'the proudest nation on the face of the earth'.

The *Cork Examiner* notes that, 'as regards potatoes, we cannot shut our eyes to the fact that the disease is extending its ravages amongst them to an extent that will not perhaps be generally known or acknowledged till the period for the digging-out of the crop'.[4]

Alarming reports

14 OCTOBER 1845

Alarming reports pour in as the potato digging begins. The blight attacking the crop throughout north-western Europe is caused by a fungus, *phytophthora infestans*. As one Irish provincial newspaper remarks, however, British government advisers 'know nothing whatever about the causes or remedy for the disease'.

The *Waterford Freeman* announces that the blight has spread to counties Kilkenny and Carlow. In Kilkenny potatoes seem healthy until boiled, when 'it was impossible to stand the horrid stench they emitted'.

Letters from Tyrone and Roscommon speak 'very despondingly' about the prospects of the potato harvest.

The *Freeman's Journal* cites a Cork report: 'There is now too much reason to fear that the general apprehension of a famine, resulting from the potato disease, is too well grounded . . . ' At a potato market every second cart-load seems affected. The state of the crop dominates conversation at Drogheda market.

The *Limerick Chronicle* reports that when twelve acres of potatoes were opened in Fedamore, 'the spade labourers left off work on finding the plant was not worth raising. This terrible epidemic, not only threatens loss of food in the present season, but loss of food for the next year.'

The *Cork Reporter* is unwilling to believe in the likelihood of famine, but 'the stoutest heart must tremble to learn how universal districts are affected'. While appearing healthy in the ground, when the farmer tests the potatoes 'he finds the murrain has entered deeply and his hopes of provision for his family, his cattle and his rent are blasted'.

The paper considers it is time for the government to act, firstly, by opening the ports to non-UK corn imports and, secondly, 'to prevent the exportation of the people's staff of life. We know that it is dangerous and, generally speaking, unwise to interfere with commerce in any article'. But to export potatoes in the present circumstances 'is exceedingly impolitic, if not cruel'.

The export of potatoes continues, none the less, with two vessels loading cargoes for Rotterdam.

From Hanover it is reported that, due to the likely shortage, the government of that German state will prohibit the export of potatoes.

An officer of Ballinrobe workhouse is accused of seducing a pauper. While he denies the charge, the woman is placed in solitary confinement pending an inquiry.[5]

17 counties affected

21 OCTOBER 1845

The potato crop is rotting in seventeen counties, according to reports.

The *Wexford Independent* notes: 'Where potatoes were believed generally if not altogether safe a week or ten days past, it is now found that they are infected and become totally unfit for use . . . What is to become of the poor people? There is serious danger that even seed for next year may not be preserved.'

The blight is universal in the north, the *Belfast Chronicle* reports.

The western correspondent of the *Freeman's Journal* writes: ' . . . I am persuaded that there exists a false sense of security in many districts where the plague has not yet shown itself. I say yet, for such is the character manifested by it in the several localities I have visited, that the field – the plot – the very ridge which today seems safe, may within two days be found to be thoroughly infected.

'I have before me as I write a dish of potatoes, some of them as fine-looking, firm and well-coloured, presenting to the casual observer all the appearances of sound and good potatoes, yet on close examination these healthy-looking potatoes present the early stages of the incipient and rapidly-advancing rot.'

In Mayo, a 'most intelligent clergyman' calculates that every third potato is rotten.

The correspondent continues: 'In the fairgreen of Screen, about halfway between Ballina and Sligo, I conversed with many of the farmers from different parts of the county. They manifested uncertainty but not alarm. I hope they may not yet have cause for alarm, but I confess that the result of careful and extensive inquiries through the three counties of Mayo, Sligo and Roscommon, leads me to fear that their confidence is the result of ignorance of the character of the disease.'

The government commissioners present their first report on the blight. Fallacious theories produce impractical advice, such as scraping nourishment from bad potatoes.

Elizabeth Smith, a Scot married to an officer and landlord in County Wicklow, writes in her diary: 'The colonel has been very much occupied with plans for the prevention of such extreme distress as the failure of the potato crop threatens the poor with . . . Energy is so wanting among these Celtick races there is no inspiring them to help themselves, and there is no other help really availing.'[6]

'Self-preservation first law'

28 OCTOBER 1845

The parish priest of Kells, County Meath, fears one family in twenty will not have a potato left by Christmas.

Dr Nicholas McEvoy continues in a letter to the *Freeman's Journal*: 'From one milling establishment I have last night seen not less than fifty dray-loads of meal moving on to Drogheda, thence to feed the foreigner, leaving starvation and death the soon and certain fate of the toil and sweat that raised this food.

'Let Irishmen themselves take heed before the provisions are gone. Self-preservation is the first law of nature. The right of the starving to try and sustain existence is a right far and away paramount to every right that property confers.

'Infinitely more precious in the eyes of reason – in the adorable eye of the Omnipotent Creator – is the life of the last and least of human beings than the whole united property of the entire universe.'

In Ireland, the *Freeman* comments: 'Famine does not arise so much from the absence of food as from the inability of the poor to purchase it; the masses of the people, therefore, must look for sustenance to the potato crop and not to the grain crops, which, however abundant, must necessarily be out of reach of men who, being without employment, must also be without money.'

The *Nation* estimates that half the crop, 'on which millions of our countrymen are half-starved every year, is this season totally destroyed, or in progress of destruction.'

A leading article written perhaps by Mr Mitchel, who has succeeded Mr Davis in the *Nation* office, agrees with a correspondent's slender expectations of aid from 'the English government, with their commissioners and chemists, who indulge in learned speculations on the *cause* of the calamity, while they leave us to feel its *effects*'.

It urges the landlords to take some effective step 'such as may convince the terrified people that they are not watched over by enemies . . . or landlordism has reached its latter days, and will shortly be with the feudal system and other *effete* institutions in its grave'.

The *Nation* observes that some continental countries, notably Belgium, have prohibited the export of grain, meal and flour. 'We have no domestic government or legislature to provide such a remedy; and, as for the English government, is not Ireland their store-farm? . . . So long as this island is a 'foreigner's farm' that remedy is out of the question.'

The *Freeman's Journal* believes the Irish people would not need outside help, if their produce could be retained for domestic use. 'Our potatoes are being exported in greater and less quantities – our corn is being shipped in large quantities.'[7]

British famine inconceivable

The *Freeman's Journal* asserts that famine would not be tolerated in Britain.

'If the condition of the English people manifested symptoms so deplorable as those which every day develop themselves in connection with our own, the English ports would not be permitted to remain closed against foreign corn for a single day – one quarter of corn, one barrel of flour would not be permitted to be exported from that country.'

The *Freeman* endorses Daniel O'Connell's call, made at a special meeting of Dublin Corporation, to provide employment on railway construction. In this way the people's self-respect would be maintained. 'Many hundreds, should famine really overtake us, would endure starvation to death ere they would batten upon the doles of public charity.'

It also agrees with O'Connell's rejection of a proposal to withhold payment of rents. Instead, the Liberator wants absentee landlords taxed at 50 per cent and resident landowners at 10 per cent. As the *Nation* point out, however, 'a parliament composed of absentees will never tax themselves to one-half nor one-tenth of their income'.

A letter from an Edenderry Poor Law guardian, Richard Grattan, is read to the Dublin meeting. He warns that the potato blight has struck part of Kildare and the adjoining King's County [Offaly].

'I anticipate nothing short of the most widespread and destructive *famine* that history has yet placed on record, unless immediate measures be adopted by the English ministers to provide against the approaching calamity.'

O'Connell proposes a deputation to the Lord Lieutenant, Baron Heytesbury, to urge the government to conserve grain stocks by halting distillation and brewing; to suspend the export of food outside the UK (but not to England where most of it is going); and to allow the importation of duty-free corn.

Peel tells his cabinet the time has come to repeal the hitherto sacrosanct Corn Laws. The Tory party splits and the Irish crisis will slip into the background as the Corn Laws become the dominant issue in British politics. The Famine is perceived as 'the invention of agitators on the other side of the water'.

Heytesbury receives a delegation from the Mansion House committee. His non-commital reply provokes the *Freeman's Journal*: 'They may starve! Such in spirit, if not in words, was the reply given yesterday by the English viceroy to the memorial of the deputation, which . . . prayed that the food of this kingdom be preserved, lest the people thereof perish.'[8]

Land system blamed

11 NOVEMBER 1845

The Mansion House committee, a Dublin pressure group, asks Sir Robert Peel to raise a loan of £1.5 million for the relief of Irish distress. Lord Cloncurry, its chairman, requests that the loan be applied 'in the first instance' to increasing the quantity and lowering the price of food.

The *Nation* publishes a leading article entitled 'The Famine'. Pointing out that commissioners have advised on how to preserve some remnant of the potato crop, it asks what commission will report on 'the political results to us and our children of the perilous year that is before us? . . . Without a government that can govern – without a legislature to legislate on our own soil, our fate may become whatever blind chance determines, if there be no native energy in the country to bring order out of chaos and give a positive direction to its own future. If there be such energy all may be well.'

The *Nation* warns that both landlord and tenant will be affected by this approaching calamity. 'The first blow on the rich will be the inevitable reduction of rents. Heretofore, they have taken from the farmer and the peasant all but a bare subsistence. They will take all but a bare subsistence now again. But that "all" is diminished. The "subsistence" must come mainly out of the corn – that is, out of the rent – out of the landlords' revenue.'

Hunger is the province of the marginalised, however. The plight of landless labourers and cottiers scarcely features in this analysis.

The *Nation* blames the land tenure system, not the blight: 'In other countries it will be a temporary privation; here it may be an absolute famine because, living habitually within one degree of starvation, the people can endure no more but must perish or fall back on the rents.'

The imminent repeal of the Corn Laws is welcomed. None the less, many Irish farmers with profitable leases and hundreds of small gentry may be ruined. 'In the end all will, perhaps, fall on the great proprietors, but only after wide and bitter suffering.'

Let the landlord class suffer, some angry tenant may declare. 'Alas, friend,' the *Nation* concludes, 'in this strange network of society, one of the hardest problems to resolve is how to punish the wicked, without also punishing the innocent.'

A meeting in Belfast calls on the government to open the ports to food imports.

Informed by Commissioner Lyon Playfair 'that the case is much worse than the [British] public supposes,' the prime minister arranges for the secret purchase of £100,000 worth of Indian corn in the United States'.[9]

'Half crop lost'

18 NOVEMBER 1845

Desolation is brooding over the land, according to a Fermanagh correspondent.

The workhouses, built to accommodate 100,000 paupers, are still three-quarters empty. But tenant farmers on holdings above £4 rateable valuation are now liable for Poor Law rates as well as their rents.

No tax is so odious to the farmers, writes Martin Browne, parish priest of Balla, County Mayo: 'For they consider it at variance with the principle of justice and charity to be obliged to support a staff of officers connected with the poorhouse and a few mendicants, who never resided in their district.'

That scenario will change as the crisis escalates.

The *Freeman's Journal* notes the British cabinet has held four special meetings to consider the food situation in England, which 'is only threatened with high prices or at most with very partial scarcity', and none on Ireland.

At a repeal banquet in Mayo, Archbishop MacHale sounds off about the 'infidel colleges' and never mentions the threatened Famine.

The Lindley-Playfair commission concludes 'that one half of the actual potato crop of Ireland is either destroyed or . . . unfit for the food of man'.

Pointing out that six million acres lie uncultivated, the *Nation* calls for employment on drainage and land reclamation schemes.

Members of a relief commission are nominated representing various departments, including the commissariat branch of the British army, the constabulary, the coastguard service and the new Poor Law. The commission is to organise food depots and co-ordinate local relief committees for the coming spring.

A correspondent from Blacklion, County Cavan, is not impressed: 'Would to heaven that our English rulers, in lieu of issuing their second humbug commission, would forthwith adopt measures to prevent the unfeeling proprietors and petty landlords from forcing their poor tenants to sell their oats to meet their rack rents . . . '

Most western landlords show little sympathy for their tenants. On some estates the pounds are filled with cattle seized for rents, and the farmers are obliged to sell their corn to redeem the livestock. In Ballinasloe it is 'melancholy to view with what insatiable avidity the agent, the bailiff and a whole host of understrappers are prowling among the wretched tenements of the poor tenantry, seeking and driving for rent'.

On the other side of the country, it is reported from Annamoe, County Wicklow, that 'Mr Barton is going to buy up all the oats in this neighbourhood at market price, and in the spring or summer to return to those who may want it for their own use at the first cost price. Would to God his example may be followed by our wealthy gentlemen.'

The people of Kells, County Meath, are said to be quiet and orderly, but their fears for the coming season are intense.[10]

Protestant clergy praised

25 NOVEMBER 1845

The *Freeman's Journal* praises the concern shown by the Protestant clergy. Letters from clergymen of the Established Church to the Mansion House committee 'manifest earnestness to depict the true condition of the poor and zeal to obviate their impending miseries'.

They betoken a new order of things, the *Freeman* announces hopefully: 'A desire upon the part of the Protestant clergy to be recognised as having a part with *all* the people among whom their lot is cast.'

It publishes a letter from Robert Gregory, of Coole Park, County Galway – the father of Sir William Gregory MP – as evidence that half the potato crop has failed.

Fr James Hughes writes from Castlebar: ' . . . when I mentioned to the people that the offensive stench proceeding from the hot boiled potatoes diminished much as they cooled, a woman observed that they always eat them when cold, for they never go to their meals except with feelings of disgust. These few days past I have heard innumerable persons declare that they had not enjoyed one satisfactory meal of potatoes for nearly the last fortnight.'

The *Ballinasloe Advertiser* remarks that respectable farmers have, to little advantage, resorted to every plan outlined by government commissioners to check the progress of the rot. 'As for the poor, God help them, they are in many places absolutely doing nothing from sheer despair . . . '

The *Clare Journal*, a conservative paper, says this despair is ignored by the unconcerned and by 'meally-mouthed gentlemen like the Ennis board of guardians, who would not indeed wish to disturb my Lord Heytesbury, over his wine and walnuts, by telling him the honest truth . . . The heart sickens at such disregard for the lives of the people.'

The rector of Miltown Malbay, Fr McGuane, recalls an 1822 famine 'which scourged his district so terribly'. He now fears disease and hunger will 'thin the people'.

A correspondent reports that potato digging has ceased in The Neale, Ballinrobe, as the crop already dug is rotting in pits. 'The panic is general, and I see a wildness in the countenances of some of the people.'

On the other hand, some farmers in Clara, King's County, are giving conacre potatoes to the poor for half the agreed sum. The local correspondent rejoices at such generosity. 'Let the landlords but do the same and spare the tenants, and with the aid of Providence there will be sufficiency for all.'

Alas for the Mansion House committee and its resolutions, the *Nation* comments; 'and alas for the unhappy country that has no power within it to take a step for its own salvation . . . Those who are de facto our rulers value our opinion of our own affairs at no higher rate than the howling of the winter wind.'

But Archbishop Daniel Murray joins the committee in its 'holy work' and encloses five guineas.[11]

Working on railways

The Earl of Devon wants to put Paddy working on the railway.

In a letter to the *Times*, addressed mainly to Irish landowners, the earl emphasises the need to create employment as 'no man conceives the idea of feeding, gratuitously, the whole agricultural population of Ireland'. The former land commissioner asserts that 'there is scarcely a square mile of land in Ireland which does not call for some improvement'.

Urging the construction of railways, Devon adds paternally: 'If Paddy is fairly put into the right way, he will be ready and willing to earn more money, and to get better food for himself and family by a more energetic exertion of his bodily powers than circumstances have hitherto called upon him to make. This visitation of Providence may teach us all some useful lessons; if we profit by them rightly, good may arise out of the present evil.'

He hopes for the lasting improvement of Ireland and a consequent advantage to the empire.

A meeting in Ennis, chaired by the high sheriff of Clare, shows little sympathy for the people.

The parish priest of Balbriggan, County Dublin, informs Archbishop Murray that the state of the potato crop 'is extremely unfavourable and forebodes the most melancholy and fearful consequences. I have conversed frequently with many intelligent persons on this all-important subject; and from all I heard and from what I have seen and know myself, I may state that in all this district there is not at this moment more than a fourth of the potato crop safe from disease.'

Fr John Smyth's panic-stricken parishioners, fearing the potatoes would soon be diseased, are feeding them to livestock. 'What cannot be consumed in this way are sold to starch manufacturers for whatever price they are pleased to offer – several mills are now in progress of being built in this neighbourhood for this purpose.'

Reflecting on the fate of the destitute, Fr Smyth pays a rare tribute to the workhouses: 'The poor labourer and cottier will not have as much potatoes as will bring them to the end of the year – and what is then to become of them; when will they get money to buy meal for their famishing families? Their only resource will be the poorhouses; and oh what a blessing that we have even that to fall back on in such a crisis.'

The *Waterford Freeman* denounces the 'murderous recklessness' of the British government in not preventing the export of food from this famine-threatened land.[12]

O'Brien warns government

9 DECEMBER 1845

William Smith O'Brien, MP, warns the British government that the Irish people will not lie down and die.

Addressing a weekly meeting of the Loyal National Repeal Association, O'Brien says that, while opposed to anarchy, he considers it the government's duty to provide work for the people. It would be in the interests of the English – 'the greatest moneylenders in Europe' – to use surplus revenue to create Irish employment.

O'Brien describes an experiment in Limerick workhouse to extract food from contaminated potatoes. The diseased part is cut away and the remainder mixed with corn meal proves to be more palatable than the usual pauper diet.

This quixotic landlord of ancient Irish lineage urges his poor fellow-countrymen to practise self-reliance, 'but above all to do anything rather than ask [for] English charity'.

Besides meal and flour, the government should purchase supplies of cured fish, O'Brien continues. 'By doing this through the medium of the several boards of guardians, they might give a stimulus to our neglected and comparatively unproductive fisheries, and contribute to the improvement of the districts inhabited by fishermen, of whom there are not less than 80,000 – a good provision for an Irish navy (great cheering).'

The *Tablet* believes it does not matter a hair's breath to Ireland whether the government is headed by Sir Robert Peel or Lord John Russell.

'The same system of treacherous and simulated benefits has long been common to both. The same principle of bureaucratic centralisation, which they apply with such zeal and earnestness to England, is the end and object of both these ministerial personages with regard to Ireland . . .

'Duped by the unanimous consent of all their leaders in Parliament and in the press, ignorant, or unheeding the reasoning and protestations of the Irish leaders, this dull English nation of ours will confirm itself in a persuasion already widely entertained, that treacheries conferred with flattery are benefits.'

Frederick Lucas, the founder-editor of this English Catholic journal, declares with foreboding: 'God grant that this policy of smooth deception be not pregnant with infernal results. God grant that the people of this country, thus insidiously deluded, do not firmly and irrevocably make up their minds that the discontent with which these monstrous evils are received in Ireland is a symptom of unalterable unreason and ingratitude; that the removal of Irish grievances is a proved impossibility . . . '[13]

Voice of poor

16 DECEMBER 1845

A Waterford newspaper describes the press as the voice of the poor.

The *Chronicle and Munster Advertiser* asserts: 'We and the press of Ireland must do our duty. We must give the alarm and, as it were, keep firing the signal guns of distress, and ringing the alarm bells continuously, until the dreadful danger is made known to those who may render assistance.'

But by crying 'wolf, wolf' the popular press may be perceived as indulging in the Irish propensity to exaggerate.

The *Roscommon Journal* believes employment would do more to 'tranquillise' Ireland than all the police in the United Kingdom.

The parish priest of Kilkee, County Clare, urges the government to develop fisheries along the western seaboard. Fr Michael Comyn says many visitors have remarked on this neglect, 'especially when we consider the unparalleled privations of a densely crowded population'. Deep-sea fishing is impossible without a safe harbour and with only canoes (currachs).

He suggests the construction of a harbour in Doonbeg, the provision of fishing smacks and the setting up of curing stations. As the railway network is extended, it will soon be possible to reach all parts of the country within hours.

Fr Comyn describes the fisheries potential as a mine of wealth, 'which, if developed, would avail in alleviating, and in fact entirely obliterating, the saddening cry of destitution that periodically moans over the country'. Its ravages were never so dreaded as with the approach of this calamitous season.

Dublin Corporation asks Queen Victoria to recall parliament.

An address to the queen concludes: 'We assure your Majesty that we are second to none in attachment to your person and throne, and if we have approached your Majesty with the sad recital of the wretchedness of your people in Ireland, we have been impelled to it by an imperative duty as the representatives in municipal council of the inhabitants of the metropolis of that portion of your Majesty's dominion, where for many years your subjects, although living in the midst of plenty, were nevertheless on the brink of famine . . . '

The queen is requested therefore to summon parliament to pass measures to avert the threatened calamity and save her Irish people from the scourge of famine.[14]

Cries of famishing children

23 DECEMBER 1845

The cries of famishing children are already ringing in the ears of the parish priest of Kells.

Fr McEvoy informs the Mansion House committee that 'the ghastly forms, fed upon a stinted allowance of unwholesome food, are even now beginning to emerge from the obscurity of their damp and darksome hovels, affrighting by their languishing looks the passing stranger of our town'.

He prays that the God of mercy will give our rulers 'bowels of compassion to inspire them to avert, by timely and adequate measures, horrors threatening to be widespread and destructive as any recorded in the annals of famine and pestilence'.

On the other hand, the rector of Ringagonah, Dungarvan, cautions against holding out 'any prospect of *gratuitous* pecuniary relief to those whose potato crop has partially failed'.

Daniel O'Connell writes to his deputy, Smith O'Brien: 'My attendance on the Mansion House Committee has made me acquainted with the frightful certainty of an approaching famine; and you know pestilence always follows famine, the prospect is really frightful especially in the north of Ireland.

'If the government does not act promptly and most bountifully in affording ample means of employment and placing within the reach of the labouring classes a sufficient quantity of food, to be paid for out of money they receive as wages, unless, I say, that government comes forward energetically with some plan of this kind, it is impossible to calculate the numbers of people that will perish in Ireland within the next twelve months of famine and pestilence.'

James Haughton, a Quaker philanthropist, preaches temperance to the Dublin working class. Despite Fr Mathew's crusade, 'thousands are still degrading themselves by seeking after low and debasing pleasures in the public house . . . True happiness is to be found in the cultivation of our moral and intellectual nature.'

On Christmas Day paupers in the North Dublin Union workhouse are given a dinner of beef, bread and soup.

The number of inmates has risen to 1,844. The guardians discuss a complaint made by the Protestant chaplain against a Catholic school-mistress 'for having refused to permit two Protestant children to attend him and obliging him to take them away by force'.

The chairman, Alderman Michael Staunton, a newspaper proprietor, observes that it is an inappropriate season for a clergyman to speak intemperately. A motion reprimanding the teacher is carried after an amendment calling for her dismissal was defeated narrowly.

In County Kerry, six cattle and thirty sheep are slaughtered for the poor of Killarney at Christmas by order of the Earl of Kenmare, 'while her ladyship has taken care that a large supply of blankets and cloaks should be provided for the aged female poor'.[15]

Eating rotten tubers

30 DECEMBER 1845

A doctor warns of the poisonous effects of contaminated potatoes. Sir James Murray reports that a Dublin labourer and three of his children are in hospital after eating rotten tubers.

The man supports seven children, without their mother, on 40d a week. Having bought cheap potatoes, he eats them ravenously with three of his children. 'After two or three such meals the four creatures were seized by severe pains and cramps of the stomach, followed by partial paralysis and acrimonious secretions.'

A County Donegal correspondent fears that half the people of Killybegs will die from eating bad potatoes. Alexander Browne informs the Relief Commission in Dublin Castle: 'I have not a sound potato out of thirty barrels. They are so bad that they sickened the cows and pony so much that they would not eat their hay.' Heaps of putrid potatoes can be seen in the neighbouring villages.

The *Tipperary Vindicator* reports that around Borrisoleigh the poorer people are counting the potatoes they give to their children, while leaving the table hungry themselves.

The *Cork Examiner* blames the consumption of bad potatoes for the prevalence of fever.

The poor have resigned themselves to the mercy of God, according to the *Nation*. It wants not 'sickly charity', but Irish MPs to attend parliament and demand a large advance of money, to be raised by an absentee or property tax. A law should be passed, too, to prevent usury.

Above all next year's crop must be provided for: 'Let us have but one starving year unless God, in his mercy, be pleased to visit us with a recurrence of the disease.'

The victims themselves interpret the disaster in social, not religious terms: 'Is ní h-é Dia cheap riamh an obair seo/daoine bochta do chur le fuacht is le fán.'

The *Nation* preaches a Sinn Féin doctrine: If Westminster fails Ireland, nationalists should fall back on the Repeal Association. 'We are well aware that this is dangerous ground. We see before us the angry frown of power, convulsed at the prospect of seeing the duties of the constituted authorities usurped by the popular will.'

Charles Gavan Duffy, the proprietor/editor of the *Nation*, continues: 'But if parliament abdicates its functions in a time of terror and danger, anarchy must be guarded against by the next practicable means . . . For our parts, we would suffer much toil, much sacrifice – much to see the true hand of legislation regulating the property, providing for the wants, and moulding the destiny of the country.'

Charles Trevelyan sanctions a salary of £700 a year for John Pitt Kennedy as secretary to the Relief – or 'Scarcity' – Commission.

Michael Keogh, of Kellystown, County Dublin, writes to Captain Kennedy, an advocate of waste land reclamation and former secretary to the Devon Commission, reminding him of that body's valuable suggestions for employment.[16]

Relief limits set

6 JANUARY 1846

The British government does not want to end up feeding the hungry in Ireland, where in 'normal' times an estimated 2,385,000 people are destitute for half the year.

On arrival in Dublin Sir Randolph Routh, of the Relief Commission, writes to Charles Trevelyan at the Treasury: 'Claims will be made on account of the distress of the people, rather than from their want of food proceeding from losses of the potato crop. There must be a distinction clearly kept.'

Marianne Nevill, who owns estates in Counties Kildare, Wexford and Cork, suggests that the people eat yams. She has written for a supply from the West Indies.

A meeting of farmers and labourers in Charleville, County Cork, sends a report to Dublin Castle, which reads in part: 'Widow Sheedy had 13 barrels dug out sound; out of the entire, though she has adopted all the remedial measures hitherto recommended, she has two barrels fit for pigs – not one fit for human food.'

A Dublin correspondent appeals to Horace Greeley, of the *New York Tribune*, for American aid: 'Society is so selfishly and antagonistically organised that men generally try to keep their souls at ease while pursuing their legitimate callings, yet the excitement here is daily growing more intense and the time is not distant when a terrific outbreak must be the consequence.'

The *Waterford Chronicle* reports that recruiting sergeants are busy. 'The farmers are in dread of the potato failure, and they will not employ labourers; consequently, many poor Irish unfortunates are thrown by the force of bitter adversity into the ranks of the English army.'

A Poor Law commissioner is censured for refusing to examine a witness because she could not speak English. A member of the Gort Union Board of Guardians complains that, during a workhouse inquiry, one of the assistant commissioners, a Scotsman, excluded testimony 'because the witness could only speak her native language'.

An epiphanic deputation from Dublin Corporation presents an address to Queen Victoria in Windsor, concerning what the *Observer* calls 'the alleged famine in Ireland'.

The queen's reply offers no practical measures of relief. The *Freeman's Journal* forbears comment – except to note the apathy of her ministers towards Irish misery – 'because we believe that no sentiment of that nature finds a place in the bosom of the Royal Lady, whom they have made use of to give expression to their own indifference'.

The delegation is entertained by the lord mayor of London, however. Replying to a toast, the lord mayor of Dublin, Henry Arabin, remarks that until recently the Irish nation was an object of ridicule in England.

'If Englishmen were placed in the same situation as the people of Ireland, instead of asking as he had done that day in the address presented to her Majesty, Englishmen would demand and be sure to obtain what they sought.'[17]

Clare evictions

13 JANUARY 1846

A priest writes to the Repeal Association about 'extermination' on the Vandeleur estate in west Clare.

Fr Michael Meehan describes the eviction of eight families – forty-four people – just before Christmas. Their homes were then levelled. 'The persons fortunate enough to be left undisturbed on the land, and who are in any way connected or related to the ejected tenants, use every effort to hush the complaints of the exiles, lest the landlord may take anger and turn more of them out.'

Fr Meehan notes that Crofton M. Vandeleur's estate comprises sixty-four square miles. If leases were granted on the easily reclaimable bogland, Kilrush would not be swarming with hundreds of idle ejected tenants. 'Mr Vandeleur, like every other rich man, can go to the Continent when, in April or May, want begins to appear and to moan in the highways, as happened in the summer of 1841' – leaving the government and the middle classes to feed the poor.

Commenting on the Kilrush evictions, the *Freeman's Journal* asserts: 'The law of landlord and tenant, as it now exists in Ireland, must be altered.' It penalises the humble and the weak because they are weak and humble. The peace of the community will continue to be shaken until the spirit of justice is infused into the law.

'These laws urge the the landlords into unfeeling exactions and stimulate the outraged into criminal resistance.'

The *Freeman* goes on to argue that land reform is in the interests of both tenant and proprietor. The landlord is less to be blamed than the odious system on which his power is constructed. The paramount evil afflicting Irish society is the despotic authority with which the law invests the owner of land.

Social disorder springs from insecurity of tenure: 'If ever the Irish peasant lifts his hand against the law, it is only when the quiet fruition of the very swine's leaving is torn from him, and what are speciously called the rights, but more truly the wrongs, of property are violently and recklessly exercised.'

A 'good landlord' story. Since the failure of the potatoes, Thomas Brehon, of New Ross, County Wexford, has arranged for each of his twenty workmen to purchase two shillings worth of bread for their families every week.

The master of Tullamore workhouse – disposing of a humbug – finds that the manufacture of starch from diseased potatoes is altogether unprofitable. Meanwhile, 'the application of destitute strangers is becoming more frequent'.[18]

Limerick 'insurrection'

Insurrectionary activity is reported from County Limerick. 'An audacious multitude' of 1,200–1,500 men assemble on the lands of Sir Capel Molyneaux, of Knocksentry, near Castleconnell, to prevent the serving of eviction notices.

Some are armed, the others carry farm implements. The insurgents camp for 48 hours, fortifying themselves with bread and whiskey and firing shots to intimidate the bailiff and local constabulary.

The military is called out from Limerick city. Initially the insurgents stand their ground as a force of 200 soldiers, a troop of dragoons and twenty policemen approach. 'The surrounding hills were covered with people, who began to conceal their firearms, but made a strong show of pitchforks, spades and shovels.'

As the magistrate reads the Riot Act for a third time, the army and constabulary charge. The insurgents retreat; some are seen at a distance wielding their implements and shouting defiance. But they disperse, 'fortunately without a collision'. Three prisoners are taken with stones in their hands.

'This proceeding on the part of the peasantry has struck consternation into the peaceable portion of the community', according to the *Limerick Reporter*.

On Sunday night, as four policemen from Annacotty patrol near General Sir Richard Burke's gate, they come upon ten armed men. The insurgents, refusing to surrender, open fire and wound two constables – one mortally. Police from Limerick city scour the district without arresting anyone.

The Clare gentry reassemble. After a meeting in Kilkee to consider public works was disrupted by Fr Michael Comyn and his parishioners, Cornelius O'Brien, MP, convenes a caucus in Ennis.

It united, the *Freeman's Journal* observes, Catholic and Protestant, Tory and Repealer, for the purpose of alleviating the sufferings of the poor and of procuring employment for the industrious labourer. 'But the meeting was especially remarkable because it was the first county assemblage in Ireland which, without affording grounds for the charge of exaggeration, has pronounced that the potato crop has been an unquestionable failure.'

With the parliamentary session about to open, the meeting outlines proposals for employment on land reclamation and railway construction. 'The men of Clare in this deplorable conjuncture make no appeal to the charity of England, but they put forward large demands upon her justice.'

Paraphrasing the meeting's submission to the lord lieutenant, the *Freeman* points out that many Irish railway projects await parliamentary sanction. It suggests setting up a tribunal in Dublin to discharge the functions of Commons select committees. The building of Irish railways is too important to be 'entrusted to the indolence or the ignorance of strangers'.[19]

£500,000 relief required

27 JANUARY 1846

The Relief Commission tells the Treasury what it does not wish to hear. In a report critical of British government relief policy, the commissioners assert that Irish landlords cannot be relied on 'to any considerable extent'. Secondly, 'a very large sum of money', not less than £500,000, is required from public funds to meet the probable emergency.

The government plans to spend 10 per cent of that figure. Furthermore, it sees its role in relief operations as 'stimulating, directing and supporting but not superseding' the landowners' duty. The chairman of the commission, Edward Lucas, is replaced by Sir Randolph Routh.

The report quotes the estimate of Professor Robert Kane that 700,000 tons of potatoes should be withdrawn for use as seed for next year's crop, and an equivalent amount of substitute food provided. 'We are aware that an abundant crop of oats, not diminished by the usual exportation, affords means within the country, and probably within every district, of supplying the deficiency to those who have means wherewith to make the purchase.'

But it would cost £2,100,000 to buy oats for the peasantry. 'A less costly description of food as for instance Indian corn, a supply of which we are informed may shortly be expected, would of course cause a diminution in this estimate.'

The report adds: 'The poorhouses will, without doubt, be found a most important means of relief and we consider it a most providential circumstance that such an extensive resource is available against the calamity – more widely extended and more serious in its nature than any that has affected the Irish poor since 1817.'

Moreover, the present potato failure 'and the minute sub-division of land in which it prevails lead us to entertain the greatest doubt whether any adjustment of Public Works can be made to meet the need wherever it may occur – and it must be met or death from famine may be the result'.

Charles Hamilton and John O'Connor, JP, writing from County Meath, urge the commissioners to reconsider the rule that labourers on public works be paid below the standard rate. Unless the wages enable a man to feed his family, it would be better to state openly that workhouses are the only form of relief which the government is prepared to offer the starving population. 'The commissioners appear to consider that there cannot be distress to any great extent in a district where there is to be found a vacancy in the poorhouses. But in using this test we think they have not sufficiently considered that the Poor Law is a new institution; the people look upon availing of its provisions as a last resource.'[20]

Indian corn arrives

3 FEBRUARY 1846

The supply of Indian meal from the US, purchased by the British government, arrives secretly in Cork.

The Relief Commission has been reorganised to administer temporary relief supplementary to that provided in the workhouses. The duties of the commission are to advise the government, through the Treasury, about Irish distress and to co-ordinate the activities of local relief committees.

The main duties of these voluntary bodies will be to encourage employment, raise subscriptions and purchase and distribute, at cost price, Indian corn from depots established by the Relief Commission and manned by commissariat officers.

The purchase of food in ordinary use is forbidden to avoid competition with private enterprise, the sanctity of the market being very much part of British political thinking.

The purpose of the limited stocks of imported corn is not to replace private traders but rather to control them. The government believes 'that under judicious management of this supply the markets would be so regulated as to prevent an exorbitant price for native produce.'

However, the Relief Commission, the Treasury and the Home Office – the government departments involved – are anxious mainly that the whole burden of coping with Irish misery should not be thrown on them.

Charles Trevelyan writes to the new commission chairman, Sir Randolph Routh: 'The landlords and other ratepayers are the parties who are both legally and morally answerable for affording due relief to the destitute poor . . .

'The measures to be adopted by you, and the officers employed under you are, therefore, to be considered as merely auxiliary to those which it is the duty of persons possessed of property in each neighbourhood to adopt.'

While the Irish landed interest is expected to finance and distribute relief, responsibility for administration remains with the British government.

Even though many of the landlords are absentees or insolvent, Trevelyan insists: 'That indirect permanent advantages will accrue to Ireland from the scarcity, and the measures taken for its relief, I entertain no doubt . . .

'If a firm stand is not made against the prevailing disposition to take advantage of this crisis to break down all barriers, the true permanent interests of the country will, I am convinced, suffer in a manner which will be irreparable in our time.'[21]

Priest weeps for his people

10 FEBRUARY 1846

A meeting in west Clare is adjourned when a priest breaks down describing the state of his parish.

At the meeting in Miltown Malbay courthouse to consider employment for the people, Fr Edward Barry, PP Kilmurry, 'became so overpowered at the thoughts of the distress and wretchedness he had for the last month witnessed, that he lost all power of utterance and had to resume his seat in a flood of tears'.

Censuring absentee landlords, the *Waterford Freeman* reports that 5,000 people are being 'consigned to the jaws of hunger' in Dungarvan.

Charles Clements informs to the Relief Commissioners that, with the destruction of the potato crop, the large farmers of County Meath are remitting the rent for patches sublet to cottiers.

The cottiers live in clusters of cabins, or clachans, and grow potatoes for their families on a strip of conacre. They are without employment from the end of the potato-digging season until the start of planting.

During those winter months the farmers employ only their 'bound' labourers, who are hired by the year but 'do not form more than one-tenth of the labouring population. Potatoes obtained from conacre afford the only means of subsistence to the labouring population generally during this season of almost total idleness, and upon the failure of this stock they will become perfectly destitute.'

The *Tablet* explains that the common appendix to a London advertisement – 'No Irish need apply' – arises less from considerations of race or religion, than from unsuitability as servants in England. It illustrates this by describing the condition of Irish labourers in English towns: often herded together in filth and ignorance, and at war with the natives.

The *Nation* asserts: 'We will take home and employ and educate our poor exiles in good time; and drive away (please God) the tribe of English-born corruptionists, who live and thrive at the expense and the ruin of a country which they despise.'

Thomas Meagher writes to the Relief Commissioners from Cappamore, County Limerick, suggesting land reclamation projects for the vast unemployed population of his parish. An expenditure of £12,000– £13,000 would establish 500 or 600 families in the neighbourhood of the Slieve Phelim mountains.

If the government showed 'a little determination' towards the landlords – whose absolute rights of property might be infringed – 4,000 acres could be brought into cultivation 'which are now only a receptacle for wild fowl. Alas, there are too many such receptacles in the country, which might be made receptacles for human beings and afford them food and raiment in abundance.'[22]

Mitchel's warning

17 FEBRUARY 1846

John Mitchel gives vent to his savage indignation with a leading article in the *Nation* entitled 'Famine'.

He writes: 'Nearer, nearer wears the day that will see fell Hunger, with stalking Plague in its train, over this devoted land. From almost every county in Ireland come reports of more and more urgent alarm and terror, as the earthed-up potatoes are uncovered, and found masses of loathsome rottenness.

'From Clare, from Galway, from Meath, we hear of calculations of how much of the people's food remains eatable, and how long it will last. In one district they reckon that there is enough sound food to sustain the population for a week – in others, perhaps a fortnight.

'And the men of Clare may comfort themselves with the knowledge that some time in the course of the ensuing spring or summer perhaps, one small fishing pier will be commenced upon their coast. Galway, we learn, is getting an additional military force; their port lies wide open for the food to go out; and if no provisions are coming in, there is at least a war steamer in their harbour. Then as for Westmeath, a man was to be hanged there yesterday; if there is to be no adequate means of supplying them with food, they shall, at worst, have plenty of justice.

'They are debating the question of free trade in parliament just now; and the state of the potato crop in Ireland furnishes orators on this side and on that with many plausible topics of discourse by which they may embarrass the Premier, or sustain his views, as the case may be. Meanwhile, the Duke of Norfolk prescribes curry-powder, and the Lord Lieutenant of Ireland assures the commercial world that there are absolutely none of last year's potatoes now remaining in store in that part of the "united kingdom" committed to his government.

'Oh, Heaven! do these men know what potatoes are – what famishing men are? Have they any conception even yet that there may soon be certain millions of human beings in Ireland having nothing to eat; and that the problem will be what to do with them? A problem which must be solved, and that right soon, or it will solve itself in some terrible manner.'

Echoing a different Ulster voice, the *Downpatrick Recorder* praises government efforts to create employment: The Bill authorising the Commissioners of Public Works to make additional grants up to £50,000 and other 'measures ought to stop the mouths of agitators; and the peasantry of Ireland are not so devoid of discrimination as not to perceive the difference between an English government which takes means to feed and clothe them, and those who despoil them of their hard-earned pence and shillings' – a reference to the 'O'Connell Tribute'.[23]

'Impending calamity'

24 FEBRUARY 1846

Daniel O'Connell begs the House of Commons 'to stop the impending calamity' in Ireland.

He cites the report of the Devon Commission to show that the people are not to blame for their poverty. He notes that more than two million quarters of grain and nearly $2\frac{1}{2}$ million cwt of meal were exported to Britain last year. While Ireland produces such abundance, the inhabitants are starving: 'So blessed was she by Providence, so cursed by man.'

The Liberator sums up: 'I have shown you that there are no agricultural labourers, no peasantry in Europe so badly off – suffering such privations as do the great body of the Irish people. In no part of Europe, I repeat, is there such suffering as in Ireland.

'There are five millions of people always on the verge of starvation . . . They are in the utmost danger of a fearful famine, with all its concomitant horrors.'

O'Connell denies that he has come to ask for money. 'I am here to say Ireland has resources of her own. You have a revenue from the woods and forests of Ireland.'

He suggests borrowing money on the rents of Irish landlords (hear, hear, and loud cheers). 'It is the business of the landlord to protect the tenant. Somebody must pay. Surrounded by sickness and famine and death, in all its worst forms, are we to be mincing the matter – raising nice questions as to the position and liability of the landlord? The tenantry must perish, or the landlords must contribute.

'You may tell me there is a poor law and poor-houses. My reply is that one and the other were meant for ordinary seasons – that they were never calculated to meet famine and disease. The poor-houses may make good hospitals for the sick, and you may want them. Fever is raging in Cork; it has broken out in Kilkenny; it prevails in Killarney. There is fever in Limerick, and it is daily carrying off its victims in the lanes of Dublin . . . Famine is coming, fever is coming, and this house should place in the hands of government power to stay the evil.'

O'Connell supports government measures, but they are only 'miserable trifles'.

'Once more', the *Nation* comments, 'the grim phantom of Irish misery has been held up before the averted eyes of our legislators. They will not look at their hideous work. They seem, in words, to admit the coming dearth, disease and death – speak with conventional phrases of sympathy about it – hint obscurely at some beggarly relief they have been providing – and then wave their hands, and bid the spectre vanish.'

'Speranza' vaporises from the German:

> . . . *For Destiny tolls the hour*
> *Hear ye it not afar?*
> *When oppression shall sink 'neath the power*
> *Of the last great Holy War.*[24]

Relief committees formed

2 MARCH 1846

The Relief Commissioners issue instructions on the formation and duties of temporary committees. Their main function is to raise funds with which to purchase and distribute the food imported by the government. The money provided by local subscription can be matched by an equal amount from funds placed at the disposal of the Lord Lieutenant.

However, 'gratuitous relief shall be afforded only to those persons who are entirely incapable of giving a day's work, and who have no able-bodied relative on whom they are dependent, and these cases only in which their reception in the workhouse of the union to which they belong, is, from want of room, impracticable.'

A correspondent writes from Newcastle on the Tipperary-Waterford border: 'It is really frightful to contemplate the condition to which most of the inhabitants even now are reduced. The stench emitted from the (potato) pits which are thrown open is such as is calculated to infect the country with a devouring pestilence.'

Thomas Gill, superintendent of roads for the Kenmare district, says he has never met men less able to work. 'This, I think, proceeds from their inability to provide a sufficient quantity of food, many of them cannot procure two sufficient meals of sound potatoes in the day, and when men are pinched in such food it is impossible to expect they can give a satisfactory return of work.'

Charles Trevelyan sanctions public works worth £4,100 in the Nobber district of County Meath. One half of the cost is to be issued as a grant and the other as a loan.

He is directed by the Lords of the Treasury 'to add that if any proprietors will be benefited by these works in a greater degree than the other cess payers, their Lordships rely upon the Lord Lieutenant causing a proper communication to be made to the proprietors in question, with a view to induce them to contribute a sum of money proportioned to the superior interest they have in the works.'

Mrs Smith, of Baltiboys, writes in her Wicklow diary that 'we hardly ought to be so cheerful with starvation at our door here . . . With potatoes at their present price it would take nine shillings a week to buy sufficient of them for the labourer's family; he can earn at best but six shillings and there are all his other necessities. The managers who buy up the flour and meal and sell it out in the very small quantities the labourers can only buy, nearly double the cost price on the poor purchaser, and if they give credit, charge usurious interest besides – a system that ruins hundreds.'

The *Tyrone Constitution* fears for next season's potatoes. Experiments have shown that contaminated seed and planting in blight-affected areas will produce a diseased crop.

Four cases of arms are imported for a clergyman in Killeshandra, County Cavan.[25]

'Infidel colleges' blamed

9 MARCH 1846

The archbishop of Tuam blames 'infidel colleges' for the Famine. Mirroring the mind-set of bigoted Protestants, this fiery Roman Catholic prelate appears to worship an Old Testament God. While they view the Famine as divine retribution for obdurate popery, John MacHale directs his wrath against the undenominational colleges planned for Belfast, Cork and Galway.

In his Lenten pastoral, Dr MacHale instructs the faithful to fast – an unnecessary injunction for the half-starved peasantry. Moreover, 'the duties of charity – of an active, benevolent and practical charity – you will, I trust, fulfil towards all, whatever may be their religious creed.'

He condemns the sins of fraud and bribery, of force and perjury, committed at elections.

But the 'Godless' colleges are the main target of his pastoral: 'There is spreading abroad the same jealousy of the holy influence of religious orders, and the same rage to transfer from them to laymen – nay, to heretics and infidels, mixed up with apostate priests, if they can be purchased – the education of the rising youth of Ireland, such as preceded the melancholy catastrophe of the French revolution. There is ringing in our ears the same jargon of liberality, and the same denunciations of a distinct and exclusive creed, with which the true faith was then sought to be annihilated.'

One wonders if the 'Lion of the West' has Archbishop Murray of Dublin in mind when he adds: 'There has been no schism, however inveterate – no heresy, however deadly, of which ecclesiastics were not found the abettors.'

Dr MacHale asks if they think it harmless to have their sons educated by 'schismatical masters'.

He compares those who speak of the economic benefits of the third-level colleges to Judas: 'The land mourneth, the people are on the verge of famine in punishment of the sins of their infidelity, and the remedy that is suggested to heal the evil, and the means which they have recourse to appease God's anger, is to lend themselves to an active co-operation in that very infidelity which so signally brings on them the chastisement of Heaven . . . Do not for a paltry relief derived from the erection of infidel colleges, suffer the worse religious pestilence and famine described by the prophet to desolate a land whose faith was hitherto untarnished.' If control of education passes from spiritual to secular control, 'a foul stream of literature will continue to issue from those putrid sources, the infidel colleges, covering your clergy, your convents and your hearths with their irreligious outpourings.'

Unsurprisingly, there is difficulty in procuring a site for the Galway college.

The archbishop regrets not providing an Irish version of his pastoral, which is just as well as this harangue would depress the people further.[26]

100,000 famishing

16 MARCH 1846

William Smith O'Brien tells the House of Commons that 100,000 Irish people are famishing. He has seen families sitting down to a meal of potatoes 'which any member of the house would be sorry to offer his hogs'.

The Home Secretary, Sir James Graham, introduces a Bill to make temporary provision for the treatment of the destitute affected with fever in Ireland. Dysentery has broken out in almost every Irish county, 'attended by fever in many instances'. The Bill will empower the Lord Lieutenant to establish a Board of Health in Dublin. A medical officer is to be appointed in each Poor Law Union, on whose representation the boards of guardians are to provide temporary fever hospitals.

The guardians are to defray expenses out of the poor rates. The scheme sounds fine at Westminster, but ignores the difficulties of rate collecting in Ireland.

An MP, citing the Irish physician Dominic Corrigan, points out that what the people need is wholesome food.

Dr Corrigan thinks 'sickness should not be made a chain to drag a man into a poorhouse'. In a pamphlet on famine and fever, he writes: 'The generation that has thus suffered cannot again be what it has been . . . and the offspring will inherit for generations to come the weakness of body and apathy of mind which famine and fever had engendered.'

Smith O'Brien, a landowner in County Limerick, wants parliament to compel absentee Irish landlords to return to their estates, instead of squandering fortunes abroad. He suggests the introduction of a property tax and compensation for tenants who improve their farms. Rather than appeal to English generosity, 'what Ireland claimed from a British parliament was just legislation – which should compel the landed proprietors to do their duty to the people.'

Some 300 tenants are evicted on the Gerrard estate in Ballinglass, County Galway. Prosperous by Irish standards, they are evicted – with the assistance of constabulary and troops – to turn the holdings into a grazing farm.

The Clonmel correspondent of the *Tipperary Vindicator* is at a loss for words to describe 'the utter want and destitution of thousands of the labouring population. Many families are literally without the means of existence.'

Sub-constable Michael Connell informs Inspector W.H. Pierse, Tullamore, about a disease-free field of potatoes in his sub-district.

Rooskey (County Roscommon) Relief Committee requests help for the starving.

The *Nation* observes: 'The Irish people, always half starved, are expecting absolute famine day by day; they know that they are doomed to months of a weed-diet next summer . . . and they ascribe it, unanimously, not so much to the wrath of heaven [*pace* Archbishop MacHale] as to the greedy and cruel policy of England.'[27]

Starved and half-starved

23 MARCH 1846

Ireland is to be coerced. In a four-page supplement on the Irish Coercion Bill, however, the *Nation* notes the increase of infanticide in Victorian England. A leading article asserts that the 10,000 armed policemen maintained here under the pretence of keeping the peace are in reality part of an army of occupation.

But Henry Grattan, jun., observes with pain the outrages committed in various parts of the country recently.

T.M. Ray, secretary of the Repeal Association, concludes his St Patrick's Day message: 'Firmness, temperance, perseverance, peace and union, and Ireland will again be a nation.'

A relief committee estimates there are nearly 1,000 individuals in a state of abject poverty in Kilkee, County Clare.

They 'are what would be understood in England as starved, and what is understood in Ireland as half starved. Their cheeks are hollow and transparent, the mouth enlarged, the nose pinched in, the eyes glassy or else of a watery clearness. They scarcely utter any complaints; they do not beg of anyone walking around the village, but follow him silently in a crowd.'

The Board of Works is to employ fifty men at ten pence a day. Yet such is the compassion of the poor that they have asked through their pastor, Michael Comyn, that instead of fifty at ten pence, 100 should be employed at five pence. 'The people say their greatest anxiety is to be able to buy a little meal for the children; they will continue to eat the diseased potatoes themselves as long as any remain, but they cannot bear to hear the cries of the starving children.'

Patrick Hayden, secretary of the Carrickbeg relief committee in west Waterford, informs the Relief Commission that three people have died of starvation.

The Marquis of Clanricarde draws attention to the hoarding of Indian corn meal by speculators intent on profit.

Lord Londonderry makes a statement about the Ballinglass evictions: 'seventy-six families, comprising 300 individuals, had not only been turned out of their houses but had even – the unfortunate wretches – been mercilessly driven from the ditches to which they had betaken themselves for shelter and where they were attempting to get up a covering of some kind by means of sticks and mud . . . these unfortunate people had their rents actually ready.'

Mrs Smith writes in her Wicklow diary: '. . . the famine is coming, has begun on the plains and must reach the hills, and though those immediately belonging to our small knot of good landlords may feel little of it, all around are already in misery, the poor broom man among them, who while walking up from the gate with me, his load upon his back, told me he had no work, no food, and was reduced to one meal a day, himself and his wife and five children.'[28]

Some depots open

Letters pour into the Relief Commission expressing alarm at the rising level of destitution.

William Monsell, of Tervoe, County Limerick, seeks permission to use the constabulary to issue Indian corn meal at cost price in Patrickswell and Clarina. The police are to be paid 2s 6d extra a day.

Mountmellick Board of Guardians suggests the provision of subsidised or free food for the poor.

George Wyndham plans to spend £5,000 improving his lands in Clare and Limerick. He has received 160 applications from tenants for emigrant passage to Canada. He calls for a regulated system of emigration, with the government, the landlord and the colonial authority each bearing one-third of the cost.

Due to local pressure, Peel's Indian corn goes on sale at food depots in Cork, Clonmel and Longford. The *Illustrated London News* reports that, on the depots being opened in Cork, 'the crowds of poor persons who gathered round them were so turbulently inclined as to require the immediate interference of the police, who remained there throughout the day. Among the poor, who were of the humblest description and needing charitable relief, the sales were but scanty.'

Nevertheless, the *Cork Examiner* estimates that 4,480lb of corn meal were sold on the first day at one penny a pound. Due to the clamour to buy Indian corn, particularly in small amounts, many depots remain open from 6a.m. to 9p.m.

The *Illustrated London News* writes complacently: 'We feel gratified to learn that a steamer has been despatched from Cork to Dublin laden with 600 sacks of Indian meal. One half is to be despatched by the Royal, and the other by the Grand Canal, to the interior. It must be acknowledged that Her Majesty's government are executing their duty promptly and with energy.'

While the *Freeman's Journal* publishes recipes from North America, those who subsisted on boiled potatoes have little experience of cooking anything else. They have no ovens and few utensils, and in many cases cannot read the cooking instructions published by the Relief Commission in English.

The corn has caused stomach upsets and, with its yellow colour, is already becoming known as 'Peel's brimstone'. It needs to be ground twice to produce digestible meal. Charles Trevelyan considers this an unnecessary expense. 'I cannot believe it will be necessary to grind Indian corn twice,' he remarks to Commissioner Routh. 'Dependence on charity is not to be made an agreeable mode of life.'

Viscount Castlereagh, county lieutenant, detects no signs of scarcity, distress or shortage of work in Down.

A police inspector in Loughrea, County Galway, reports on a mass meeting to dissuade farmers and merchants from allowing wheat and other provisions to leave the neighbourhood. He warns of looting unless relief is forthcoming.[29]

Starvation feared

6 APRIL 1846

The voice of the poor is seldom recorded. In a letter to the Relief Commission, however, the rector of Freshford encloses a note from John Mansfield 'as a specimen of the numberless cases of urgent distress' in the Kilkenny village.

The rector, Luke Fowler, writes: 'Every day the distress becomes more urgent and extended here, amounting to all but starvation in numerous cases. My house is beset with miserable people, who I know have no sustenance or means of procuring it.'

While Mansfield's hand-writing is ornate, his spelling and punctuation are irregular: 'Reverand Sir Pardon me for letting you now my great distress I did not earn one Shilling This 3 weeks I had not one Bite for my familly since yesterday Morning to eat And iam applying to you As a good Charitable gentle man to lend me a little Reliefe as I have a promise of Asituation in the Rail way in the coarse of a month which with the help of the lord I will pay you the first Money I will earen . . . '

Mr Mansfield has pawned his coat and clothes belonging to his wife. Unless he receives help, the family will die of want. The Rev Fowler vouches for the truth of this statement.

From Caherconlish, County Limerick, Dr Noble Seward writes that the poor are on the verge of starvation. One man informed him: 'I'm ashamed to tell you my wife, seven children and myself only eat one meal of potatoes yesterday. Another this day. We had two eggs in the house last night which my wife was obliged to get up and give the children to prevent them crying. And our last meal of potatoes is now in the house.'

Poverty and starvation were depicted in his face, the doctor notes. He finds the poor have a great aversion to entering the workhouse. Several people came to him within the last few days and told him they were starving, that they were willing to work but could not get employment.

Richard Pennefather, Under Secretary, says he has been informed by a gentleman of the highest respectability in Ballyclerahan, County Tipperary, 'that the people are starving – that there are not more potatoes in the parish than would do for seed – that when a miserable pittance of potatoes was boiled for the food of the family, the children were fighting for the few sound ones among them, and the wretched parents compelled to eat those that were not fit for food for the commonest animal.'

This village is situated principally on land owned by the Established Church. The property has been divided and sub-divided to extract the maximum rent 'until you come to the miserable occupier of the hovel.'

The poor of Edenderry, King's County, are in a pitiable condition, James Colgan, PP, tells the Relief Commissioners.[30]

Hunger marches

13 APRIL 1846

Hunger leads to peaceful protests in Counties Clare, Kerry, Kilkenny, Tipperary and Wicklow. In Clare, however, the poor 'are manifesting an alarming inquietude and expressing a determination not to starve whilst food can be procured'.

The consequences of the potato failure are being experienced even on the east coast. As poverty tightens its grip on Bray, forty men stage a sit-down protest at Loughlinstown Workhouse. The guardians inform them that no assistance will be forthcoming until they become destitute and thus eligible, with their families, for the poorhouse. But Sir George Hodson, chairman of Rathdown Board of Guardians, does take steps to form a local relief committee.

Inspector W.J. Waraston describes a protest in Kilkenny: 'About 100 men of the lowest orders of the labouring class assembled at the Poor House of this town to demand employment or food for themselves and families. They stated that they were starving and many of them declared they had not had food for two days, and could not obtain employment, and that they were willing to earn if they could get work, and unless they were afforded relief they would have recourse to violence.'

Mr R. Sullivan, JP and poor law guardian, remonstrates with them on the 'impropriety of their conduct . . . as many as wished would be admitted into the Poor House if found to be proper objects, on presenting themselves to the Guardians when assembled in the Board Room'. This offer is declined.

In Ballylongford, County Kerry, a band of men proceed to the parish priest's house and announce 'they would take some of his fat cows from him for food if they did not soon get relief'. A constable reports that about fifty labourers, headed by Patrick McElligott, warned Fr Daniel McCarthy that, unless employment or some relief is forthcoming, they will be reduced to plundering. They make similar complaints to Stephen Sandes Esq and William Hickie JP before dispersing.

John Lewis JP, Newport, County Tipperary, informs the Inspector General of the Constabulary about a notice which appeared on the chapel gate at Birdhill: 'It most earnestly requested that the labouring class of Birdhill meet on Tuesday next, quietly and peaceably to go to their resident magistrate – Mr Going – to know from him if there is any employment or relief to be given to prevent the forthcoming famine which is at hand with a great number; there is no time to be lost.'

Forty or fifty people are received by Mr Going, who said he will do all in his power for them.

The *Cork Examiner* reports that within the last three weeks forty-six houses, the homes of 277 people, were levelled on the property of the Marquis of Waterford. Each family was given £2 to quit.[31]

Irish alienation

20 APRIL 1846

William Smith O'Brien believes there would be no Famine if Ireland was self-governing. While accepting the British monarchy, this Protestant patriot rejects Westminster rule.

He tells the House of Commons during a Coercion Bill debate that the Irish people are alienated, perhaps irrevocably, from this parliament. He finds the linking of repressive legislation with relief measures disingenuous.

'How different would have been the conduct of an Irish government and an Irish parliament,' O'Brien asserts. 'An Irish government would have summoned an Irish parliament to meet in November last, to consider the steps necessary to meet the unforeseen calamity; instead of coupling measures of coercion and relief . . . out of the resources of Ireland they would have made preparations to prevent famine among the people.'

O'Brien will hold British ministers responsible for premature loss of life. Already three people have died. He cites the *Roscommon Journal*: 'On Sunday morning a poor man was discovered within half a mile of this town, stretched by the ditch, and apparently some hours dead.' An inquest jury found that the man died from destitution and hunger.

In Limerick a man has died of starvation on the public works. Fellow workers subscribed a penny each – one-twelfth of their hard day's earning – for his family.

It is monstrous, O'Brien continues, to talk about the rights of property when the people are starving. In Limerick, Clare and Kerry many families are surviving on one meal of bad food a day. He describes a meeting of several thousand labourers in his County Limerick constituency. With the help of the Catholic clergy, 'who on all occasions exerted themselves for the preservation of the peace', the people were persuaded to disband without any attack on property.

In reply, the Home Secretary, Sir James Graham, says no official account has yet been received of any death from destitution.

Perhaps he is not aware of the letter which the Relief Commissioners in Dublin received from John Smith, of Clifden, on March 23rd. Smith said it was his 'melancholy task to relate that the first victim that has fallen a sacrafice [sic] for want is the father of five children – and probably some of them and his wife may follow. The government are awfully responsible . . . '

The Home Secretary claims the government – unlike O'Brien's fellow landlords – is doing its utmost. An Irish parliament could not have dealt with the crisis more generously than the British parliament has done.

Mrs Smith, the Scottish diarist living in Wicklow, records that as yet O'Brien is only laughed at. 'Legislate for Ireland, a nation of lunatics. Reason with Irishmen! Everyone of them stark staring mad from the peer to the peasant.'[32]

Exports deplored

A commissariat officer considers four million people will have to be fed during May, June and July before the new potatoes are fit to eat. General Edward Pine Coffin, stationed in Limerick, urges the British government to buy and store the grain which is being exported. He considers it inconsistent to be importing supplies of Indian corn 'into a country which is at the same time exporting its own resources'.

The Relief Commission intends to hold onto its meagre supply of Indian meal until the summer – leaving the poor at the mercy of speculators.

It is quite impossible for the government to support half the population of Ireland, Sir Robert Peel tells the House of Commons. People in 'the wilds of Galway or Donegal or Mayo' must look to their landlords.

The majority of resident landlords are contributing benevolently, according to Smith O'Brien. Appealing to the government to act generously, he estimates that spending £500,000 on public works would be a more realistic grant than the £50,000 allotted.

O'Brien remarks: 'The circumstance which appeared most aggravating was that the people were starving in the midst of plenty, and that every tide carried from the Irish ports corn sufficient for the maintenance of thousands of the Irish people.'

In no part of Ireland has the potato failure caused so much distress as in his native County Clare. Clarecastle is described as the most hungry village in the county.

A boat laden with flour and Indian meal is plundered on the River Fergus by fourteen armed men. Richard Russell recovers fifty-one bags of flour, belonging to his father, hidden near the Hurlers' Cross on the Limerick-Ennis road.

Outside Clonmel, four or five thousand of the unemployed and destitute poor attack Mrs Shanahan's mill in Marlfield and carry off several sacks of flour. The military is called out to protect property. As the soldiers march through Clonmel, with mounted artillery, they are passed by at least 250 carts laden with flour for export (the property mainly of Messrs Grubb and Sargent) coming from Cahir, under a heavy escort of cavalry and infantry. The *Limerick Reporter* observes that Clonmel appeared as if under siege. The crowd disperses before the army reaches Marlfield.

In Tipperary town, the police act with forbearance while a dray laden with flour is seized by hungry people.

Another commissariat officer writes to Trevelyan: 'The barges leave Clonmel once a week [for Waterford], with the export supplies under convoy which, last Tuesday, consisted of two guns, fifty cavalry and eighty infantry escorting them on the banks of the Suir as far as Carrick.'

The Irish peasant sells his produce, even when his children are crying with hunger, to save them from eviction. To pay the rent is the first necessity of life in Ireland.[33]

Priests console people

4 MAY 1846

The people have only the clergy to console them, according to a Mayo priest.

Fr Patrick MacManus informs the Relief Commission that typhus fever, diarrhoea and dysentery are rife in Kilgeever. 'There is but one resident gentleman in this parish – Mr James Garvey, of Tully; there are no magistrates, none but the clergy to convey the wants of the people.' Nevertheless, a relief committee has been formed: 'We seek not alms, we solicit employment. But, whatever the mode of relief be, we again repeat our hope that the people will not be allowed to starve.'

Clergymen report destitution in Leitrim and the midlands. George Shaw writes from Annaduff Rectory, Drumsna: 'The parish of Annaduff consists of nearly 10,000 acres and has more than 6,000 inhabitants; and there is not a single resident landed proprietor to assist, by his presence and personal co-operation, in any benevolent undertaking.'

Mr Shaw points out that the potato crop has failed for several seasons in his parish, and impoverished the small farmers and labourers even before the present crisis. 'It is lamentable to see the crowds of able and willing labourers standing idle for want of someone to hire them. Potatoes can scarcely be had at any price.'

Fr D. Flanagan says there are upwards of 4,000 people in the Robertstown-Rathangan-Edenderry-Carbury region: 'living many of them in miserable sod hovels and endeavouring to exist on a few scanty meals of extremely bad potatoes. There is no employment – no gentry to alleviate distress or sympathise with them.'

In the patient neighbourhood of Robertstown, 'I see more immediately than many the wants of the people. My duties call me frequently amongst them. I witness therefore their distress and feel it keenly . . . '

From County Limerick, Fr James Walsh reports that 2,300 people are in need in the parishes of Kilready, Emlygrennan and Ahenessy, but local farmers have raised £165 to buy meal by taxing themselves one shilling an acre.

The Rev C.B. Gibson says nearly half the 7,000 people of Mallow, County Cork, are utterly destitute. The secretary of the Cobh relief committee requests help for 2,500 people surviving on one meal a day.

In County Wicklow the diarist, Elizabeth Smith, and her husband visit an elderly couple maintained by their son, who earns sixpence a day. His landlord keeps 'the idle blackguard out of charity'. Mrs Smith comments: 'Idle, who could be busy, underfed, under-clothed, under-housed, crushed body and soul by the extreme poverty.'

She adds: 'Mrs Kearns, a farmer's wife, brought us instead of their rent the most earnest supplication for food for the support of her family. She has one day's provision in the house.'[34]

Destitution widespread

11 MAY 1846

In Clonoulty, County Tipperary, Fr Thomas O'Carroll, spends two hours in his chapel distributing Indian meal to the poor.

A special reporter of the *Freeman's Journal* writes from County Clare that the means of the people are nearly exhausted, 'and they are in the utmost consternation at the prospect of utter destitution facing them full in the face'.

In the village of Doonass he found the parish priest, Fr McMahon, a curate and two gentlemen dispensing meal. 'There were the representatives of at least 1,000 human beings collected about the place, all eager to get their bags filled with meal, in order to carry it off to their famishing children and families. Would that some landlords and legislators had witnessed the scene. The faithful clergy assisting their flocks in the trying hour of need, whilst the landlords, who are morally bound to take care of the persons from whom they derive their incomes, remain in listless apathy and leave the people to their fate.

'There are in the parish of Doonass over 250 families utterly destitute of food or the means of procuring it, and were it not for the exertions of the Catholic clergy these unhappy people would at the present moment be without even the scanty allowance which is afforded them. I cannot omit mentioning a gratifying fact, namely, the Rev Mr Allen, a Protestant clergyman, has been most active in this parish in assisting the Rev Mr McMahon and his curates . . .

'I have never witnessed anything like the scene presented at Doonass: the creatures crowded round the windows of the house – the doors had to be closed; it was pitiable to hear the implorings of the mothers and daughters beseeching the reverend gentlemen to let them go at once as their children, fathers, or families were waiting for food.'

From Petworth in Sussex, George Wyndham writes to Dublin Castle defending the removal of seventy-seven families from his property in County Clare. No person was evicted without the offer of being sent to Canada at his expense. 'This offer was made from a desire that neither the neighbouring landlords nor the country should be encumbered by them.'

According to his information, there is no scarcity of provisions in Ireland: 'The cry is said to have been got up for political purposes.'

Thomas Brereton, resident magistrate, reports that in Lorrha and Durra in County Tipperary 300 men proceeded to several gentlemen's houses and demanded employment or food. They were led by Anthony Moylan, 'a great agitator' who has attended Repeal meetings all over the country.

They 'stated that they would take the cattle off the fields if their demands were not complied with. They carried a loaf of bread on a large pole . . . Their demeanour was quiet yet very determined.' Mr Brereton adds: 'I know there are several families in those parishes in distress.'[35]

Hunger in Belfast

18 MAY 1846

Hunger extends to Belfast. The Rev Mr Courtenay and Mr Francis Ritchie inform the Poor Law guardians 'that distress and destitution bordering on starvation exists in Ballymacarret electoral division'. Belfast workhouse can still provide accommodation.

Elias Thackeray, Vicar of Dundalk, speaks of the need to relieve the poor, not only from bodily want but from anxiety. On the authority of forty years' connection with the district, he identifies a road-building project as the best form of relief. The employment 'would remove from their anxious minds the uncertainty which now rests upon them [as to] how they are to support themselves and their families for the next three months.'

The vicar is a relation of William Makepeace Thackeray and, as a captain in the Cambridgeshire Militia, commanded the escort which brought Tone to Dublin after his capture in 1798.

Colonel Thomas Leigh Goldie reports deep animosity in County Clare between the peasantry and gentry, who are unwilling to subscribe to relief funds or join relief committees.

The secretary of Corofin relief committee, John Cullinan, writes that subscriptions are insufficient to give any adequate assistance. The privations of the poor cannot be exaggerated. They are consuming seed potatoes – a 'most calamitous' development. A depot to retail Indian meal at cost price is requested.

Patrick Hayden seeks aid to relieve the 'dreadful destitution' in Carrickbeg, County Waterford, which has over 3,000 inhabitants.

John French, Dean of Elphin, suspects meal and potatoes are being hoarded by gombeen men in Roscommon.

Great distress is reported from Templecrone, County Donegal, where the people seek the removal of Lord Conyngham's unsympathetic agent, Robert Russell.

In County Tipperary, Joseph Tabuteau, of Cashel, suggests reducing wages on the public works after complaints by farmers about difficulties in hiring labour.

Inspector J. Malone reports a 'food and labour march' on Borrisoleigh by 150 labourers from the mountains.

The Thurles guardians note 'that from the great destitution now prevalent through this entire union, caused from want of employment and food, great fears are entertained of a popular outbreak'.

Famine is already at our doors, according to the Earl of Mountcashel, in a letter to the Relief Commissioners marked urgent. He writes from Kilworth, County Cork, that the people have already borne privations with 'laudable patience, but when many are reduced to three meals in the week, and their children go crying for hunger to bed, it becomes necessary to seek for prompt relief'.

The poverty of Cape Clear Island with a population of 1,300 is likely to be great, Fr Edward Spring warns; 200 are already destitute.[36]

Food depots open

25 MAY 1846

The government Indian corn goes on sale in food depots. At 1d a pound, it is by far the cheapest food available and the depots are besieged. But Whitehall intends to restrict Irish relief to the corn purchased on the orders of Sir Robert Peel. It is to be sold to the people in a once-off operation. Indignant relief committees are told that the aim of the depots is to control the price of food; 'they are not intended to feed the whole population and are not adequate to do so'.

The *Galway Vindicator* reports starvation in the city. At the insistence of Fr Peter Daly, a woman near her confinement is called before the local relief committee. She and her husband have not eaten for two days, and he is now 'ill through starvation'.

Fr Daly declares that if it was an isolated case, while he had a coat on his back, he would allow no fellow creature to perish with hunger. But hundreds of his parishioners are in the same condition and he has no means of helping them. A quarter of the population of 45,000 is dependent on public charity.

The parish priest of Graiguenamanagh, County Kilkenny, Martin Doyle, reports that farmers are not sowing their usual amount of potatoes. 'The poor, who heretofore made efforts to sow a little, seem now indifferent altogether.'

The *Morning Chronicle* has sent a special reporter to County Clare, who writes: 'I cannot tell you how melancholy a sight it was to me, in walking and riding through the county, to see a band of thirty or forty people appear in sight; young men, young women and children, with probably two or three carts containing a few articles of bedding, furniture, etc. The men for the most part just rising into manhood – active, clean-limbed young fellows, with every mark of intelligence and energy in their features.'

They are on their way to the US, via Canada. It is difficult to conceive the force of the bonds which the peasant snaps asunder when he makes up his mind to quit the village of his forefathers. Existence and hard labour are all he expects in North America.

The *Sligo Champion* observes that it is not the destitute who are swelling the tide of emigration but 'the better classes of the peasantry', who have given up their farms while they have the money to enable them to emigrate.

A meeting in Downpatrick, County Down, is told that a number of the poor are starving; £270 is subscribed to a local relief fund.

William Smith O'Brien, who has raised the cry of 'ourselves alone', is imprisoned for refusing to serve on a House of Commons committee. He is in jail, the *Nation* comments, 'for asserting the right of his country's representatives to be representatives of their country; he is in jail for declining to attend to England's business, while Ireland's business is cobbled, patched, botched by Englishmen'. [37]

Board already overwhelmed

1 JUNE 1846

The Board of Works, hopelessly under-staffed and deluged by applications, is already overwhelmed. While the Treasury has allotted £50,000, applications for works to cost £800,000 have been received.

The authority which Charles Trevelyan exercised over the distribution of food for relief, through the Commissariat, is now applied to the administration of public works; item by item, Irish relief plans come under Treasury scrutiny. Furthermore, public works are to be 'of such a nature as will not benefit individuals in a greater degree than the rest of the community and therefore are not likely to be called for from any motive but the professed one of giving employment.' It sounds like a road leading to nowhere. Commissary General Routh observes: 'Something more direct, more immediate is necessary.'

Ireland experiences a kind of famine each year between the old and new crops. The height of the season of 'normal distress', greatly intensified by the potato failure, is approaching. In many parts of the country holdings are left uncultivated as crowds flock to relief committees eager for paid employment. Larger numbers than can be employed force themselves on to the public works.

The *Cork Reporter* finds the street where the relief committee meets impassable. Bands of half-clothed, half-famished men walk up and down, 'silently appealing to public commiseration' and kept at bay by the police. Their haggard looks give no idea of privations suffered secretly in lanes and garrets. But the poor tenement-dwellers are comforted by the Society of St Vincent de Paul.

The relief committee of Clonrush, County Galway, has obtained £65 from the Lord Lieutenant. The committee says there are no resident gentry in the area but myriads of squatters, 'the refuse and evicted tenantry of other districts. There are 236 families, amounting to 1,307 individuals, totally unemployed, without provisions and therefore daily becoming victims of famine.'

In County Wicklow, Elizabeth Smith and a large party picnic on the top of Blackmore Hill – where rebels camped in '98. 'One of the pleasantest sights of the day was our group of attendants over the fragments – men who never taste meat twice in a year truly enjoying what we had left of our luxuries; the saddest was . . . a little ragged frightened boy, who had collected on a stone the shakings out of the table cloth, and who was piling up crusts of bread with one hand and holding bare bones to his mouth with the other – the impersonation of famine.'

Fr O'Carroll, of Clonoulty, County Tipperary, notes in his diary that 'the crops are very promising and people are beginning to feel less apprehensive with respect to the anticipated failure of the potato crop this year too.'[38]

Much has been done

The *Freeman's Journal* acknowledges that much has been done to alleviate Irish misery. The exertions of local committees have gone far to stem the approaches of famine. The Treasury has, after innumerable delays, advanced nearly £134,000, thus permitting public works to start in many districts. Railway projects have been sanctioned.

In ordinary times the people would be comparatively prosperous. 'In the present year all are insufficient to overcome the calamity with which the land is everywhere oppressed.'

Castlebar poor law guardians praise government action. 'Although there is a large supply of food in the country, still a great part of this is in the hands of parties who trade in usury; and had not steps been taken, by the introduction of maize and Indian corn, to keep the market price at a fair standard, the price of food would be entirely beyond the reach of the humble classes.'

The *Castlebar Telegraph* refers to the 'princely liberality' of George Henry Moore, of Moorehall, who is to spend £1,000 on useful public works. Mr Moore has also purchased £800 of oaten meal and is now distributing it to his peasantry; the only remuneration he requires is the improvement of their cottages.

In King's County, Head-constable Corcoran has compiled a list for Lord Rosse and the Cloghan relief committee showing that 1,100 people are bordering on starvation in the neighbourhood of Banagher. Nevertheless, Dr Daniel Vaughan, PP Killaloe and Bridgetown, County Clare, has arranged for the purchase of 100 tons of seed potatoes in Banagher.

Fever and scarlatina are rampant in Tullamore, where a workhouse fever ward has been opened.

In Nenagh, the relief committee lacks funds and the workhouse is nearly full.

While Sir Randolph Routh describes the official corn imports as 'almost only a mouthful', Deputy Commissary-general Hewetson informs Trevelyan: 'I am assured that in all the localities where our meal is in use, the general health of the people has wonderfully improved . . . The mass of the peasantry are really grateful to the government for their timely inter-position.'

John Smith, of Clifden, Co Galway, reports heart-rending scenes when Indian meal is being sold at the coastguard station. His account is corroborated by the chief coastguard officer, who says people travel ten miles expecting to get a portion free of charge, 'but which I could not give – not being armed with authority'.

In the Burren region, destitution has increased due to the number of people squatting on commonages; sixty-one families are reported to be in 'a very wretched state' on Kilnaboy Common. The Corofin relief committee has collected £206–13–6; subscribers include: Marquis of Conyngham (£15), Dowager Lady O'Brien (£10) and Patrick Cahir, tenant farmer (£5).[39]

Starvation victim

15 JUNE 1846

In west Waterford a man dies of starvation surrounded by his seven children crying for food. Two men give 2s 6d each to buy a coffin for Mr Fitzgerald. The *Waterford Freeman* asks: 'How long will the noblest of God's creatures, honest men, be doomed to want food and to famish in the midst of plenty in their own nature-blessed, but misruled country?'

The *Freeman's Journal* comments: 'As we penetrate the summer the diminishing resources of the country become too apparent, and the sharp cry of distress rings harshly and imploringly on the ear. We read of death by starvation in Dungarvan . . . of distress spreading to a frightful extent in Mayo and Kilkenny – so intense and sudden in the latter county that the farmers generously, and on the spot, contributed £30, and the landlords – nothing.'

Thousands are seeking employment on the public works. The rector of Killeshandra, County Cavan, complains to the Relief Commissioners that the works tickets sent to him excluded the poorest labourers.

In Kilkee, County Clare, the rector deplores the arbitrary power of gangers. The Rev James Martin encloses a petition from a labourer, James Carrig. The petitioner was dismissed apparently because he worked one day for a man who 'gave him a basket of black potatoes for his little children . . . Then when petr. was murmuring for having him dismissed, Sullivan [the overseer] desired him to go to the priest and that if he gave him a ticket he would take him in the work, which petr. did obtain from the priest and got one day's work afterwards. Your petr. having pawned his coat for which he only got 2s to buy provisions for his family. And that himself and them are living these three days back on one meal a day. Your petr. is surprised that any committee would allow this imposter Sullivan to go on in this manner when they have a power to discontinue such infernal practice.'

In County Cavan, on the fair day of Kilnaleck, a notice is posted on trees warning against buying potatoes and taking them to County Meath. The inspector of police suggests that a few printed notices be circulated cautioning the public not to interfere in regulating the market rates.

Captain Gordon reports that large quantities of potatoes are in the possession of landed proprietors and extensive farmers in County Meath, but they are sent mostly to the Dublin market. The poor cannot plant much potatoes because they have only half the supply of last year. Moreover, 'the conacre system is given up this year by landlords, so that no ground can be procured by those poor that have seed, because the landlord is afraid that the crop may again fail.' What will be the fate of those who are just able to struggle through the present distress?[40]

Martins bankrupt

22 JUNE 1846

The 'King of Connemara' fails to help his subjects. John Smith, of Celerna, Clifden, informs the Relief Commission that the principal landowner of the region, Thomas Barnewall Martin, MP, has refused to subscribe to the relief fund.

The Famine is tearing away the veil of romance surrounding the patriarchal Martins, who are bankrupt after generations of high living and the collapse of agricultural prices in the post-Napoleonic era.

Their estate comprises 196,540 acres. Thomas Martin, a son of 'Humanity Dick', was called the King of Connemara in the days when visitors to Ballynahinch Castle included Maria Edgeworth and Thackeray.

The secretary of the Clifden relief committee says 'many families are now bordering on starvation reduced to one meal in the twenty-four hours, and even this procured with difficulty and only by resorting to the pawn office'. There is a sufficient supply of food in the district but the poor have not the means to purchase it.

Fr Roche, CC Clifden, states that he attended a sick woman (Widow Byrne) who has since died. It can be proved on oath that she died of starvation.

Sir James Dombrain, Inspector General of the Coast Guard, reports crisis conditions along the coast of Galway and Mayo. He disputes the assertion of Sir Randolph Routh, chairman of the Relief Commission, that the food scarcity is part of the annual cycle of distress along the western seaboard.

Constabulary Sub-inspector John Bindon Corbet, Ballinrobe, reports an attempt by a group of 'distressed paupers' to gain access to public works.

Indian meal to feed 12,000 daily is required by Killarney relief committee. Killorglin relief committee appeals for assistance to prevent mass starvation.

The number employed on roads by the Office of Public Works has soared to 127,000. Projects are underway in fifteen counties, but by far the greatest concentration of labourers – 47,972 – are at work in Clare, where irregularities are reported in their payment; 150 men force themselves on to relief works in Ballyvaughan.

Colonel Harry Jones, OPW commissioner, complains that the surveyor of the Shannon works at Drumsna, County Leitrim, could get only 150 of the 1,200 labourers required because relief committees are issuing work tickets indiscriminately and encouraging sloth.

The Mayo county surveyor, Henry Brett, complains that Hollymount relief committee has approved 670 labourers to work on the Ballyglass mail coach road instead of the 300 agreed.

Colonel Arthur Knox Gore, of Belleek Manor, Ballina, says he cannot answer for the consequences if relief works are not provided for the destitute poor between Newport and Achill Island.[41]

People 'rescued'

Deputy Commissary-general Edward Pine Coffin writes that the country people declare they have 'been rescued from a state of frightful misery, or, to use their own strong but common expression, that "only for the government meal, thousands would have been now dying by the roadside".'

In Wicklow town, Perrin and Nolan, millers, threaten to cease importing corn if the rumoured reduction of government meal to uncompetitive prices proves true.

Peel repeals the corns laws – virtually abolishing duties on imported grain. The laws had kept bread prices needlessly high by excluding cheaper foreign corn, chiefly for the benefit of the landed gentry. This reform will make little difference in the west of Ireland, where, as Trevelyan has remarked, bread is scarcely ever eaten by the poor.

Patrick Harley, PP Aran Islands, reports the reappearance of blight in the new potato crop. On the mainland, 500 families go hungry in Spiddal.

Captain S.R. Pole, Banagher depot, reports that an attempted march on Banagher by 800 men in search of food and employment was dispersed by Father Walsh, PP Lusmagh.

In County Westmeath, hard-pressed labourers are falling into the clutches of usurers known locally as 'mealmongers'. James O'Reilly, Moygoish, says twenty families are starving, with 100 facing starvation.

In Sixmilebridge, County Clare, Mr McMahon deplores the rejection of his application for a post on the public works and the appointment of a schoolmaster named Hamilton, who has 'debauched' McMahon's daughter.

The *Ballyshannon Herald* reports on a procession by mainly women and children through the Donegal town, 'preceded by a wretched looking creature carrying a long pole, from the top of which was suspended a loaf of bread'. They halt occasionally and the leader explains the loaf symbolises that, although there is plenty of food in the country, it is beyond the reach of the poor because of its price and their lack of employment.

He proposes three cheers for 'several persons' who are reserving their potatoes for the use of the town and three groans for those who continue exporting to Liverpool. The procession proceeds next to the workhouse, where the destitute are told they cannot be admitted without a recommendation. It is feared that the vessel being loaded with potatoes will be attacked. Police are constantly on deck.

In County Antrim, the Ballymacarret relief committee has employed 200 families to break stones for seven weeks, and is providing them with Indian meal, soup and bread in lieu of wages.

In Killeagh, County Cork, one-third of the population of 10,000 is 'without food', the rector and parish priest assert in a joint appeal.[42]

Russell becomes premier

6 JULY 1846

Lord John Russell becomes Whig prime minister. Charles Trevelyan writes to Sir Randolph Routh, of the Relief Commission: 'I think we shall have much reason to be satisfied with our new masters.' The Chancellor of the Exchequer, Charles Wood, is a firm believer in *laissez-faire*. Routh comments: 'You cannot answer the cry of want by a quotation from political economy.'

In Cong, landlords cannot provide relief because their properties are in the hands of creditors. The parish priest, Michael Waldron, says the poor are eating their winter cabbage to survive. He appeals for public works on behalf of 'a most peaceable people'.

Fr Michael McDermott writes from Strokestown, County Roscommon: 'I cannot describe the alarm which is felt in this town in consequence of the high price to which provisions have risen this day. The people wear a sullen aspect and are giving expression to their discontent in a very menacing tone. Nothing is heard in the market but threats and murmurs. Potatoes – lumpers – are four shillings per hundred[weight] – oatmeal 17 shillings. In this state of things there is no employment nor relief fund. So in the name of God do something for us . . . '

In an initialled note, Routh asks: 'Why is there no committee in this town, and why is there no subscription even of shillings and sixpences or of some collection at church? Something to prove the disposition of the people to make an effort in their own behalf, to which the government will so readily contribute.' There are depots in Carrick-on-Shannon, Roscommon and Longford, where Indian corn meal can be procured at £10 a ton.

The chairman of the local relief committee is Major Denis Mahon, of Strokestown House.

Fr Patrick O'Gorman, PP Clarecastle, says the villagers of Clareabbey and Killone are starving because of bureaucratic delays to public works.

In Roundstone, County Galway, two supplies of Indian meal are exhausted. A meeting chaired by Dr Kiernan reflects anxiously on 'the display of destitution and apparent starvation exhibited on the two last days' sale of the Indian corn meal; the desperate energy with which the unfortunate poor exerted themselves to obtain a supply and when they were told that all was sold, the mixed emotions of gloom, silence and noisy clamour with which they retired to their cheerless homes, without food to eat, altho' they pawned their clothing and sold their little livestock to purchase this Indian meal.'

The meeting concludes there is no likelihood of obtaining subscriptions in Roundstone because of its remoteness 'and the very few persons of respectability [property] residing in it'. Considering the destitution of the people, an application should be made to the government to reduce the price of meal to a minimum and distribute it free of charge to the 'extreme poor'.[43]

More food imported

13 JULY 1846

The supplies of Indian corn are beginning to run low. As July is expected to be the month of most distress, the government purchases a further supply. An additional 3,000 tons, believed to be inferior to the American corn, is bought from Mediterranean countries. Trevelyan warns Routh the government will not purchase a third quantity.

Even though the Relief Commission recommends that the food depots should remain open until September 1st, the new Whig government decides to close them on August 15th – leaving Ireland to the mercy of market forces.

Trevelyan believes 'the only way to prevent the people from becoming habitually dependent on government is to bring the operations to a close. The uncertainty about the new crop only makes it more necessary . . .

Whatever may be done hereafter, these things should be stopped now, or you run the risk of paralysing all private enterprise and having this country on you for an indefinite number of years. The Chancellor of the Exchequer supports this strongly.'

In the meantime, the Relief Commission continues to top up local funds. For instance, when Major Denis Mahon informs Dublin Castle that Strokestown relief committee has collected £85 – £20 contributed by himself – Routh recommends a grant of £60.

In the barony of Carra, County Mayo, 226 families out of 900 are in want.

The Rev William McClelland, secretary of Tisrara and Dysart relief committee, says something must be done or the people in this part of County Roscommon will starve. He complains about lack of co-operation from the landlords and the Catholic clergy.

Some landlords are extremely reluctant to assist. Mr McClelland has addressed a third letter to each of them. 'Should my third appeal prove ineffectual, I shall by the beginning of next week report the names of such as I find it impossible to move in this charitable business.'

There is only £15 in the local relief fund. Mr McClelland concludes: 'Had the priest of Dysart announced from the altar that subscriptions would be received by a person I had nominated as my treasurer hard by the chapel, the £15 would now be £30. But neither priest nor people in Dysart have co-operated with me and they are likely to suffer for it.'

Nor is the hunger confined to the west. Fr John Aylward writes from near Castlecomer, County Kilkenny, that 3,000 are destitute in Fassadinin. 'Many families without an inch of land, without work, without food and at this moment staggering thro the streets with hunger. As we have no gentry in this very poor district, I hope the government will take into their humane consideration the very sad condition of my poor people. This parish abounds with the meanest and most filthy cabins in any part of Ireland – beds without covering and the backs of the poor people almost as bare.'[44]

New crop fails

Sir Randolph Routh, who is receiving daily reports from throughout the country, informs Charles Trevelyan: 'Disease is reappearing.' He adds: 'The reports of the new potato crop are very unfavourable. All letters and sources of information declare disease to be more prevalent this year than last in the early crop.'

Fr James O'Driscoll, secretary of the Kilmichael (County Cork) relief committee, applies to use a government grant to provide Indian corn at a reduced price or gratuitously to the destitute, who have pawned clothing and bedding and are subsisting on cabbage.

In Clare, the Corofin relief committee has been selling Indian meal to the poor at a reduced price since April. John Cullinan, secretary, recording that 142 tons of meal have been sold at a loss of £500, requests a grant to feed 40,000 dependants in the seven parishes of the barony.

The parish priest of Ahascragh, County Galway, having failed to persuade the local gentry to form a relief committee, observes that many would have starved but for the Calcutta Fund.

Public anger is reported from Kinvara, where landowners are demanding compensation for public works on their properties. Charles Lynch, of Clonbur, reports two deaths from starvation.

Ballingarry (County Limerick) relief committee encloses two threatening notices from 'Captain Starlight', ordering farmers to provide employment. In Kilfinane, a pay clerk is robbed of labourers' wages.

The parish priest of Firodah, County Kilkenny, reports that several of his parishioners are living on weeds.

In Foxford, County Mayo, the peasantry are subsisting on one meal of oatmeal a day, having sold their belongings or borrowed from usurers at 20–50 per cent interest. They are reluctant to enter the workhouse after the death of some inmates.

Fr Thomas O'Connor, secretary of the Frenchpark relief committee, reports that the new potato crop has failed; a large proportion of the baronial population of 28,859 is surviving on one meal a day.

The Castlerea relief committee records 'abject distress' in the town, where the distillery has closed. The entire population of the townland of Arou, 1,116 souls, are reduced to pauperism.

The Ballaghaderreen relief committee, having received £54 in subscriptions, sends for three tons of Indian meal. It points out that the population of the town is nearly 1,500: 'many of whom are unable to work and are completely destitute – no credit being now given in the country as was heretofore the custom, those poor persons who depended on it in other years and have no means of obtaining provisions are in a deplorable state . . . '

The committee urgently requests a grant. Dublin Castle replies asking for a subscription list with a certificate of bank lodgement.[45]

'Fearful destitution'

27 JULY 1846

Police report the reappearance of potato blight in Counties Down, Monaghan, Derry, Donegal, Longford, Kildare and Sligo.

In King's County, two-thirds of the crop is affected by advancing disease; 100 unemployed labourers are in a 'most pitiable condition' in Banagher.

In Castlemartyr, County Cork, the blight has 'manifested itself to an alarming extent in the early potato crop'.

Help is sought for 4,000 destitute families in Clifden, many of whom are ill after eating eighteen sacks of rotten meal.

The secretary of the Ballyhea relief committee, Fr Richard Ryan, warns the Relief Commission 'for the last time' that the people are starving. Two mass meetings have been dispersed by a justice of the peace and the parish priest with promises of employment.

Also from County Cork, Carrignavar relief committee reports the discharge of 138 labourers after the landlord, Mr Roche, failed to contribute £20 as promised.

From County Mayo, the parish priest of Clare Island and Innisturk, Peter Ward, writes that unless immediate relief is provided 200 families will fall victims of starvation. He grieves to say that the landlords, Lord Lucan and Sir Samuel O'Malley, 'are disposed to let the people die without the least desire to subscribe one farthing'.

'Fearful destitution' prevails in the parishes of Lisronagh and Donaghmore in County Tipperary. The landlords are all non-resident, the Rev Robert Carey – rector and chairman of the local relief committee – informs the Relief Commission. 'About six weeks since I addressed to each a printed circular, one third of whom at once most generously responded to the call, by taking upon themselves the relief of the destitute on their respective properties. The remaining two-thirds have either taken no notice of the application or have replied to the effect that it was not in their power to assist us.'

Mr Carey names the landed proprietors who have ignored two appeals for famine aid. They include Lord Clonmell.

Two priests and twenty-nine parishioners of Cloonoghill, Kilturra and Kilshalvy, County Sligo, 'most respectfully' inform the commissioners of the extreme destitution of many of the poorer classes in the district, where there are no resident landlords and no public works. 'From our want of means we fear that any subscriptions we may be able to collect will appear so trifling in your eyes as scarcely to justify our demand of relief which we are however most urgently compelled to make.'

Dublin Castle preaches self-reliance: 'State that aid can only be recommended as an auxiliary to local funds, but that if a list of subscriptions be forwarded, however small, with a certificate of lodgement, a grant in aid will be recommended.'

In the meantime, the poor must go hungry.[46]

Young Ireland secession

3 AUGUST 1846

O'Connell and Young Ireland split

The Young Irelanders leave the Repeal Association, led by William Smith O'Brien. O'Connell's 'peace resolutions' are the means of either whipping his young critics into line, or getting rid of them. He insists that a pledge repudiating the use of physical force in all circumstances be adopted by every member of the association.

The great political debate in nationalist circles is not about the Famine, but what direction the Repeal movement should take. The Liberator is intent on a new Whig alliance. Although no one is seriously contemplating force at this time, the peace resolutions are unacceptable to Young Ireland.

Fr Thomas O'Carroll's diary reflects the controversy. At a dinner in Cashel attended by twenty-nine clergymen and the archbishop, 'champagne and claret were passed about rather freely. Many of the clergy with whom I conversed appeared very sanguine about a meeting which they are to hold in Cashel on Thursday next, the object of which is to record a vote of undiminished confidence in O'Connell and declare their abhorrence of the physical force doctrine of the Young Ireland heresy.

'Though I concur in the objects of the meeting, still I do not purpose attending it or contributing a pound, as I am disposed to think that the resolutions about to be adopted will imply a censure on the conduct of Smith O'Brien and only tend to widen the unhappy differences that are at present distracting the councils [sic] of the popular party.

'Besides I consider the manner and conduct of John O'Connell [a son of the Liberator] during last Monday's and Tuesday's debates in the Conciliation Hall extremely dictatorial and overbearing. Should I go to Cashel entertaining these views and perhaps provoked to give expression to them, I would be put down as a black sheep and persecuted as such – merely because I dared to dissent . . .'

The relief committees have collected £98,000 – to which the British administration has added almost £66,000.

A coastguard inspector intended going to Achill with Indian meal for sale, until he learned that those most in need are too poor to purchase it.

John Manseragh, secretary of Tipperary town relief committee, says labourers are living on one meal of Indian corn a day.

W.B. Cooke, of 'Repeal Villa', Oulart, County Wexford, accuses the Relief Commission of humbugging the 'Paddies'. He prays: 'From the insolence and ignorance of foreign legislators, alien commissioners and domestic cutthroats, good Lord deliver us.'

Sir Randolph Routh instructs his officials not to answer this letter.[47]

Crop wiped out

Almost overnight the new potato crop is wiped out.

Fr Theobald Mathew, 'the Apostle of Temperance', writes flatteringly from Cork to Charles Trevelyan. He first thanks him for helping his orphan nephew, then continues:

'I am well aware of the deep solicitude you felt for our destitute people, and your arduous exertions to preserve them from the calamitous effects of the destruction of the potato crop last season. Complete success crowned your efforts. Famine would have desolated this unhappy country were it not for your wise precautions.

'Divine providence, in its inscrutable ways, has again poured out upon us the vial of its wrath. A blot more destructive than the simoom of the desert has passed over the land, and the hopes of the poor potato-cultivators are totally blighted, and the food of a whole nation has perished.

'On the 27th of last month I passed from Cork to Dublin and this doomed plant bloomed in all the luxuriance of an abundant harvest. Returning on the 3rd instant I beheld, with sorrow, one wide waste of putrefying vegetation. In many cases the wretched people were seated on the fences of their decaying gardens, wringing their hands and wailing bitterly the destruction that had left them foodless.

'It is not to harrow your benevolent feelings, dear Mr Trevelyan, I tell this tale of woe. No, but to excite your sympathy on behalf of our miserable peasantry. It is rumoured that the capitalists in the corn and flour trade are endeavouring to induce government not to protect the people from famine, but to leave them at their mercy. I consider this a cruel and unjustifiable interference.

'The gentlemen of the trade have nothing to do with Indian corn; it is, I may say, a creation of the government, a new article of food, wisely introduced for the preservation and amelioration of the people of Ireland. Insidious efforts were even made to prejudice the people against this new food. Thank God they were in vain, and it is now a favourite diet; and 10,000 blessings are hourly invoked on the heads of the benefactors who saved the miserable from perishing.'

But Trevelyan, supported by the Whig political economists, persists in his policy of non-intervention.

Sir James Dombrain, of the Coastguard Service, reports that, in a tour of 800 miles during the first week in August, 'all is lost and gone'; the stench from rotting potatoes is 'perceptible as you travel along the road'; in Cork the stench is 'intolerable'.

Colonel Knox Gore, lieutenant of County Sligo, finds 'from Mullingar to Maynooth every field was black'. A steward of the Ventry estates writes that 'the fields in Kerry look as if fire had passed over them'. The blight is reported to be universal in Ulster, and in Longford, Galway, King's County, Westmeath and Dublin.[48]

Relief operation ends

17 AUGUST 1846

With the poor at the end of their resources, the operations of the Relief Commission are wound up.

The *Nation* comments: 'This day ends the commission of one set of government Relief Commissioners. Today they close their office, balance their books and retire from their labours. The distress arising from last year's deficient potato crop is passed by: the state alms-givers shut their doors; because it is the 15th of August, and the new crop ought to be crowned with abundance.

'And on this very day a cry of Famine, wilder and more fearful than ever, is rising from every parish and county in the land. Where the new crop ought to be, there is a loathsome mass of putrefaction: the sole food on which millions of men, women and children are to be fed, is stricken by a deadly blight before their eyes; and probably within one month those millions will be hungry and have nothing to eat.

'Yes, there have been, by this time, accounts received from every county in Ireland; and they all concur in representing the blight as being, even at this early period of the season, almost universal; for one family which needed relief during the past season there will now be three. Last year government had to bethink themselves how to provide against a very general deficiency – this year they will have to consider how a starving nation is to be fed.'

Whatever machinery of public alms-giving there is must not only be continued in operation, but have its powers and means increased, says the *Nation*; 'and it will be well, indeed, if with all possible efforts and furtherances in this direction, they may be enabled to stay the advancing Plague and rob Death of his prey.'

British officials, on the other hand, consider that last year's aid programme should foster better relations between the two countries.

Sir Randolph Routh avers: 'A practical relief of this description, distributed to a nation in small issues, to reach the poorest families, is an event of rare occurrence, even in history . . . a deep feeling of gratitude has risen up in return for the paternal care of her majesty's government.'

Sir Edward Pine Coffin writes that 'an arduous task is ended, at least for the present occasion, and it now only remains to make some kind of disposal of our large residue, and close the accounts.' He hopes to depart for England before the end of next month.

However, 'the gratification which I have felt at the successful conclusion of this new and difficult duty is more than counterbalanced by the gloomy anticipation of the coming season. The prospect of the present potato crop is so uniformly bad, that I can scarcely enter into any details on the subject.'[49]

Harshness 'greatest humanity'

24 AUGUST 1846

The new Whig government believes the Irish people need to be taught a lesson in self-reliance. 'There are times when something like harshness is the greatest humanity,' echoes the London *Times*. In Ireland many relief committees deplore the decision to close the food depots at a time of unprecedented distress.

But the Whig ideologues consider a dangerous precedent was set last year: Sir Robert Peel's relief measures created an expectation that the government would again supply food. Lord John Russell has no intention of allowing his government to repeat the experiment. He states: 'It must be thoroughly understood that we cannot feed the people. It was a cruel delusion to pretend to do so.' Repeated state intervention would not only paralyse private enterprise, but increase Irish dependence on Britain.

In the second year of the Famine, therefore, the Whigs compromise. They assure Irish merchants there will be no government interference in the import of food into the eastern part of the country. They will, however, intervene in the west – where there are fewer traders anyhow – if it proves to be absolutely necessary.

Responsibility for overseeing the distribution of food is placed in the hands of the Treasury, confirming the importance of Charles Trevelyan and the Chancellor, Sir Charles Wood. The depots, now confined to the west coast, are to be used only as a last resort. The sub-depots, superintended by the constabulary and coastguard last year, are not to be reopened as they had 'embarrassed the accounts considerably'. Central depots are to be controlled by the Commissariat Office under Sir Randolph Routh.

Furthermore, the influence of the view that the Irish crisis is providentially determined can scarcely be over-estimated. Wood, the man in charge of the purse strings, believes in a retributive yet beneficent providence: 'A want of food and employment is a calamity sent by providence'; 'except through a purgatory of misery and starvation, I cannot see how Ireland is to emerge into a state of anything approaching to quiet prosperity.'

Trevelyan agrees: 'Even in the most afflicting dispensations of providence, there was ground for consolation and often even occasion for congratulation.' To Wood, the government is the agent and not the initiator of these sanctions.

Providentialist thought requires that, ultimately, Ireland be left to the operation of 'natural causes'. While the Irish administration contains many earnest and conscientious men, their political masters in London will merely tinker with the food supply.

But for economists imbued with the ethos of evangelical Protestantism, the Famine is a God-given opportunity to transform Irish behaviour. They regard the potato as the root of all Irish evil: a 'lazy root', grown in 'lazy' beds by a 'lazy' people. To push the feckless Irish up the ladder of civilisation, the degenerate potato should be replaced by a higher food source like grain.[50]

Poor seek employment

The 'poor day labourers' of Templecarrig, Delgany, County Wicklow, seek work. Their memorial is presented to Dublin Castle by George Hudson, JP and member of the Bray relief committee.

Writing from the Kildare Street Club, Mr Hudson points out that he is the only resident gentleman in the Bray relief district no. 6. 'Instead of being assisted by those from whom I expected aid, I have been opposed in every possible way, and in many cases most vexatiously so, in endeavouring to get for the poor that employment which a paternal government seemed to wish they should get.'

He has taken on extra men and increased the wages of his labourers from six shillings a week to 7s., 7s.6d. and 8s., 'according to the number of their family'.

The proposed relief work would benefit the neighbourhood, and provide Mr Hudson with a safer road to drive from Templecarrig House into Bray.

In their submission, the labourers – William McDaniel has signed for those who cannot write – describe conditions. A few of the poorest families had been receiving a stone of Indian meal per week gratuitously from the Bray relief committee, which is now charging 10d. a stone. 'If it was not for the goodness of one or two gentlemen and the farmers in our neighbourhood, many of us must have perished.'

A number of landholders, headed by Peter La Touche, certify that this is a true statement.

Meanwhile, in County Roscommon, the tenants of Cloonahee, Elphin, petition Thomas Conroy, the hated agent of Denis Mahon: 'Our families are really and truly suffering and we cannot much longer withstand their cries for food. We have no food for them, our potatoes are rotten and we have no grain.'

Promised employment by Major Mahon, the tenants were turned away by a Board of Works supervisor so that relief works will not be completed too quickly.

They continue menacingly: 'Gentlemen, you know little of the state of the suffering poor . . . are we to resort to outrage? We fear that the peace of the country will be much disturbed if relief be not immediately, more extensively afforded to the suffering peasantry. We are not for joining in anything illegal or contrary to the laws of God or the land, unless pressed to it by HUNGER.'

A sub-inspector of constabulary writes from County Cork: 'A stranger would wonder how these wretched beings find food . . . Clothes being in pawn there is nothing to change. They sleep in their rags and have pawned their bedding.'

From St Mullins Lower, County Carlow – where prior to the temperance movement faction fights were a common occurrence – it is reported that 'there are 500 ablebodied men having nothing to do and, if not now, very soon to be without provision.'[51]

Works replace depots

7 SEPTEMBER 1846

Dublin Castle reorganises public works which are to replace food depots as the principal means of famine relief.

It lays down the terms on which relief work is to be given: 'No person to be employed on relief works who could obtain work elsewhere; wages to be 2d. less than that given in the district for other work; persons thus employed to be paid according to the amount of work they actually performed.'

Road-building is the preferred option, rather than bringing the vast stretches of unproductive bog into cultivation. The government fears that drainage schemes would benefit some landlords and not others.

But the worst feature of this form of relief is that hard physical labour requires a high-calorie diet, which is precisely what the famished workers lack. Moreover, in an effort to confine aid strictly to the destitute, stringent tests are imposed on applicants. As a result people are often so weak from hunger before qualifying that they are unfit for employment.

A healthy man can earn about a shilling a day on the roads, although few make more than 8d. Furthermore, market forces, now given free rein, are working inexorably against the poor; with no brakes on speculation, those few traders who have secured supplies of Indian meal can charge what they like for it.

The Rev William Crosthwaite, secretary of the Carrigbue relief committee, County Cork, asserts that, with the poor facing starvation, a refusal of the Office of Public Works to provide relief works on grounds of insufficient distress is unacceptable.

James Hamilton, Fintown, County Donegal, warning that gratuitous relief would demoralise the labouring classes, applies for a low-interest loan to improve his estates.

Complaints are received from Athleague, County Roscommon, about the waste of public works funds through the employment of the influential and well-off as stewards on high wages.

There is a rush for labour tickets. Major Mahon, deputy county lieutenant and secretary of Strokestown relief committee, requests 1,000 tickets.

Fr Felix MacHugh, Drumahair, Co Leitrim, says labourers on road works have not been paid for sixteen days.

Martin Joyce, Kilconnell, Co Galway, is dismissed after sustaining an eye injury while breaking stones on relief works.

The secretary of the Ballymoe relief committee reports seven deaths from typhus fever.

In Clifden, many walk up to ten miles in search of a day's work and return home in the evening, not having tasted food for eighteen hours. 'Can it be doubted then that famine exists?' a local doctor asks Dublin Castle.[52]

'Nation of jobbers'

14 SEPTEMBER 1846

In Clonoulty, County Tipperary, a curate tears down an 'inflammatory notice' posted on the chapel gate. It urged the people to assemble on the fairgreen to devise some means to keep themselves from starvation. Fr O'Carroll records in his diary that the constable was afraid to pull it down.

He speaks to two parishioners in the sacristy 'on the necessity of something being done immediately to mitigate the distress and inspire confidence, as the people are in a great ferment about food. It is much to be feared that outrages will take place.'

Fr O'Carroll considers, however, that the extent of the distress is being exaggerated at present. Some disorderly fellows, taking advantage of the alarm, are going about the country inciting the poor to seize the cattle of the gentry. But the potato crop is a total failure in all parts through which he has passed recently.

'In pursuance of the notice, about 200 persons tumultuously assembled today in the appointed place and it is difficult to say what amount of mischief might have resulted, had they been not dispersed by Mr Mackey [the parish priest]. Parties went from house to house last night requiring the labourers to attend the meeting today. It is well for those folk who take such a delight in calumniating the Catholic priesthood, that we still retain so much influence over the people – it is generally exerted for their protection.'

A fellow curate arrives late for dinner with a gun which he removed from a peasant engaged in target practice. 'It is really provoking to witness the efforts which the youth of this parish are making to possess firearms . . . It is quite a usual thing for servant men and paupers employed on the public works to club a portion of their earnings in order to purchase a gun. If this system be much longer tolerated, the young men of the country will be certainly demoralised and these arms will be converted to a very bad purpose. Many of these people are looking forward to an outbreak.'

On the other hand, Fr O'Carroll is disgusted with the conduct of some of the comfortable farmers. They were asked to provide the relief committee with information about the poor in their localities and furnish lists of families requiring employment on public works.

'Instead of co-operating to carry out this charitable object, they recommend none but their own friends and dependants, many of whom were admitted to have money funded in the saving banks, whilst others were known to possess corn and cattle.

'We Irish are essentially jobbers,' Fr O'Carroll declares. 'I was slow to believe that there were so much baseness and corruption in the Irish character, as I have seen manifested lately in the meetings of and the applications to our committee for employment on the public works.'[53]

Painful witness

A Mayo priest finds it difficult to witness the sufferings of his people. Fr Peter Conway, of Partry, regrets being unable to feed them.

Writing from Louisburgh, Fr Patrick MacManus estimates that a great number of the 12,000 population require employment. It is frivolous to exclude people on the verge of starvation from public works unless they have tickets.

A police report from Ferbane, King's County, asserts that, although generally considered troublesome, the labourers of the district appear grateful for all that has been done to provide employment and food for them.

Jonas Studdert, a west Clare proprietor, says want of money has already induced many to plunder the potato fields of their neighbours. Kilkee resort is crowded in summer but forsaken in winter. The poor who have flocked in from the surrounding countryside are now without food, employment or any support.

In Carrigeen, County Kilkenny, farmers contribute £45 to a relief fund compared with the landlords' £26.

The redoubtable John Smith, of Clifden, asks the authorities: 'Can I believe that you will allow thousands to starve from your negligence . . . We have daily men carried off the road from absolute starvation . . . How long is mismanagement to exist?'

Thomas Tully, a Poor Law guardian in the Loughrea union, complains about extortioners who are exacting from the poor a security to pay 50 per cent above the market price of food.

Ballyhogue relief committe, County Wexford, tells of poor families which brought waste land into cultivation but are destitute since the loss of the potato crop. 'Some families have no one to earn for them yet won't take Workhouse relief, fearing that when they get out they would not have land or cabin to go into.'

C.K. O'Hara, the principal landlord in his part of Sligo, has employed 350 men and spent £500 on meal during the last six months. His funds are exhausted and he cannot support the poor of other estates.

Fr John Golden writes from Kildorrery, County Cork: 'The district is generally wretchedly poor and very densely inhabited and with two exceptions, Mr Oliver and Mr Bowen, has no resident gentry. I feel the greatest alarm and uneasiness respecting the preservation of the peace if something is not immediately done for us.'

J.J. Heard, Justice of the Peace and chairman of Kinsale relief committee, warns that the people must starve or plunder unless they are employed. A meeting of labourers dispersed at his suggestion, 'but made no secret of their determination to help themselves if they were not enabled to procure food by their labour'.

There are disturbances in Youghal as a crowd attempts to hold up a ship laden with oats for export.[54]

'Develop agriculture'

28 SEPTEMBER 1846

A County Limerick landowner wants the poor to be employed developing agriculture, rather than on useless public works.

William Monsell, of Tervoe, Clarina, outlines his views in a letter to the Chief Secretary, Henry Labouchere. He estimates that for the next ten months work must be found for 500,000 men – mainly in the south and west – and this cannot be done for less than £5 million:

'Wherever it comes from, and however it is employed, this money must be spent; a vast number of those who will receive it never touch money from the beginning to the end of the year, except in the purchase and sale of their pigs; they barter and labour with the neighbouring farmer for potato land, and the produce of that being gone they have nothing . . .

'They have been year after year standing as it were with one foot hanging over the precipice; with starvation yawning beneath them. Into the fearful gulf they must fall if they do not get employment.'

Monsell predicts a series of years of distress. A large proportion of the money necessary for the support of the starving people during their transition from one sort of food to another must be raised from the land. The farmers are asking what they shall grow next year instead of potatoes.

The present relief measure requires the expenditure of vast sums of money on unproductive labour. Monsell's second objection to the Act (10th Vic.) is that 'it involves congregating together large masses of people upon public works – where the evil-disposed so often give the tone to the whole lot – and the consequent demoralisation of the labouring classes. And under the same head may be stated the great hardship of making the poor labourers walk long distances to their work, rendering it almost impossible for them to have their meals brought to them in the middle of the day.'

He asserts that a large amount of the money granted last year was diverted from its stated object of helping the destitute. While the government cannot compel drainage or fencing, it can compel the owner of land to employ the poor, and make those who refuse to employ them on productive labour pay for their employment on public works.

The legislation for relieving distress draws no distinction between good and bad landlords. 'The one man has made his tenants comfortable and few of them require relief. The other has ground them to the earth and they are starving.' It taxes improving landowners and tenant farmers for the sins of those who neglect their duty.

The benevolent Mr Monsell is unlikely to be heeded by a government whose liberality does not extend to Ireland. But he is thinking of standing for parliament – and following Dr John Henry Newman into the Roman Catholic Church.[55]

'Give us food'

5 OCTOBER 1846

'Give us food or we perish' is now the loudest cry in this unfortunate country, according to the *Belfast Vindicator*.

'It is heard in every corner of the island – it breaks in like some awful spectre on the festive revelry of the licentious rich – it startles and appals the merchant at his desk, the landlord in his office, the scholar in his study, the lawyer in his stall, the minister in his council-room and the priest at the altar.

'It is a strange popular cry to be heard within the limits of the powerful and wealthy British empire.'

In other countries there are wants, the *Vindicator* concludes; in isolated Ireland alone is there a want of the necessities of life. 'Nothing but a state of being, in which the crimes of civilisation and barbarity had united to banish the virtues of both, could reduce a whole nation to a huge, untended poorhouse, from which one only prayer ascends – "Give us food or we perish".'

A police officer warns of 'the most direful consequences' in Skibbereen unless immediate employment is provided on public works. But the relief given this year is more stringently administered, frugal and difficult to obtain.

An extract from the report of Sub-inspector George Pinchin: 'I beg to impress on you the great failure of the potato crop, want of employment and consequent destitution that exists to an alarming extent in this part of the country amongst the working classes. A stranger would be at a loss to imagine where these wretched beings find means (small as they are) to procure occasional food; on inquiry it would be found that the clothing of these miserable creatures are the resources used, through the agency of a pawn office, that enables them to do so; and it is a fact that the majority of them exist upon one meal a day (such as it is).'

Fever is raging in this County Cork town, the constabulary report continues. It is caused by lack of cleanliness and not having a change of clothes. The poor are compelled to sleep in the rags they wear by day, as their bedding has also been pawned. 'The produce of means so procured cannot last long . . . The accounts from the islands of Cape Clear and Shirkin are horrifying, even the fisheries in those places (this season) produce little or no fish.'

A Justice of the Peace finds people are 'actually starving' in Kinsale. On learning that crowds are gathering, Thomas Cuthbert and a 'brother magistrate' ride through the district. They meet three large assemblages whose demand is for food or work.

The local relief committee gives £20 worth of Indian meal in payment for work repairing old roads. 'When our small fund is exhausted, we fear the very worst consequences unless active measures of relief are adopted.'[56]

Repealer blames Union

O'Connell's secretary urges landlords, in a forlorn hope, to join the Repeal Association.

W.J. O'Neill Daunt, of Kilcasan, County Cork, writes to his fellow landlords: 'You should struggle to recover for yourselves and for your countrymen the exclusive control of your and their concerns; which for the last forty-six years have been mismanaged by foreigners, always incompetent and often hostile.

'It may be asked, why agitate Repeal at a period when our attention is engrossed by the heavy dispensation with which Providence afflicts the land? I answer – because the Union is essentially connected with all Irish distress, either as a cause or as an aggravation. It is the direct source of much of the evil that our country suffers; and it aggravates all evils that spring from other sources, by diminishing or annihilating our power of self-protection.'

He asserts that in no self-governing country 'do the sufferers in periods of scarcity experience, from any portion of their fellow subjects, the heartless barbarity with which a part of the English press has treated the starving Irish population'.

(*Punch*, for instance, publishes cartoons week after week depicting the Irishman as a filthy, brutal creature, a would-be assassin begging for money, under the pretence of buying food, to spend on weapons. It is comforting to treat Ireland's desperate appeals as merely another whine from a professional beggar. 'It is possible to have heard the tale of sorrow too often,' the *Times* remarked on August 3rd.)

Sir James Graham, who had been Home Secretary in the Peel administration, is critical of the policies adopted by the Whig government. He confides to Sir Robert Peel: 'The real extent and magnitude of the Irish difficulty are under-estimated by the government, and cannot be met by measures within the strict rule of economical science.'

Meanwhile, a revised set of instructions for local relief committees is published. They stipulate that food can be sold only in small quantities and to people who have no other means of procuring it. Providing food gratuitously is to be avoided as far as possible. It can be given only to those who are incapable of employment on the public works and if the local workhouse is full.

Furthermore, underlining a reliance upon private enterprise, the relief committees are ordered to charge the local market rate for corn. In an era of high prices, this is of little benefit to the poor. When committees in Cork and Kerry reduce prices below the market rate, however, local traders complain to the government that their prices are being undercut.

Grain will not be sent to Ireland or any depots opened until the government believes is it absolutely necessary. Moreover, Scotland – where there is also a scarcity – is to be supplied with imported food before any can be sent to Ireland.[57]

Panic seizes people

19 OCTOBER 1846

Panic seizes the country and people clutch wildly at public works as their only hope of staying alive, now that the potato has failed again.

Hungry peasants and eager farmers cause riots at presentment sessions – meetings called to consider projects.

In Hospital, County Limerick, a Board of Works officer is 'hunted like a mad dog by the whole country population' because it is believed that Mr Kearney prevented works being started in the district. He reports that armed police had to intervene before he could drive off in his gig, 'under awful groaning and pelting of stones . . . Several hundred disencumbering themselves of their coats, shoes and stockings . . . followed me for four miles, but thanks to a good horse I got off with my life.'

In one month, the number employed on relief works has risen from 26,000 to 114,000 men. Approximately 363,400 men, women and children – or 10 per cent of the total work-force – will soon be employed on the public works; in Clare, the average daily number is set to rise to 26 per cent of the labour force.

While the administration of the relief works grows more centralised, the method of financing them is decentralised. The road works carried out last spring and summer cost £476,000, half of which was a grant from the government. The post-August relief works scheme will cost £4,848,000 – to be borne by the localities in which they are carried out.

In spite of the enormous expenditure and increase in Board of Works staff, however, the public works fail to stem the rising tide of hunger. The demand for employment continually outstrips supply, while the wages of those who do obtain work are insufficient, as the price of Indian meal spirals towards 3s. a stone.

When inclement weather prevents work, labourers are sent home and receive only a half day's pay. Therefore, last month's minimum wage is already insufficient to feed a family. The average daily wage paid on the public works is 7d. – even lower than the punitive rates envisaged by the Board of Works and Treasury.

A notice calling a meeting to demand that public work pay be increased to 1s.6d. a day is posted at chapels in Carrigtohill, County Cork: 'The clergy from the altars . . . adjured their flock not to attend and the meeting failed.'

The most frequent complaints of the poor against the system are the slowness in paying wages, the delay in starting public works and the imposition of task work. As the labourers become weaker, they are less capable of completing enough task work to earn an adequate day's pay.

The delay in starting a public work can be as long as five weeks. The *Limerick Reporter* asks: 'Are the Irish people to starve? Scarcely in any district have the works which were passed at the presentment sessions as yet received the sanction of the Treasury and the Board of Works.'[58]

Hunger stalks Belfast

26 OCTOBER 1846

It is distressing to hear the number of poor going about this town saying they are starving, a correspondent writes in the *Belfast Vindicator*.

A Castlewellan correspondent considers there is no real sympathy among the landlords for the people.

The able-bodied men stand idle, while their wives and children grow weak:

'Owing to the extraordinary wetness of the season, turf cannot be procured – coals are out of the question, and the poor have thus the double pressure of hunger and cold to bear up against; while the rich wrap themselves up in their own importance and shun their dependants as a plague.

'The continual cry among the small farmers is, "What in the world are we to do!" The rent is being called for, in some instances, with merciless perseverance. Add the prospect of being turned out of their holdings, to that of depriving themselves of the means of sustenance, and you will be able to form an opinion of the feelings of the poor farmers in this district.

'The bodings of the cottiers and day labourers are melancholy in the extreme; their accustomed food is gone, and no substitute forthcoming. Their usual wages would require to be trebled to be of any sufficient service whatever; it is provokingly barbarous to offer them 8d. or 10d. per day, and yet none of the farmer class is able to pay more.'

'A County Down man' concludes that the landlords of the locality should not be allowed to 'shab' away to England and leave their tenants to the mercies of 'heartless, ignorant bog-bailiffs and screwing agents, whose pay depends on the amount wrung from the unfortunate class committed to their charge'.

The impact of the partial potato failure of 1845 and the virtually total loss this year is disrupting the relationship between farmers and their bound labourers. Traditionally, such labourers have been willing to work in exchange for a potato patch and a cabin and a few so-called privileges. But with their potato gardens withered by the blight, money wages have become essential if they are to avoid starvation. The widespread refusal of farmers to pay wages is forcing labourers to surrender their plots and flee to the public works or, as a last resort, to the workhouses.

Furthermore, there is a massive default by unbound labourers in the payment of conacre rents. Cottiers and small farmers are compelled to dispose of their stock.

Archbishop Michael Slattery of Cashel writes to the Viceroy, Lord Bessborough, appealing for an end to the delay in starting public works.

The Rev G.M.Massy, of Charleville, County Cork, confirms that the method of appointing the army of stewards and overseers on the public works is being grossly abused. People who have influence with members of relief committees are appointed, 'without the slightest reference either to qualification or character'.[59]

Despair sets in

2 NOVEMBER 1846

The poor seek refuge in the newly-built workhouses, until now shunned as degrading.

The country has been divided for administrative purposes into 130 Poor Law unions. Edward Twistleton, the chief Poor Law commissioner in Ireland, forwards urgent requests from western unions for loans to keep their workhouses open. An assistant commissioner says that, given the state of the country, it is almost impossible to collect any rate or tax in the Connacht unions.

But Sir George Grey, the Home Secretary, does not want to deviate from established practice. Adequate rates must be struck and collected at all costs.

Castlebar board of guardians turns forty applicants away because of lack of funds; ninety are refused admission in Cahirciveen due to scarcity of food. The following unions are already in financial difficulties: Ballinrobe, Carrick-on-Shannon, Castlebar, Mohill, Scarriff, Sligo, Swinford, Tralee and Westport.

Although Swinford poorhouse is full, as many as 200 people a day continue to seek admission or help: 'Multitudes of starving men, women and children soliciting with prayers just one meal of food.'

The master of the workhouse gets drunk. While considered a bad example to the male paupers, he is related to most members of the board and therefore unlikely to be removed.

Coastguard officers find people apparently dying due to a 'total absence of food' in remote western districts such as Killeries, Clifden and Ballinakill. The inspector-general, Sir James Dombrain, deciding that they must not be allowed to starve, allows the free issue of Indian meal on a doctor's certificate.

Sir James distributes 11,663lb in this manner, for which he is rebuked by the Treasury. He had no authority, he is informed, to give meal away free. Instead, he should have called on the leading people in each distressed district to form a relief committee and raise a fund by private subscription, which might be increased by a government donation.

Dombrain points out: 'No committee could have been formed. There was no one within many miles who could have contributed one shilling . . . The people were actually dying.'

The general feeling is one of despair. A commissariat officer in Westport finds the subjection of the masses extraordinary. A large crowd marches to Westport House and asks to see Lord Sligo. When his lordship appears, someone cries 'kneel, kneel' and the crowd drops on its knees before him. The Mayo town is described as 'a nest of fever and vermin'.

In Banagher meal-dealers, hungry for money, 'buy up whatever comes to market and offer it again in small quantities at a great price which a poor man cannot pay and live'.[60]

British incomprehension

9 NOVEMBER 1846

The English know as little about the west of Ireland as of west Africa. This is the opinion of army commissariat officers serving in Irish relief.

For instance, senior British officials fail to grasp the place of the grain harvest in Irish life. Corn is not grown to eat but to pay the rent and, for the Irish peasant, failure to pay his rent means eviction.

'If the people are forced to consume their oats and other grain, where is the rent to come from?' a commissariat officer asks in Westport. It is a long way to Whitehall, where Charles Trevelyan writes: 'I cannot believe there is no store of food in Roscommon from the oat harvest.'

Commissary-general Routh is told that he asks too much for Ireland. The food scarcity, he is reminded in a Treasury minute, extends over the whole of western Europe and the UK. Nothing ought to be done for the west of Ireland which might send prices still higher for people 'who, unlike the inhabitants of the west coast of Ireland, have to depend on their own exertions'.

The London *Times*, in an editorial entitled 'Sermon for Ireland', preaches that this year 'the Irishman is destitute, so is the Scotchman and so is the Englishman . . . It appears to us to be of the very first importance to all classes of Irish society to impress on them that there is nothing so peculiar, so exceptional, in the condition which they look on as the pit of utter despair . . . Why is that so terrible in Ireland which in England does not create perplexity and hardly moves compassion?'

Indeed. Well might Lord Monteagle, the humane Limerick landowner, doubt 'if the magnitude of the existing calamity and its dangers are appreciated in Downing Street'.

Trevelyan – who has moved into lodgings to devote more time to scrutinising the deluge of applications for public works from Ireland – claims that 'government establishments are strained to the utmost to alleviate this great calamity. My purchases are carried to the utmost point short of transferring the famine from Ireland to England.' At least the Permanent Secretary at the Treasury admits there is a famine in Ireland and not in Britain.

He then lectures Lord Monteagle on political economy: 'It forms no part of the functions of government to provide supplies of food or to increase the productive powers of the land.'

Trevelyan sees a bright light shining through the dark cloud which at present hangs over Ireland. 'The morbid habits are gradually giving way to a more healthy action. The deep and inveterate root of social evil remains, and I hope I am not guilty of irreverence in thinking that, this being altogether beyond the power of man, the cure has been applied by the direct stroke of an all-wise providence . . . '

He sees the blight as a heaven-sent opportunity to convert the land from a potato economy to grain cultivation.[61]

Quakers organise

16 NOVEMBER 1846

A meeting of Quakers in Dublin leads to the formation of the Central Relief Committee of the Society of Friends.

The Friends in New York begin their well-organised Irish relief work. Subscriptions from the rich are raised through the president of the Merchants' Bank and from the poor through Bishop John Hughes.

At home as the destitute stream into the workhouses, Baltinglass is declared full.

The government has committed itself to acting as a supplier of last resort west of the Shannon. In the rest of the country, ministers and relief officials consider themselves bound by a policy of non-intervention. This leads to exorbitant food prices.

Relief Commissioner Randolph Routh tells a delegation from Achill Island 'it was essential to the success of commerce that the merchantile interest should not be interfered with'; the government is determined to act in accordance with the enlightened principles of political economy.

The leader of the delegation, Fr Malachy Monahan, points out that the people of Achill know nothing about political economy. Routh insists there is nothing more essential to the welfare of a country than a strict adherence to the principles of free trade. He fobs off the delegation by inferring that Edmund Burke would oppose any interference with trade, even in present conditions.

Fr William Flannelly, of Clifden, County Galway, denounces 'the slowness and the bungling of officials and the greed of the merchants and hucksters'. Forbidding relief committees to undersell the market means protecting 'famine prices'.

At a meeting in Dublin, David Creighton, a Presbyterian minister, seconds a motion by Archbishop Daniel Murray criticising the government which 'allowed the poor to perish sooner than interfere with the interests of the general trader'.

Privately, however, Routh can no longer disguise his disillusionment with government policies and accuses the Treasury of not having made sufficient provision for Ireland. The purchase of foreign corn began too late in the season to expect the arrival of sufficient quantities before Christmas. Routh considers the export of 300,000 quarters of oats 'a most serious evil'.

Charles Trevelyan admonishes Routh: 'We beg of you not to countenance in any way the idea of prohibiting exportation. The discouragement and feeling of insecurity to the trade from such a proceeding would prevent its doing even any immediate good; and there cannot be a doubt that it would inflict a permanent injury on the country.'

This rigid adherence to *laissez-faire* economic doctrines ensures a gap in domestic food supplies before the arrival of Indian corn ordered from America. By its refusal to prohibit exports, the British government seems prepared to allow a large proportion of the Irish people to starve.[62]

Public works failing

The public works relief scheme is failing to provide the destitute poor with adequate means of subsistence.

Those employed are paid, irregularly, from 6d. to 8d. a day – with the price of Indian meal rising to 2d. a lb. Mallow relief committee describes the wages as 'arbitrary cruelty' and declares 'the men on the works are starving'.

The labourers are not paid because there are no pay clerks to pay them; works are not started because there are no engineers to lay them out; task-work is not measured because there are no stewards who can be entrusted with the calculation.

Lord Monteagle (Thomas Spring Rice) describes to Lord Bessborough his difficulties with Board of Works' staff. On his Mount Trenchard estate, the first official resigned and the second 'walked out in the midst of our troubles, with works to be laid out on which human lives depended'. He paid the labourers out of his own pocket. A mass of discontent is being created.

'You must have pity on us,' the new Commissioner for Relief Works writes to Lord Mounteagle. 'We are perfectly unable to meet the requirements for engineers. The inspecting officers are all failing us.'

Officials are worked hard – 'up until 2 and 3a.m. and up again at 7a.m.,' writes Colonel Harry Jones. At presentment sessions they meet with opposition and insults from a 'yelling mob'; they have to travel long distances and are subjected frequently to severe wettings. 'Some resign from inability to support the strain, some from intimidation . . .'

The public works are suspended in the Tulla district of County Clare because of 'a system of insubordination and outrage, which endangers the lives of the officers and overseers, and deters the poor and peaceable inhabitants from labouring on the works'.

In Rosbercon, County Kilkenny, the starving are being driven 'frantic by repeated delays' in starting relief works.

A Board of Works inspector observes that County Limerick is 'regularly riddled with roads'.

The rector of Castlebar writes: 'Never has such a calamity befallen our country. The whole staff of life is swept away; the emaciated multitudes are to be seen looking in vain for food, with hunger depicted in their countenance.'

Fr Cornelius O'Brien, PP Lorrha and Doorha, informs the editor of the *Tipperary Vindicator* 'of another victim of starvation'. Daniel Hayes, who survived for several days on the refuse of vegetables, was found dead. 'Our relief committee has been formed and sanctioned three weeks, and the names of persons in need of employment returned to the proper officers; but scarcely any notice has been taken of our returns. Ere many days I fear there must be need of an increase of coroners and a decrease of civil engineers, if matters go on in this way.'[63]

'The people are starving'

30 NOVEMBER 1846

The poor of Spiddal, County Galway, are in an appalling condition. Fr Francis Kenny tells the story of Thomas Mollone, who had been working for four weeks on the new road from Costello Bay to Oughterard. Weakened by hunger and fatigue, on his way home from work last Friday he lay down and died within eighty perches of his cabin.

To earn a miserable subsistence for himelf, his wife and six children, he walked six Irish miles each morning 'through a wet pathless mountain and the same journey back in the evening, after carrying dripping sand on his back during the day, with only one meal and that same a scanty one'.

Those who live near the public works are little better off; they labour from morning till night to earn 6d. With 3,000 thus employed in Galway, unsurprisingly there is some violence towards overseers. 'The people are starving and consequently prepared for any mischief.'

The *Waterford Chronicle* reports an inquest on Mary Byrne, who fell down and died of exhaustion in Enniscorthy. Pregnant and deserted by her shoe-maker husband, she had been admitted to the local workhouse. After the birth of her child, however, they were turned out 'for not being natives and, consequently, having no claim on the union'. The *Chronicle* remarks that the poor laws 'have dried up the charitable drain'.

The *Nation* has begun publishing a list of landlords who are reducing rents. The *Clare Journal* reports that the Marquis of Conyngham has instructed his agent, Marcus Keane, that an abatement of 25 or 15 per cent should be made according to the tenants' circumstances.

But farm work is being neglected as the people flock to relief employment. The Board of Works inspecting officer for Clare observes that, on a journey of fifty-six miles, he saw only one plough at work preparing the ground for wheat.

In the midlands, cart-loads of flour and oatmeal are attacked by crowds of men, women and children.

A meeting of 10,000 labourers in Castletownroche, County Cork, resolves not to buy goods of English or Scottish manufacture 'until the export of Irish provisions shall be stopped'.

The *Liverpool Times* fears that the influx of Irish paupers will both depress wages and place an added burden on the poor rates. On particular days the roads leading from Liverpool to Manchester and other populous centres are covered with Irish families.

The paper notes that there are two classes of emigrants: the emigrants of hope and those of despair. The latter category migrates to Britain. 'An Irishman will endure what no one else would endure rather than leave his native country; but still there is a limit to his powers of endurance, and the increasing crowds which are now pouring into this country prove that this has been passed.'[64]

Anarchy rules

7 DECEMBER 1846

Anarchy is setting in. Bands of starving people roam the country begging for food, 'more like famishing wolves than men'. In the relatively prosperous county of Westmeath, a Board of Works officer reports that he has 'half-clad wretches howling at the door for food'.

Employment lists become a farce as mobs force themselves on to the public works. Women are breaking stones at 4d. a day. In County Limerick, masses of hungry people with spades and pickaxes 'are perfectly unmanageable'.

The weather compounds the misery. Already the winter is being described as the most severe in living memory. Snow has continued to fall throughout November, while a north-east wind sweeps across Europe. Crowds of starving, half-naked men, women and children huddle on the works, exposed to the cold and rain.

In Cork 5,000 beggars prowl the streets, dying – according to Fr Mathew – at the rate of 100 a week.

Farmers, unable to pay by money instead of potatoes, are turning their labourers adrift. The land lies neglected, a Board of Works inspector writes, 'partly from the inability to get seed and partly from the feeling that if they do sow it the landlord will seize the crop'.

The relief department of the Board of Works in Dublin issues circular no. 38, which proposes to assist small farmers while they cultivate their plots. It is suppressed by the Treasury. Trevelyan explains: 'It is quite impossible for my lords to give their sanction to parties being paid from public funds for the cultivation of their own land.'

In County Mayo the parish priest of Kilconduff, Bernard Durcan, deplores the apathy of the Whig government. He finds it impossible to estimate the number of Famine victims.

Nearly the entire population of the united parishes of Kilconduff and Meelick – 10,987 people – depended on the potato. Yet not more than 400 men have been employed in the two parishes, and the public works system is so defective even that number receives little relief. In despair, the people are abandoning their homes and fleeing the country.

Censuring O'Connell's judgment, Fr Durcan believes there should be no question of supporting a government that would not fling its 'wretched blighted theories to the winds when the people are starving – open the ports, establish depots for the sale of food to the poor at moderate prices' and employ the destitute.

There are no resident landlords in Kilconduff, the priest continues. 'We made an effort to create a fund by subscription for the purpose of keeping a supply of provisions in Swinford, to be sold to the poor in small quantities.' Not one of the absentee landlords responded. 'They are not, however, idle. Their bailiffs are on the alert, distraining the rent, and the [cattle] pounds are full.'[65]

Evidence of Quakers

The sufferings of the Irish poor might be dismissed as exaggeration were it not for the sober evidence of the Quakers. One of the first objects of their Central Committee is to obtain 'trustworthy information respecting the real state of the more remote districts'.

Accordingly, William Forster, a respected English Quaker, visits the west and north-west accompanied by Joseph Crosfield. They witness a heart-rending scene outside Carrick-on-Shannon workhouse: 'Poor wretches in the last stage of famine imploring to be received into the house; women, who had six or seven children, begging that even two or three of them might be taken in.' Their husbands earn an inadequate 8d. a day. Children are worn to skeletons.

A widow with two children, who for a week had subsisted on one meal of cabbage daily, are admitted. They are in so reduced a state that a guardian remarks to the master of the poorhouse that the youngest child will trouble them but a short time.

A great number is refused admission as there are only thirty vacancies. Some of those rejected look so wasted it is doubtful if they will reach their cabins alive.

Mr Forster distributes 40lb of bread. 'The ravenous voracity with which many of them devoured it on the spot spoke strongly of starvation, or of a state nearly approaching to it.' One woman, however, eats only a small portion of her bread because she has five other children at home.

'Throughout this journey, it was William Forster's observation that the children exhibit the effects of famine in a remarkable degree, their faces looking wan and haggard with hunger, and seemingly like old men and women . . . To do the people justice, they are bearing their privations with patience and fortitude, and very little clamorous begging . . . Forster has completely formed the opinion that the statements in the public newspapers are by no means exaggerated.'

A member of the board of guardians remarks callously to him that the poor 'were dying like rotten sheep'. Two clergymen say that while they are at their meals, 'poor famishing wretches appear before the windows and groan in the most pitiable manner'.

Mr Forster, who has experience of managing soup kitchens for the English poor, offers to provide a boiler and give a donation to start a soup kitchen in each place he visits. Except for Castlerea, County Roscommon, this largess is accepted gratefully. In Castlerea a priest refuses because he fears the town would be overwhelmed by destitute hordes from the countryside.

Five or six thousand starving people march into Listowel, County Kerry, shouting 'Bread or Blood'. Despite the pleas of the parish priest, Jeremiah Mahony, they refuse to disperse. Fr Mahony faints with exhaustion from his exertions. The townspeople remonstrate with the peasants, who agree to leave.[66]

Skibbereen conditions

21 DECEMBER 1846

Famine is raging in Skibbereen union. Since November 5th, 197 have died in the poorhouse, the principal cause of death being 'the prevalence of a fatal diarrhoea, acting on the exhausted constitutions of the persons admitted'.

Nearly 100 bodies have been found in the lanes or in derelict cabins, half-eaten by rats.

The guardians want to open soup 'shops', but the Poor Law Commission insists that relief is to be provided only inside the workhouse.

The *Cork Examiner* describes the horrors of Famine: 'Disease and death in every quarter – the once hardy population worn away to emaciated skeletons – fever, dropsy, diarrhoea and famine rioting in every filthy hovel and sweeping away whole families – the population perceptibly lessened – death diminishing the destitution – hundreds frantically rushing from their home and country, not with the idea of making fortunes in other lands, but to fly from a scene of suffering and death – 400 men starving in one district having no employment, and 300 more turned off the public works in another district on a day's notice – seventy-five tenants ejected here, and a whole village in the last stage of destitution there – relief committees threatening to throw up their mockery of an office in utter despair – dead bodies of children flung into holes hastily scratched in the earth without shroud or coffin – wives travelling ten miles to beg the charity of a coffin for a dead husband, and bearing it back that weary distance . . . every field becoming a grave and the land a wilderness.'

James Hack Tuke reports on a Quaker visit to County Donegal.

In Dunfanaghy, where the sea is teeming with fish, the people starve because they have no one to teach them how to build seaworthy boats. In Dungloe, the crowds are crying with hunger and cold. While thousands of acres of reclaimable land lie neglected, thousands of anxious men are unable to procure work.

The Quakers find the inmates of Glenties workhouse half-starved and half-naked. 'The day before they had but one meal of oatmeal and water, and at the time of our visit had not sufficient food in the house for the day's supply. The people complained bitterly and begged us to give them tickets for work, to enable them to leave the place and work on the roads. Some were leaving the house, preferring to die in their own hovels.

'Their bedding consisted of dirty straw, in which they were laid in rows on the floor; even as many as six persons being crowded under one rug; and we did not see a blanket at all. The rooms were hardly bearable for filth. The living and the dying were stretched side by side beneath the same miserable covering. No wonder that disease and pestilence were filling the infirmary, and that the pale, haggard countenance of the poor boys and girls told of sufferings, which it was impossible to contemplate without pity.'[67]

Ennis poorhouse full

28 DECEMBER 1846

Christmas Eve: Ennis poorhouse is full. Captain Edmond Wynne, inspecting officer for west Clare, reports that 'police are stationed at the doors to keep the numerous applicants out, therefore no relief can be expected from that quarter'.

The relief committees are broke. Captain Wynne warns: 'Without food we cannot last many days longer; the public works must fail in keeping the population alive. What is to become of the thousands to whose cases the relief works are totally inapplicable?'

The public works in Clare Abbey have been closed because of an assassination attempt on Wynne's principal overseer. In accordance with regulations, the works are to remain closed until information leading to the arrest of his assailant is forthcoming. As a result the people are starving, 'but as yet peaceably'.

After venturing through this parish, Wynne writes to Trevelyan: 'Altho' a man not easily moved, I confess myself unmanned by the intensity and extent of the suffering I witnessed more especially among the women and little children, crowds of whom were to be seen scattered over the turnip fields like a flock of famishing crows, devouring the raw turnips, mothers half naked, shivering in the snow and sleet, uttering exclamations of despair while their children were screaming with hunger. I am a match for anything else I may meet with here, but this I cannot stand.'

Ennistymon workhouse is overflowing. Doctors report that deaths are increasing due to the effects of disease brought on by inadequate food, rather than actual starvation.

William Sharman Crawford, who has formed the Ulster Tenant Right Association, writes to his tenants: 'I do not take from the landlord the power of resumption, but I endeavour to limit it within just bounds. It will be said by some that this restraint is a violation of the rights of property. I say not. Property in land is not absolute ownership . . . I am only reducing to practical rules the unwritten law of tenant right, founded on the long-established custom of this part of Ireland by which its superior prosperity has been permanently established.'

Denis Mahon, of Strokestown, serves eviction notices on tenants who have not paid their rents. The tenants petition to be allowed to stay in their homes at least for the remainder of this pitiless winter. But Mahon believes most of them are troublemakers, 'who are known to be able to pay and only refuse from combination. These tenants I should be glad to get rid of on any terms.'

Sir Randolph Routh considers 8,000 tons of grain the minimum level needed before there can be any general opening of the western depots. With official stocks barely exceeding 6,000 tons, the Treasury consents finally to opening the depots 'for the sale of food as far as may be prudent and necessary.'[68]

'Ghastly skeletons'

4 JANUARY 1847

A grim beginning to this year of death.

Nicholas Cummins, a Cork magistrate, sets out for Skibbereen with as much bread as five men can carry. He is surprised to find the wretched hamlet apparently empty. He enters some of the hovels to ascertain the cause.

'In the first, six famished and ghastly skeletons, to all appearances dead, were huddled in a corner on some filthy straw, their sole covering what seemed a ragged horsecloth, their wretched legs hanging about naked about the knees.

'I approached with horror and found by a low moaning they were alive – they were in fever, four children, a woman and what had once been a man . . . In a few minutes I was surrounded by at least 200 such phantoms, such frightful spectres as no words can describe, either from famine or from fever.'

Their demonic yells are still ringing in his ears, Mr Cummins writes in a letter addressed to the Duke of Wellington and published in the London *Times*. 'In another case, my clothes were nearly torn off in my endeavour to escape from the throng of pestilence around, when my neckcloth was seized from behind by a grip which compelled me to turn, I found myself grasped by a woman with an infant just born in her arms and the remains of a filthy sack across her loins – the sole covering of herself and baby.'

That morning the police opened a house on the adjoining lands and two corpses were found, half-devoured by rats. 'A mother, herself in a fever, was seen the same day to drag out the corpse of her child, a girl about twelve, perfectly naked, and leave it half-covered with stones. In another house, within 500 yards of the cavalry station, the dispensary doctor found seven wretches lying unable to move under the same cloak. One had been dead many hours, but the others were unable to move either themselves or the corpse.'

Sir Randolph Routh blames the landlords. The proprietors of the Skibbereen district, he tells Charles Trevelyan, draw an annual income of £50,000.

One of the reasons why the British government does no feel bound to send food to Skibbereen is because there are ample provisions in the locality. On Saturday the market was supplied with meat, bread and fish. This contradiction is occurring all over Ireland. Trevelyan insists that the resources of the country should be drawn out, failing to realise that those resources are utterly inaccessible to the wretches dying in the streets and by the roadsides.

The starving in such places as Skibbereen perish not because there is no food, but because they have no money with which to buy it. But it is the payment of rents which separate the people from food in the first instance.

The British Association for the Relief of the Extreme Distress in the Remote Parishes of Ireland and Scotland is formed.[69]

'Lie down and die'

11 JANUARY 1847

William Edward Forster joins his father and a Quaker delegation in County Mayo. He finds Westport is 'like what we read of in beleaguered cities, its streets crowded with gaunt wanderers sauntering to and fro with hopeless air and hunger-struck look; a mob of starved, almost naked women, around the poorhouse, clamouring for soup tickets; our inn, the headquarters of the road engineer and pay clerks, beset by a crowd of beggars for work'.

Connemara has changed since a previous visit. In Leenane the boatmen are pale and spiritless, 'so different from their wild Irish fun when I made the same excursion before'. On that occasion one woman whose cabin he visited did say: 'There will be nothing for us but to lie down and die.' He tried to give her hope of English aid. Alas, however, 'her prophecy has been but too true. Out of a population of 240, I found thirteen already dead from want. The survivors were like walking skeletons; the men stamped with the livid mark of hunger; the children crying with pain; the women in some of the cabins too weak to stand.'

The young Mr Forster is struck by the patience of these sufferers. In Bundorragha men have been at work for up to five weeks on the roads. Due to the negligence or mistake of some officers, no wages were received until this morning – but still only with pay for a few. 'It was wonderful, but yet most touching, to see the patient, quiet look of despair with which the others received the news that they were still left unpaid. I doubt whether it would have been easy to find a man who would have dared to bear the like announcement to starving Englishmen.'

In Clifden, 'of burials without coffins we heard many instances; and to those who know the almost superstitious reverence of the Irish for funeral rites, they tell a fearful story. In two cases, my father told me he had had applications for money not to keep the people alive, but for coffins to bury them.'

Rumours about the 'arming of the peasantry' are hardening many English hearts. But James Hack Tuke, on returning from the west, writes that it is the sons of large farmers who buy guns for the protection of property; the starving, even if weapons were put into their hands, have not the strength left to use them.

The *Northern Whig* records that 'it would be impossible to exaggerate the awful destitution that exists in the town of Clones and neighbourhood . . . No day passes but some victims of this frightful calamity are committed to the grave. The number of deaths in Clones workhouse during the last week has been twenty-five at the lowest . . . The workhouse contains upwards of 100 over the regulated number, and most of them were all but starved before they obtained admission. Their exhausted frames were then unable to bear the food doled out to them, and hence they are at this moment dying in dozens.'[70]

Irish Confederation formed

18 JANUARY 1847

The Young Irelanders attempt to revive the Repeal agitation. Having 'reluctantly resigned all hope of reconciliation' with O'Connell, they meet in the *Nation* office – 4 D'Olier Street, Dublin – under the chairmanship of John Blake Dillon and issue an address in which they defend the principle of integrated education, denounce any alliance with the Whig government and deny they seceded from the Repeal Association last July on the issue of physical force. 'Certain members of the committee were, on one pretence or another, excluded because they held opinions opposed to Mr O'Connell.'

Divorced from the reality of Famine, the middle-class intellectuals advance nationhood as a panacea: 'The accursed Union is yet bound like a yoke on our necks, crushing down the national spirit, corrupting the public morals, draining away the very blood and marrow of the human beings, who waste and pine in dreadful famine on our teeming soil.'

James Fintan Lalor, who is emerging from seclusion in Queen's County, sees that under existing circumstances an agitation based exclusively on the national question is doomed to failure; ultimately, it must be coupled to the engine of agrarian revolution. This policy is unacceptable to most of Young Ireland, which looks on nationality as a unifying force and still hopes to win resident landlords to the Repeal cause.

None the less, while G.H. Moore, of Moorehall, and the sons of O'Connell are attending a levée in Dublin Castle, the Irish Confederation is being launched in the Rotunda, with a reluctant William Smith O'Brien at its head.

The Liberator is 'sumptuously entertained' on a visit to Maynooth College, where he receives 'the gratitude, the love, the confidence and the prayers of 500 faithful, Irish ecclesiastical hearts'. O'Connell asks has 'the government no feelings of accountability? Englishmen have now supplied the world with a crowning proof of their utter incapability of dealing with the affairs of this country.'

Meanwhile, Assistant Poor Law Commissioner C.G. Otway reports on the state of Castlebar workhouse. Since November 21st, the paupers have been left without breakfast three days a week, the master having no fuel to cook it. This means the inmates receive only one meal on those days. The sick lack the diet prescribed by their medical attendant.

The Rev Mr Gibbons sums up: 'Those able to creep are preferring to brave want abroad [outside] to dying by cold and hunger inside.'

Collecting the poor rate is proving impossible in this western union. A vast number of the ratepayers are being reduced to pauperism, while landlords claim they are unable to produce rates due to non-payment of rents. Already the local proprietor, Lord Lucan, is being called the 'Exterminator'.[71]

Victoria donates £2,000

25 JANUARY 1847

A Limerick man gets Queen Victoria to double her contribution to Famine aid. She first subscribed £1,000. But Stephen Spring Rice, secretary of the British Relief Association, tells the government it is not enough. 'It was increased to £2,000.' Baron Lionel de Rothschild, the Jewish banker, gives £1,000.

While mortality is rising in the workhouses, the organisation of Castlebar Poor Law union has broken down. Lord Lucan, chairman of Castlebar board of guardians, writes from Hanover Square, London, regretting that the paupers are without food and fuel. Contracts hadn't been signed because of the union's insolvency. His lordship, who owns 61,000 acres in Mayo with a rent roll approaching £100,000, wants the government to bail out the union. No wonder the British middle class is growing tired of Irish landlords.

Lucan's agent delivers turf and meal sporadically to the poorhouse, but no bread which those with dysentery need. As a result deaths from dysentery are increasing.

The gentlemen who comprise the board of guardians fail to strike a poor rate to maintain the paupers. Assistant Commissioner Otway recommends dismissing them, particularly after an inmate's body lay for two days in the workhouse because there was no money for a coffin. The board talks of getting up a subscription but defers any action. Finally, the medical officer (Dr Ronayne) and the clerk and master of Castlebar poorhouse pay for it out of their own pockets

It should be recorded, too, that the chairman of Ballina board of guardians is advancing £120 a week to keep that workhouse open. Edward Howley remains determined to make every sacrifice rather than allow the poor to be turned out and left to die; still it is impossible for one private individual to support 1,300.

The *Cork Constitution* reports that even respectable farmers, holding thirty acres or more, 'are obliged to consume in their families and in their stables the corn which in former years procured clothes and other comforts for them'.

Captain Wynne, the idiosyncratic inspector employed by the Board of Works in Clare at £1 a day, says the relief committees are composed of 'half-gentry, bankrupts in fortune and in character'. They 'refuse no applicant and throw the entire odium on me'.

Wynne dismisses about 10,000 workers on public relief whom he considers are not really destitute, ignoring a death threat from 'Captain Starlight'.

Crowds of country people attack bread carts in Dublin, 'devouring the bread with evident voracity'.

The Quakers open their model soup kitchen in Upper Ormond Quay.

Russell presents to the House of Commons proposals to substitute soup kitchens for public works in Ireland.[72]

Public works abandoned

1 FEBRUARY 1847

Replacing the public works with soup kitchens represents a radical change of policy. Relief by employment is to be abandoned.

New relief committees are to be nominated to distribute soup and yet another Relief Commission is to be set up.

Employing 700,000, the public works have been a costly failure and humanitarian disaster. The tide of Irish distress, Trevelyan admits, 'appears now to have completely overflowed the barriers we opposed to it . . . This is a real famine, in which thousands and thousands of people are likely to die'; none the less, 'if the Irish once find out there are any circumstances in which they can get free government grants . . . we shall have a system of mendicancy such as the world never saw'.

What is going to become of the poor between the phasing out of public works and the installation of soup kitchens? Those works are objectionable and demoralise our people, Archbishop Michael Slattery of Cashel observes, 'but at the same time they were the means of keeping them alive, although they barely did the same'. Meanwhile, 'the distress is every day increasing and persons, who three months ago were able to do without assistance, are now run out'.

From Carrickmacross, in Monaghan, Bishop Charles MacNally writes that fever and famine are making frightful ravages. 'Fourteen deaths in this parish on yesterday were reported to me. It is wonderful how the clergy can bear their unceasing labours attending on the sick and dying.'

In Kerry, Archdeacon John O'Sullivan of Kenmare acknowledges the strain in the privacy of his diary: 'I often think of betaking myself to some other country rather than see with my eyes and hear with my ears the melancholy spectacle and dismal wailing of the gaunt spectres that persecute and crowd about me from morning until night imploring for some assistance.'

As the destitute migrate eastwards, Bishop Francis Haly records that 'the deaths from starvation average more than 50 per diem' in Carlow.

The medical officer considers that Kilmallock, County Limerick, workhouse cannot accommodate more than 800 without engendering disease; it now has 1,207 inmates. Dr Morgan O'Connell, who is a cousin of the Liberator, says that people with 'famine fever' (typhus and relapsing fever) are sheltering in the Dominican priory ruins, so as not to spread the contagion among their families.

Mitchelstown workhouse, built for 900, now contains 1,533 paupers.

Skibbereen poorhouse is described as 'a plague spot'. The medical officer is nearing breakdown; seven of his staff have fever, other members resign. He asks the guardians to meet in the courthouse instead of the disease-ridden workhouse; 332 of the 1,169 paupers are suffering from fever or dysentery. Nevertheless, starving and sick people beg for admission daily.[73]

O'Connell's last appeal

8 FEBRUARY 1847

Daniel O'Connell informs the House of Commons that 15,000 premature deaths have occurred already in Ireland.

The Liberator, who looks close to death himself, confides to his friend, P.V. Fitzpatrick, that Westminster appears ignorant of the real state of horror in which Ireland is plunged: 'If it be in my power I shall say a few words this evening.'

O'Connell can barely stand in the House for trembling, or be heard in the silence of a pitying respect. He casts himself – as his British mockers have long cast him – as the Big Beggarman. He throws his country upon the mercy of England.

He estimates that 5,000 adults and 10,000 children have died, *Hansard* reports, 'and that 25 per cent of the whole population would perish unless the House should afford effective relief. They would perish of famine and disease unless the House did something speedy and efficacious – not doled out in small sums – not in private and individual subscriptions, but by some great act of national generosity, calculated upon a broad and liberal scale.

'If this course were not pursued, Parliament was responsible for the loss of 25 per cent of the population of Ireland.'

He assures the Commons he is not exaggerating. Typhus fever is desolating whole districts. Only one in ten of those attacked survives. This fearful disorder – conveyed by the louse – will soon spread to the upper classes and to England, 'for it would be brought over by the miserable wretches who escaped from the other side of the Channel'.

Several Irish landlords are doing their duty; others are not.

O'Connell continues: 'The patience of the people of Ireland could not be too much admired. It had been exhibited on all occasions, and the forbearance of the lower orders, considering their almost intolerable privations, was wonderful. It was, however, possible that they might be driven from misery to madness; and, as to the levying of rates, it was at present impossible.

'As to the reimbursing of England for her advances, he contended that she would be no loser at the present crisis, anymore than she had been on former occasions. He maintained that England had been a gainer by her loans to Ireland.'

He again assures the House that Ireland is too poor to support itself and calls on Parliament to rescue his country.

Ireland is in their hands – in their power, he concludes. 'If they did not save her, she could not save herself. He solemnly called on them to recollect that he predicted with the sincerest conviction, that one-fourth of her population would perish unless Parliament came to their relief.'

But Russell's government is unwilling to introduce measures that go against prevailing economic orthodoxies, or that would upset the powerful lobby opposed to giving additional aid to Ireland.[74]

Lone mourner

15 FEBRUARY 1847

This Diary seeks to unearth the stories of the unrecorded. Churchyards are being enlarged throughout the country.

In County Galway, a priest meets a man with a donkey and cart. On the cart there are three coffins, containing the bodies of his wife and two children. He is alone. On arrival in the graveyard, being weakened by starvation himself, he is unable to bury his dead.

Next day, the priest finds ravenous dogs eating the bodies. He hires a man to dig the grave, in which what may be literally called their remains are placed.

Conditions are horrendous in the workhouses, 100 of which contain an excess number of inmates. Deaths number approximately 2,700 a week. In Gort, County Galway, one quarter of the paupers are suffering from fever or dysentery. The Cork poorhouse, built for 2,000, houses 4,400 paupers; in one day a hundred bodies are consigned to a mass grave.

From Roscommon to west Cork the dead are being buried without coffins, frequently in unconsecrated ground.

In the House of Lords, the Earl of Lucan is censured for serving 6,000 processes on his Mayo estate.

Lord Brougham comments: 'The landlord in Mayo had thought it necessary to serve his tenants with notice to quit in the midst of one of the most severe winters that had ever been known, in the midst of the pestilence too which followed, as it generally did, in the train of famine.'

What, he asks, is the result of such wholesale clearance? A great flood of destitute Irish has begun to pour across the Channel into Liverpool and Glasgow. At Liverpool in the last five days 5,200 paupers were landed, in an advanced state of starvation and with cholera among them. Many had come from Mayo.

Harsh and pitiless, the Earl of Lucan replies that anyone who knows anything about Ireland realises the organisation of the country has broken down. Anyone who knows anything about Lucan is aware that he believes there is only one solution for Ireland – a large part of the population must disappear; and he has declared that he 'did not intend to breed paupers to pay priests'.

His lordship is chairman of Castlebar board of guardians, whose work-house children have 'death-like faces and drum-stick arms'.

To Lord Lucan the Famine horrors are convincing proof of the need to clear the land of people. He is getting nothing from his estates and considers he has contributed more than his share. Lucan's generosity in paying the expenses of Castlebar workhouse for a month is overshadowed by his policy of evicting small tenants.

Wherever the parish priest of Ballyhaunis, Eugene Coyne, goes he encounters 'the poor crying and saying that they have no person to tell them what steps they are to take in order to procure food or relieve them unless I do it, so may God relieve them'.[75]

Clare curate's day

22 FEBRUARY 1847

A day in the life of Hugh Quigley, a Clare curate, during 'Black '47':

'We rise at four o'clock when not obliged to attend a night call and proceed on horseback a distance of from four to seven miles to hold stations of confession for the convenience of the poor country people, who flock in thousands to prepare for the death they look on as inevitable. At these stations we have to remain up to 5p.m. administering both con-solation and instruction to the famishing thousands . . . The confessions are often interrupted by calls to the dying and generally, on our way home, we have to administer the last rites to one or more fever patients.

'Arrived at home, we have scarcely seated ourselves to a little dinner when we are interrupted by groans and sobs of several persons at the door crying out, "I am starving", "if you do not help me I must die" and "I wish I was dead", etc. . . . In truth the priest must either harden his heart against the cry of misery, or deprive himself of his usual nourishment to keep victims from falling at his door.

'After dinner – or perhaps before it is half over – the priest is again surrounded by several persons, calling on him to come in haste – that their parents, or brothers, or wives, or children, are "just departing". The priest is again obliged to mount his jaded pony and endeavour to keep pace with the peasant who trots before him as a guide, through glen and ravine, and over precipice, to his infected hut . . .

'The curate has most commonly to say two Masses . . . at different chapels; and to preach patience and resignation to the people, to endeavour to prevent them rising en masse and plundering and murdering their landlords. This gives but a faint idea of the life of a priest here, leaving scarcely any time for prayer or meditation.'

In Mayo, the curate of Kilgeever, Patrick Fitzgerald, witnesses a mother sending her five children to bed, almost lifeless from hunger. 'Despairing of ever again seeing them alive, she took her last leave of them. In the morning, her first act was to touch their lips with her hand to see if the breath of life still remained; but the poor woman's fears were not groundless, for not a breath could she feel from some of her dear little children; that night buried them in the night of eternity.'

At a meeting to raise funds for the Irish in a New York synagogue, the Rev Jacques Judah Lyons declares: 'We are told that we have a large number of our own poor and destitute to take care of, that the charity we dispense should be bestowed in this quarter, that the peculiar position of ourselves and our co-religionists demands it at our hands, that justice is a higher virtue than generosity, that self-preservation is a law and principle of our nature . . . It is true that there is but one connecting link between us and the sufferers . . . That link is humanity.'[76]

'Soup Kitchen Act'

1 MARCH 1847

Soup is now considered the best hope and cheapest means of keeping the Irish alive until the harvest. The Temporary Relief Act is rushed through Parliament. Known as the 'Soup Kitchen Act', it is to provide emergency rations during the summer months.

After August 15th, notwithstanding the financial difficulties which Irish unions particularly in the south and west are already experiencing, the British government is determined that the Poor Law shall become responsible for providing relief. Trevelyan maintains: 'The owners and holders of land in these districts had permitted or encouraged the growth of the excessive population which depended upon the precarious potato and they alone had it in their power to restore society to a safe and healthy state.'

The Quakers have pioneered soup-kitchen relief. In King's County, Edenderry Poor Law union is dealing with the problem of overcrowded workhouses by opening a soup kitchen in each electoral division.

Initially, the Poor Law Commissioners refuse to sanction any expenditure for what they consider as tantamount to outdoor relief – i.e., other than in the poorhouse. The Edenderry guardians respond by pointing out one of the major flaws in government policy: 'There is most poverty where there is least means of getting funds.'

But the Home Secretary, Sir George Grey, impressed by the Edenderry experiment, regards soup kitchens as an effective way of providing extensive relief cheaply. He therefore recommends that soup kitchens, organised by local relief committees, be established in areas of intense distress. By placing the soup kitchens under the control of relief committees, the government ensures that at least part of the cost will be borne locally.

In addition the Lord Lieutenant begins to issue small sums of money to the insolvent unions.

The impact of the Famine is being experienced even in the wealthiest parts of the country. The Belfast union, for example, has problems common to all workhouses at present: rapidly increasing pauper numbers (as the destitute flock to the town) and a high rate of disease within the poorhouse. Mortality among the older inmates is averaging fifty to sixty a week.

With Indian meal selling at famine prices, labourers and smallholders have no choice but to consume their seed potatoes. The ensuing deficiency of seed dwarfs last years's shortage. A commissariat officer asks the parishioners of Templecrone, County Donegal, why, instead of being idle, they do not dig their land. The answer he receives is: 'They have neither food to eat while working, nor seed to put in.'

The combined adverse circumstances result in an enormous decline in the potato acreage in 1847 – a mere one-sixth of what it was last year.[77]

Evangelical diatribe

8 MARCH 1847

A heightening of sectarian tension adds to the general misery. The Rev Edward Nangle has established a Protestant colony on Achill Island. He publishes a monthly journal, the *Achill Missionary Herald*, 'exhibiting the principles and progress of Christ's kingdom, and exposing the errors and abominations of that section of the rival kingdom of Antichrist commonly called the papacy'.

He has just issued a tract on the Famine. It starts: 'Fellow Countrymen – Surely God is angry with this land. The potatoes would not have rotted unless He sent the rot into them; God can never be taken unawares; nothing can happen but as He orders it. God is good, and because He is, He never sends a scourge upon His creatures unless they deserve it – but he is so good that He often punishes people in mercy . . . to turn them from their sins.'

This analysis, based on a fundamentalist reading of the Old Testament, is profoundly conservative. Protestants are suffering now as well as Roman Catholics, 'for although they are not dying of hunger they cannot get their rents'.

Mr Nangle, who belongs to the evangelical wing of the Church of Ireland, thinks we have incurred divine wrath by removing the Bible from schools: 'The Pope's priests hate the Bible because it exposes their false religion, and they raise a disturbance whenever people are striving to get their neighbours to read the book of God. So these wicked priests never were easy as long as the Bible was in the national schools . . .'

The second sin which has provoked God to send a scourge of famine is murder: for the last thirteen years, a month did not pass without some dreadful murder being committed.

Thirdly, Rome is guilty of idolatry: 'And when you consider that the more devout Roman Catholics, in using the Rosary according to the teaching of their priests, say ten prayers to the Virgin for every one they say to God, you will see what horrid idolatry the Church of Rome teaches. And next consider what a Roman Catholic worships when he goes to mass; he worships a wafer made of flour and water by the hands of a man . . .'

Mr Nangle also blames the grant to Maynooth College in 1845: 'As soon as ever this daring affront was offered to the Almighty He sent the rot into the potatoes, and because there was no repentance for this sin, His anger is not turned away, but His hand is stretched out still.'

He urges his readers – who fortunately do not include the Irish-speaking poor – to have done with 'Romish mummery', the 'cursed wafer made in the priest's saucepan' and 'cease to trust in the Virgin Mary, in saints or angels or masses'.

As Mr and Mrs S.C. Hall have observed, this evangelical mission is a failure: 'The principles upon which it has been conducted have not been in accordance with the divine precept of charity.'[78]

'Mistaken policy'

15 MARCH 1847

Two west Cork clergymen are a welcome contrast to the bigoted Mr Nangle. The Rev Richard Townsend, of Skibbereen, does not see the Famine in terms of divine wrath; he blames British government policy for much of the suffering and describes the local population as victims of 'a most mistaken national policy on whom the principles of political economy have been carried out in practice to a murderous extent'.

Of the parish of Schull, where deaths in a population of 18,000 number fifty a day, the rector Dr Robert Traill writes: 'Frightful and fearful is the havoc around me . . . the aged, who with the young – neglected, perhaps, amidst the widespread destitution – are almost without exception swollen and ripening for the grave.'

One visitor mistakes children of nine and ten 'for decrepit old women, their faces wrinkled, their bodies bent and distorted with pain, their eyes looking like those of a corpse'.

A commander of the Royal Navy is taken on a tour of Schull by Dr Traill. J. Cruford Caffin finds three-quarters of the villagers are reduced to skeletons: 'the men in particular, all their physical power wasted away; they have all become beggars'. He finds people dead or dying in every one of the thirty cottages visited.

The first house that Caffin enters is above the ordinary in appearance and comfort. Young people are crouched over a fire, while the parents lie in another room. The father's voice is gone; the mother's cries for mercy and food are heart-rending. The family kept their cow and sheep in the house at night, until they were stolen during the day.

In another cabin the visitors find an emaciated daughter keening over the body of her mother. In an adjoining hovel are three children belonging to the daughter, whose husband has abandoned her. She doesn't know what to do with her mother's corpse, being too exhausted to remove it herself.

The door of the next cabin is blocked with dung. An old woman bursts into tears on seeing the kindly Dr Traill. She has been unable to sleep since a stranger died in her bed. The passer-by asked to be allowed to rest and died an hour later of exhaustion. Her body lay in this hovel of six feet square for four days.

The old woman had some money. She asked neighbours' children to buy her food, but they were too taken up with themselves. She now wishes 'to depart and be at peace, and had blocked up the door that she might not be disturbed'.

About 600 people have been buried in Swinford paupers' plot this spring without 'coffin or sermon or anything denoting respect for the dead'.

At a by-election in Galway, the government candidate defeats a Repealer by four votes (510 to 506), due to 'enormous bribery, horrible perjury, unlimited exercise of landlord intimidation', according to the *Nation*.[79]

Tá sinn ocrach

22 MARCH 1847

West of a line from Derry to Waterford the cry of the poor is: 'Tá sinn ocrach' (we are hungry).

The English Quaker William Bennett finds in his travels: 'They did but rarely complain. When inquired of what was the matter, the answer was alike in all – "Tha shein ukrosh".'

He and his son set out from Dublin with supplies of seed for the west. On the way they pass hundreds of emigrants mostly on foot. 'It was an affecting sight to observe numerous whole families, with all their worldly goods packed up on a donkey cart, attempting to look cheerful as they cast a wistful glance at the rapidly-passing-by coach passengers; and thus abandoning a country which should have nourished them and their children.'

Between Boyle and Ballina, 'it was melancholy in the extreme to see women and girls labouring in mixed gangs on the public roads. They were employed not only in digging with the spade and with the pick, but in carrying loads of earth and turf on their backs, and wheeling barrows like men and breaking stones; while the poor neglected children were crouching in groups around the bits of lighted turf in the various sheltered corners along the line. I need scarcely say that the soil was totally neglected here.'

A correspondent of the *Chronicle and Munster Advertiser* records his impression of conditions in west Waterford: 'Every house you enter (with the exception of the occasional strong farmer's) presents nothing but one black mass of the most deplorable wretchedness. Not a spark of fire on the hearths of nine out of every ten of the wretched houses. And where you do see a spark of fire, you will behold the squalid and misery-stricken creatures crouching round it, like spectres, with not a human lineament traceable upon their countenances. As to food, good or bad, they have none.'

In Ring, Ballynacourty, Old Parish and Ardmore he estimates deaths from starvation at twenty to thirty a day. 'Coffin-making is the staple trade of the country; every turn you take you see them in dozens being brought to the rural districts; sometimes in cars, sometimes under men's arms, and not infrequently on women's heads. I lately met several times on the Slievegrine mountain half-naked women going home and the only commodity they were able to bring from Dungarvan was coffins on their heads.'

A farmer remarks that it is impossible to walk near Tallow 'without being frightened by the rabid, hunger-stricken faces which meet you on your way – faces which you can no longer recognise . . . '

Large sums of money are arriving from the US. Archbishop William Crolly of Armagh informs Archbishop Michael Slattery of Cashel that he has received £3,000 from Bishop John Fitzpatrick of Boston.

In Oklahoma Choctaw Indians discuss the plight of Ireland. Having suffered intensely themselves, they collect $170.[80]

'Ireland a Golgotha'

29 MARCH 1847

With a fever epidemic sweeping the country, scenes of unbelievable suffering abound. Ireland seems about to turn into a Golgotha, John Mitchel predicts in the *Nation*.

In County Armagh, 400 paupers have died in Lurgan workhouse in the past eight weeks.

There were fifty deaths in Kilkenny poorhouse last week, with 520 patients in the fever hospital.

In County Clare yesterday, a correspondent reports, 'I met fifty skeletons of cows, scarcely able to move, driven to pound for the last May rent . . . Fever in every cabin; in one house a corpse lies for the last four days; no one could be got to enter it to relieve the dying, or remove the putrified victim.'

In Rosscarbery, County Cork, a man decapitates two children while stealing food. In the same neighbourhood a woman is jailed for taking vegetables; on being released she finds her children have died of starvation.

There are nearly 1,000 prisoners in Cork county jail charged with larceny and sheep-stealing, one-tenth of whom have typhus fever.

In Kilkenny, a 13-year-old boy breaks three panes of glass in a shop window so as to be transported and taken 'from his hardship'.

In Dublin scenes of misery makes even the humane callous, the *Nation* observes. 'Many, obviously unskilled in the hard lessons of mendicancy, creep out of alleys and lanes and make mute signs, stretching out their hands with an indecision which plainly shows the struggle going on within. But the most doleful of all sights and sounds is to hear and see starving women and children attempting to sing for alms . . . Hundreds – thousands – bred to industry, have now to make fellowship with the hardened vagrants, the makers of their own sores, with broken bully and the outworn prostitute.'

In Ballaghaderreen, a child aged two dies of hunger in its mother's arms during Mass.

When a poor woman comes home to her children in Killeshan, County Carlow, one of them, maddened by hunger, bites off part of her arm.

In Donoughmore, County Cork, Fr Michael Lane writes in the baptismal register: 'There died of the Famine from November 1846 to February

1847, over 1,400 of the people (almost a third of the population) and one priest, Dan Horgan. Requiescant in pace. Numbers remained unburied for over a fortnight, many were buried without a coffin. Four men were employed to bury the dead and make graves and two, and sometimes four, carpenters to make coffins.'

In Galway, the Sisters of Mercy – with Quaker support – feed up to 600 children daily; the Presentation convent provides about 500 breakfasts.

Pope Pius IX takes the unprecedented step of issuing an encyclical, *Praedecessores Nostros*, appealing to the Catholic world on behalf of the Famine victims. He has already sent 1,000 Roman dollars to the Irish bishops.[81]

Employment reduced

5 APRIL 1847

The Treasury orders a 20 per cent reduction in the numbers employed on relief works.

This policy is further evidence of England's indifference, according to William Smith O'Brien MP, who estimates that 240,000 Irish people have died unnecessarily of starvation. Unofficially, the constabulary puts the death total during the winter of 1846–7 at 400,000. Those who survived the terrible winter are being dismissed before the opening of soup kitchens.

The *Nation* does not charge Lord John Russell with wilful murder. But 'we say of the Whig premier and his fellows this: holding the interests of England, her merchants and people, superior to our lives, they did not endeavour to save the latter, unless where the attempt would not injure the former; and that, through ignorance of the means best adapted for the preservation of the lives of our countrymen and also through ignorance of their necessities, this foreign cabinet first thrust upon us a system of relief which was a system of gradual killing, and has now changed it secondly into one of killing at fixed periods so many per cent . . .

'It may attribute to an all-just God the sorrows it has inflicted upon us – nay, Him it may blasphemously arraign for the results of its own robbing imperialism, its ignorance, its incompetence and its brutish insensibility.'

A gentler voice, the Quaker William Bennett, is an eyewitnesses to the suffering in Mayo: 'We entered a cabin. Stretched in one dark corner, scarcely visible from the smoke and rags that covered them, were three children huddled together, lying there because they were too weak to rise, pale and ghastly, their little limbs, on removing a portion of the filthy covering, perfectly emaciated, eyes sunk, voice gone, and evidently in the last stages of starvation.'

An old woman lying on straw moans piteously, imploring the visitors to give her something. 'Above her, on a ledge, was a young woman with sunken cheeks – a mother I have no doubt – who scarcely raised her eyes in answer to our inquiries, but pressed her hand upon her forehead, with a look of unutterable anguish and despair. Many cases were widows, whose husbands had recently been taken off by the fever, and thus their only pittance, obtained from the public works, was entirely cut off. In many cabins the husbands or sons were prostrate under that horrid disease [famine dropsy] – in which first the limbs and then the body swell most frightfully and finally burst.'

Reflecting that thousands are dying of hunger and its kindred horrors, Bennett asks: 'Is this to be regarded in the light of a divine dispensation and punishment? Before we can safely arrive at such a conclusion, we must be satisfied that human agency and legislation, individual oppressions and social relationships have had no hand in it.'[82]

'Next year's famine'

12 APRIL 1847

In his unmistakable, apocalyptic style, John Mitchel writes about 'next year's famine'.

His leading article in the *Nation* asserts: 'Into every seaport in Ireland are now thronging thousands of farmers, with their families, who have chosen to leave their lands untilled and unsown, to sell horses and stock and turn all into money to go to America, carrying off both the money and the industry that created it, and leaving a more helpless mass of misery and despair behind them.'

The ground remains uncultivated because of mutual distrust between landlord and tenant. The landlord is afraid that, if he provides seed, the tenant will consume the crop and not pay his rent. The tenant is in dread that, if he sows grain, the landlord will pounce on the crop as soon as it is cut.

Mitchel continues: 'And the doomed wretches, who can neither leave their country nor live in it – when grubbed up weeds will no longer sustain them, when the agonies of hunger are over, and all the bitterness of death is long past and gone, patiently make themselves at home with death – take their last look at the sun and the blasted earth, and then "build themselves up in their cabins, that they may die with their children and not be seen by passers-by". And thrice and four times blessed are they who have already perished thus, instead of being kept half alive, upon stinted rations and charity soup, to die more surely, more hideously, next year.'

An increasingly radical Mitchel warns the landlords: 'Let them not press to a decision, sooner than they can help, the momentous questions that lie unsolved between them and the occupier – that might have lain unsolved for many a day if the Famine had not visited us. Men are on all sides beginning to ask to whom, after all, this land belongs; whether the rights of property appertain only to property in rents; whether the royal patent can confer the power of awarding life or death at the patentee's pleasure; whether the tillers of the soil are to go on for ever borrowing or hiring land, instead of owning it.'

The *Nation* has looked 'in no unfriendly spirit' on the gentry's attempt to form a parliamentary grouping at Westminster. But what are they doing now, it asks, 'when the abyss is yawning for them and for their country? Oh, heaven! moving clauses in Poor Law Bills . . . Have they considered whether improvements include graveyards? Have they satisfied themselves that there will be anybody left to pay the rates, in large divisions or in small? Are they deaf and blind to the fact that the peasantry, the people, the masses, the great rent-paying machine itself, is falling fast into disorder and ruin?'

Adder-deaf and stone blind, Mitchel concludes, 'and if so then doomed to destruction irretrievable, signal and unpitied'. The social order is not to be disturbed lightly, but 'the existence of a nation is more precious still'.[83]

American aid arrives

The *USS Jamestown*, manned by volunteers, arrives in Cork with 800 tons of food. An estimated 20,000 'strangers' have crowded into the city. The people are dying in such numbers on the streets that Fr Theobald Mathew provided for 135 burials in the past week.

A meeting in Faneuil Hall, Boston, resulted in the dispatch of two warships lent by the US government.

The gentlemen of Cove address the commander of the sloop: 'Filled with sorrow and dismay at the calamitous condition of a large portion of our population, it is indeed most consoling and gratifying to us to receive such kindly and substantial evidences of sympathy from a country which we look up to with so much respect and admiration, and to know that the thousands who are now hastening from our shores are going to a land where they may calculate on a warm and hospitable reception, and where industry and integrity are sure of their reward.'

Michael Doheny, the Young Irelander, has a more realistic idea of 'the blessings of emigration'. He reports from Cashel that farms are being consolidated rapidly: 'The appendages of famine, like the pangs of death, may be differently modified in different localities, but the exhausting current of public weakness flows on and on unchangeably everywhere.'

He observes that when a family emigrates two or three of the weaker members remain behind. While the better off may leave them with a year's provision, the poor can provide scarcely a week's supply. He knows of three or four cases 'where a father and mother went away by night and left three little children, scarcely more than infants, to a person to be taken next morning to the poorhouse. It may be said this was cruel and unnatural, but those who say so little know what that father and mother may have endured – how much they struggled to avoid this awful sacrifice.'

This practice is quite widespread. Imagine the legacy of guilt and bitterness which those people carry to America. They generally intend to send for their children, if successful in the New World.

Meanwhile, fifteen vessels are preparing to sail from Limerick for British North America and the United States.

In Killaloe 100 families, averaging 500 people, surrender their small holdings to the proprietor, Francis Spaight, in return for a free passage to

Canada. The *Jane Black* sails with 500 passengers for Quebec. They are principally farm labourers from Limerick, Clare and Tipperary. The *Heather Bell* sails this evening for New York with 105 passengers, 'including several independent farmers with their families from the County Kerry'.

Some $218,040 has been collected for Ireland in the US. Even the Sultan of Turkey, upon hearing of the sufferings of the Irish, donates £1,000.

Thomas Moore sends £5 to the Bannow (County Wexford) relief fund.[84]

'Work not charity'

26 APRIL 1847

The poor resent being reduced to beggars. There is a disastrous gap in relief measures between the phasing out of the public works and the installation of soup kitchens. After a winter of forcing skeletons to work for piece rates, the destitute are now to be given soup.

Initially, the people find soup kitchens degrading; they would prefer to receive wages or cook food rations themselves. They also dislike the soup, or porridge as it is often called. They demand work, explains the *Limerick Reporter*, and 'abhor the idea of being made beggars'.

Resistance is widespread in Clare, where many were until recently employed on the public works. A crowd of several hundred people attack the newly-established soup kitchen in Meelick, smash the boiler and tear up the relief committee's book. They also destroy the boiler in Cloonlara and try to do the same in Ardnacrusha, until restrained by the police. A boiler is removed in Kilfenora, while in Corofin the local soup kitchen is demolished by people who request meal rations instead of cooked 'porridge'. Rioting breaks out in Kilrush.

A mob breaks the boiler and other utensils in Patrickswell, County Limerick. In Castlemartyr, County Cork, people threaten to 'smash all the soup boilers in the country', because they want no more 'greasy kitchen stuff but should have either money or bread'.

The soup kitchens are viewed by the government as a temporary expedient to feed a large number of people with a small amount of money. Moreover, beggars can not be choosers for long.

Alexis Soyer, the French society chef, opens a model soup kitchen on Royal Barracks Esplande, Dublin. (This place is known also as the Croppies' Acre, where the bodies of executed rebels were flung into a mass grave in 1798.) After Soyer produces 100 gallons of soup for under £1, the Relief Commissioners retain his services to open a number of kitchens.

Meanwhile, a forest appears to have been cut down to feed Victorian bureaucracy – and account for every penny spent. The commissioners have distributed 10,000 account books, 80,000 sheets and 3,000,000 card tickets. The weight of these papers exceeds fourteen tons.

From Mount Melleray Abbey on the slopes of the Knockmealdowns, Dom Mary Joseph Ryan writes: 'Even in this isolated place, on a most ungrateful and profitless mountain, we relieve from eighty to 100 wandering poor daily, besides thirty-three families around us ranging from four to ten in each, who are our regular weekly pensioners and whom we have, under God, saved from hopeless starvation.'

James Fintan Lalor addresses the landlords in a letter to the *Nation*: 'If you persevere in enforcing a clearance of your lands you will force men to weigh your existence, as landowners, against the existence of an Irish people.'[85]

Hearts grow cold

3 MAY 1847

The Famine suffering is sapping not only the vitality but the compassion of the people.

In Skibbereen, Dr Daniel Donovan is given ample opportunity to study the sensations experienced by the starving. Young and old are becoming increasingly insensitive to the wants of others, he notes, responses being dictated by the desperation of their own needs. Dr Donovan has seen mothers snatch food from their starving children, sons and fathers fight over a potato, and parents look on the dead and decaying bodies of their offspring without evincing the slightest emotion.

While the people dread that they or their relations should be buried without a coffin, they are terrified of pestilence. Corpses are lying out in the fields, Bishop Charles McNally of Clogher tells the president of Maynooth College, and 'none but the clergy can be induced to approach. I yesterday sent a coffin out for a poor creature who died in a field of fever, and have just heard that no one could be prevailed to put the body in it.'

In Kerry, Archdeacon O'Sullivan of Kenmare records there is 'nothing unusual to find four or five bodies on the street every morning. They would remain so and in their homes unburied, had we not employed three men to go about and convey them to the graveyard.'

In Tralee, a visitor is informed that the local distress is 'quite beyond their means of relief' even though the town is situated on the estate of an 'unencumbered landlord, who draws about £12,000 a year out of it but whose subscription for the relief of his starving tenants was paltry in the extreme'. The body of a child lies in the main street opposite the principal hotel, 'and the remains have lain there several hours on a few stones by the side of a footway like a dead dog'.

From Clare, Cork, Galway and Mayo come reports of the dead being buried everywhere without coffins, as the living are too weak to carry their bodies to the graveyard.

The *Times*, always ready to pounce on the sister kingdom's wound, says 'the astounding apathy of the Irish themselves to the most horrible scenes under their eyes and capable of relief by the smallest exertion is something absolutely without parallel in the history of civilised nations . . . The brutality of piratical tribes sinks to nothing compared with the absolute inertia of the Irish in the midst of the most horrifying scenes.'

It regards the Irish as 'a people born and bred from time immemorial in inveterate indolence, improvidence, disorder and consequent destitution'. It argues that money spent on Irish relief is wasted. Ireland needs 'real men possessed of average hearts, heads and hands'.

Edward Twistleton, the Chief Poor Law Commissioner, is concerned that such racist opinions in the most influential newspaper of the day are having a negative impact on British policy.[86]

Starvation gap

A starvation gap caused by the 'cumbrous machinery' of the Temporary Relief Act is confirmed.

Priests describe conditions in 'begging letters' to the *Tablet*, whose editor Frederick Lucas has launched a fundraising campaign among English Catholics.

Fr Jeremiah Molony writes from Rosscarbery, County Cork: 'My good pious people are every day dying of hunger and its consequences – fever, diarrhoea and dropsy, and their sufferings must frightfully increase during the next month because the labourers heretofore employed at the public works are almost all now disemployed, and the projected out-door relief cannot come into full operation in this parish for some weeks.'

The parish priest of Goresbridge explains why: 'The names of the poor applicants for relief are taken down; the lists are then sent to Kilkenny, from thence to Dublin and then home again; in all which places they are to undergo a revision, and if any error be discovered full time must be taken to correct it before the poor starving creatures will get one pint of porridge.'

Relief committees have been maintaining nearly 4,000 people in Loughbrickland, County Down, but the funds raised by voluntary contributions and government donations are exhausted.

Owen Madden, PP Lisacull, Ballaghaderreen, says that out of 700 families in his parish, 400 are in want and have scarcely half a meal a day to sustain them. Within the last three weeks eighteen people died of starvation.

Fr Tighe, of nearby Kilcolman Abbey, acknowledges the generosity of British people: 'It is their charities and not our wavering, faithless government that have stayed in some measure the hand of death from numbers of the poor.'

The Relief Act is coming slowly into operation, he adds, 'and a more degrading, humiliating system was never offered a nation. Only think of bringing poor people six or eight miles every morning for one pound of Indian meal. The consequence is our town is crowded every day, habits of idleness are acquired, all industrious pursuits are totally neglected, and to crown our miseries fever is spreading rapidly amongst us.' Disease spreads wherever crowds assemble – especially as the warm weather approaches.

A man would have a better chance of escaping with his life in battle than in Sligo, where every street is full of infection: each night ten to fifteen people 'far gone in fever' are left outside the hospital.

Fr Maurice Power, Killeagh, County Cork, informs his bishop that 4,500 parishioners are suffering from Famine. 'Numbers of them are lying sick of fever in their wretched cabins. We have no hospitals, nor is there any means of procuring persons to attend on the sick. And, to increase our misfortunes, we are not yet receiving any aid from what is wrongly called the Relief Act.'[87]

'Doomed land'

17 MAY 1847

A west Clare priest sees no alternative to emigration from 'this doomed land'.

Malachy Duggan, PP Moyarta and Kilballyowen, has been serving his people since the famine of 1822. He now writes to the *Limerick Reporter*: 'Hitherto the employment under the Board of Works enabled about half of those who were applying for relief to drag out a miserable existence.' But this plank, to which they clung with the grasp of death, has been withdrawn and thrown the country into the greatest confusion.

'Nothing [is] to be heard but lamentations, sighs and moans, nothing scarcely to be seen but crowds of emaciated, naked and starved creatures; flocking to every door, craving for something to prolong life, even for a few hours – but, alas, in vain. The people, however well disposed and ready to respond to the calls of charity, are not able to give them any, even the smallest relief, for such as were hitherto in comparatively comfortable circumstances, their private resources being exhausted from purchasing food during the year at an exorbitant price, are now reduced to a level with almost the most destitute, thus rendering almost universal that deluge of ineffable woe which has visited this district, sweeping away hundreds.'

Fr Duggan despairs of being able any longer to save the people. The present relief measures are rendered inadequate by delays and technicalities. Since the dismissal of men from the public works, he was enabled by the donation of a benevolent family in England to rescue many from the grasp of 'a most violent and malignant fever. But that fund is now exhausted, while sickness consigns to premature graves those who could have been saved had he the means to provide them with 'those necessaries the sick poor require'.

There is one measure which, in his opinion, 'would serve as a safety valve for the people, at least in these parishes, and that is emigration on a liberal scale . . . It is impossible that a population of 14,000 could exist under present circumstances on 10,000 acres of arable land of an inferior quality. For the next year there is scarcely any provision made – no cultivation, no tillage.'

Hemmed in on every side, the poor must perish unless some means be devised 'whereby they may be enabled to leave this doomed land, and pass to another country to obtain that which is denied them in their native home'.

Despite the mounting crisis and numerous suggestions that the poorest people need assistance to emigrate, the government refuses to deviate from its policy of minimum intervention.

At a meeting of the Irish Confederation, Charles Gavan Duffy proposes a resolution calling on Smith O'Brien 'and other Irish members who loved their country to quit the British Parliament and come home and take counsel for the salvation of Ireland'.

O'Connell dies in Genoa.

[Fr Duggan died of cholera on 19 May 1849.][88]

Exodus gathers momentum

24 MAY 1847

The panic-driven exodus from Ireland gathers momentum.

Before the Famine, the Irish were reluctant to emigrate. But now the people, terrified and desperate, flee a country which seems accursed.

The *Cork Examiner* notes that 'the emigrants of this year are not like those of former ones: they are now actually running away from fever and disease and hunger, with money scarcely sufficient to pay passage for and find food for the voyage'.

For the most part, however, only those with some stake in the land can afford to emigrate; for the landless poor, with no savings or assets, the cost of a passage to British North America – £2 – remains too high. In the words of the general manager of the Provincial Bank of Ireland: 'The best go, the worst remain.'

Getting out of Ireland is a matter of life or death. Thomas Burke writes from Roscommon: 'They are Dying like the choler Pigs as fast as they can Bury them and Some of their Remains does not be Buri[e]d for 10 or 15 Days and the Dogs eating them some Buried in mats others in their clothes.'

Letters anticipating money from America paint stark images: 'Our fine country is abandoned by all the population'; 'one ile of our Chapel would hold our Congregation on Sunday at present'; and 'for the honour of our lord Jasus christ and his Blessed Mother hurry and take us out of this'.

Bands of up to 700 people have been passing through Mayo on their way to the ports. The land, says the *Mayo Constitution*, is one vast waste; not a soul is to be seen working on the holdings of poor farmers. The numbers emigrating daily from Tyrawley to America 'is astonishing: whole villages are deserted and the houses locked up . . . Mayo will be ruined irretrievably.' For six miles around Westport there are not ten acres under cultivation.

The weak and destitute flock to institutions like Ballinrobe workhouse, which is 'one horrible charnel-house'. The paupers are not the only victims of fever, however; the dying and the dead include the master, clerk, matron, doctor and chaplain.

The Catholic clergy and people walk in procession at the funeral of the rector of Westport, the Rev Pounden, who has died of disease caught while attending to the poor of his parish.

The priests of Derry have compiled a list from the parish registers of all deaths attributable to starvation between November 1846 and April 1847. They place this list in the diocesan archive, rolled in black crepe and inscribed: 'The records of the murders of the Irish peasantry, perpetrated in AD 1846–47, in the 9 and 10 Vic., under the name of economy during the administration of a professedly Liberal, Whig government, of which Lord John Russell was Premier.'[89]

Frantic appeals

The clergy appeal frantically for help on behalf of their people, who are 'dying a slow but dire death'.

Fr Eugene Coyne writes from Clifden, County Galway, that scarcely a day passes without two or three people being found dead: 'I have often seen from eight to ten corpses meet at a churchyard in a small segment of this parish, and the persons bearing them to the grave had more the appearance of walking skeletons than human beings.'

In Ballinasloe, Fr F. Whyte has observed 'health, strength, youth, childhood and old age – all withering before the face of this frightful Famine. To its victims I broke "the bread of life"; the bread that perisheth I could not command; and frequently, indeed, I have wept bitterly in quitting the abode of misery, unable to aid its wretched inmates.'

Fr Whyte has just returned from administering the last rites to a man aged forty dying in his cabin. His wife was boiling weeds for their three children. 'We were getting the relief meal, we were struck off and now we have only these weeds to eat,' she explains. 'Good heavens,' he exclaims, 'can it be possible that man, created in the image of the living God, is forced to live on weeds.'

The poor have lost all hope, writes Mary Theresa Collis from the Presentation Convent, Dingle, County Kerry. 'The children of our school are shocking to behold. They are in a filthy, ragged condition. They and their parents have parted with every decent article they had to purchase food. We would recoil from their appearance did not compassion for their miseries induce us to attend to them. Their night and day clothing is the same. Many of them have parted with their bed covering, laying it in the earth with the bodies of their deceased members.'

The relief given by the Sisters of Mercy to starving children in Kinsale, County Cork, has been of immense benefit, Fr D. Murphy avers; 'for the past five months, hundreds of these dear little children have been thus preserved from a premature grave.'

A Patrician Brother writes from Lombard Street, Galway: 'Look at our two great schoolrooms, each 100 feet by thirty, crammed to suffocation with famishing, fainting, emaciated little creatures, some of them striving to beguile the cravings of hunger by application to the food of the mind, others pining away in listless inaction and calculating as to when or where they may get a breakfast for today, or a crumb for tomorrow; infants of three years crying to their mothers for bread, and the mothers asleep in the cold green grave.'

The brothers are concerned, not with the risks to their own health in the midst of such misery, but at being unable to feed more than half of the 1,046 hungry boys crowding into their schools.

Thanks to 'the charity of our friends in England', the Christian Brothers in Peacock Lane, Cork, are able to give one meal daily to 400 children.[90]

Coffin-ship report

7 JUNE 1847

In a great mass movement the people make their way, by tens of thousands, out of Ireland, across the ocean to America, or across the sea to Britain.

The voyage to Canada in 'coffin ships' becomes a path of horror. The philanthropist Stephen de Vere, of Curraghchase, County Limerick, travelled as a steerage passenger so 'that he might speak as a witness respecting the sufferings of emigrants'.

His report reads (in part): 'Before the emigrant is a week at sea, he is an altered man. How can it be otherwise? Hundreds of poor people, men, women and children, of all ages from the drivelling idiot of ninety to the babe just born; huddled together, without light, without air, wallowing in filth, and breathing a fetid atmosphere, sick in body, dispirited in heart; the fevered patients lying between the sound, in sleeping places so narrow as almost to deny them the power of indulging, by a change of position, the natural restlessness of the diseased; by their agonised ravings disturbing those around them and predisposing them, through the effects of the imagination, to imbibe the contagion; living without food or medicine except as administered by the hand of casual charity; dying without the voice of spiritual consolation, and buried in the deep without the rites of the Church.'

The food is generally unsuitable and seldom sufficiently cooked. Passengers are compelled frequently to throw their salted provisions and rice overboard because they are not given enough water for cooking and drinking – never mind for washing.

The captain sells liquor indiscriminately to the passengers once or twice a week, 'producing scenes of unchecked blackguardism beyond description'. On arrival in Quebec, de Vere succeeds in having him fined for using false water measures.

Forty vessels with more than 13,000 refugees are detained for quarantine at Grosse Île, extending in a line two miles down the St Lawrence. About 1,200 fever cases lie in sheds, tents and the little church on the island; an equal number of sick wait to be taken off the ships.

The *Looshtauk* reaches Quebec after a voyage of seven weeks. Besides typhus, scarlet fever raged on board killing all the small children.

Dr George Mellis Douglas, Grosse Île's medical superintendent, is over-whelmed by the influx of sick and dying: 'I never contemplated the possibility of every vessel arriving with fever as they do now.'

According to a correspondent in the *Freeman's Journal*, 'the scene in New York is truly lamentable. The Irish are there, walking and begging in the streets, in as numerous groups as you will find them in Liverpool.'[91]

Fever threatens all

14 JUNE 1847

The wealthy are immune to starvation but not to fevers, particularly typhus.

Every rich person who contracts fever in this town dies, a *Cork Examiner* correspondent warns. The rich should look to the frightful condition of pestilence-carriers, for their own if not for humanity's sake. 'By night some of them, though not actually recovered from fever but driven by the gnawings of hunger, leave the fetid straw on which they were stretched and go around the town clamouring for something to eat at the houses of the wealthy classes.'

Fr Mathew's cemetery is full, 10,000 bodies having been interred there since last autumn – 'exclusive of those buried from the workhouse'.

Crowds are flocking into Mallow since the new relief committee started to issue free rations. Poor creatures place a little straw at a hall-door or outside some public building, and remain there until they die.

The Belfast General Relief Fund is providing grants to relief committees in the south. In addition a day asylum has been established in Belfast; it is now admitting 900 people daily, an estimated two-thirds of whom are described as strangers from outside the city.

The Carmelite, John Spratt, organises an interdenominational relief committee in Dublin, where 'to perpetuate the kind feeling now so liberally evinced in favour of our starving people by those of every class and creed in the distribution of relief there shall be no religious distinction whatever'.

In Limerick, the Christian Brothers in Sexton Street, with the support of Quaker families, have a cauldron of stirabout ready for the boys each day.

The Presentation Convent in Cork city has provided over 50,000 breakfasts for girls since January, with the help of 'our English brethren'.

The English Catholics have stood by us, writes Fr James Brown, of Ballintubber, but 'we are betrayed by government'. His parish is living on weeds. 'We have sent up our estimates to government and were to be relieved in four days. Fourteen days have passed and no relief. I procured meal for £60 on my own credit. It is all gone . . . Our dead are buried without coffins, and a parish once of 600 families is now reduced to sixty.'

In Paris, a committee led by Archbishop Denis Auguste Affré and Count Charles Montalembert co-ordinates assistance to the Irish, 'a people to which France is bound by so many memories'.

The Irish branch of the Society of St Vincent de Paul – which includes John O'Connell, the Liberator's son, and Charles Gavan Duffy, editor of the *Nation* – distributes aid collected by the parent body in France.

The poet 'Speranza' invokes the lesson of revolutionary France in the *Nation*.

The students and staff of the Irish College in Rome do without meals to raise money.[92]

Grosse Île

Most of the Irish disembark at Grosse Île because the fare to Canada is lower than to New York and the regulations governing the transport of passengers are less strict. The Famine devastation now extends to this quarantine station thirty miles down river from Quebec.

A medical officer observes 'a stream of foul air issuing from the hatches as dense and as palpable as seen on a foggy day from a dung heap'.

Stephen de Vere notes: 'Water covered with beds cooking vessels etc. of the dead. Ghastly appearance of boats full of sick going ashore never to return. Several died between ship and shore. Wives separated from husbands, children from parents.'

Even though the Catholic archbishop of Quebec has addressed a circular to the Irish bishops, asking them to 'use every endeavour to prevent your diocesans emigrating in such numbers to Canada', at least 45,000 more are expected.

Imposing a quarantine for fever is 'physically impossible', according to Dr Douglas, the line of ships awaiting inspection being now several miles long. There is no room on the small island to make quarantine effective. Therefore passengers are to perform their quarantine on board, after the fever cases have been removed.

But so great is the number of sick that 'a fatal delay of several days' occurs before fever cases are taken away; infection envelops the poor emigrants as the healthy and ill, dying and dead, are cooped up together under the Canadian sun. The *Agnes*, for instance, which arrived with 427 passengers, has only 150 alive after a quarantine of 15 days.

Dr Douglas warns the authorities of Quebec and Montreal that a typhus epidemic is bound to occur. With quarantine regulations abandoned as hopeless, up to 5,000 so-called healthy people have left Grosse Île; out of these, '2,000 at the least will fall sick somewhere before three weeks are over'.

In Quebec, 'emaciated objects' are soon crowding the doors of churches, the wharves and the streets, 'apparently in the last stages of disease and famine'. Fever sheds are put up at St Roch in the face of violent opposition from citizens, who throw down the first buildings erected.

Montreal is the main destination, however. Steamer-loads of emigrants, at the rate of 2,304 in twenty-four hours, come up from Grosse Île. They are discharged sick, bewildered and helpless; some lie on the wharves dying; others throng the streets with 'troops of children'. The Board of Health issues urgent recommendations: 'the pestilential odour from the emigrants' clothes alone makes it undesirable' that they should be landed in the centre of the city.

In Montreal, the sick are nursed by the Sisters of Charity. Seventeen 'Grey Nuns' and seven priests die ministering to the Irish, who are expiring at the rate of about thirty a day.[93]

Poor Law Act

28 JUNE 1847

Parliament prepares to throw the financial burden of Famine relief exclusively on Irish taxpayers by passing the Poor Law Amendment Act.

A Poor Law designed to help approximately 100,000 paupers will be forced shortly to provide relief to $1\frac{1}{2}$ million people.

The Poor Relief (Ireland) Act empowers boards of guardians to grant outdoor relief to the aged, infirm and sick poor and to widows with two or more dependent children. Able-bodied men can secure relief only if destitute and solely as inmates of the workhouse, although exceptions will be allowed for limited periods.

This latest measure to assist the Irish poor will become an agent of depopulation. Firstly, Sir William Gregory's clause precludes anybody holding more than a quarter of an acre from receiving public relief; small farmers and their families will thus be forced off the land and into the poorhouse or emigrant ship.

Secondly, leaving Irish ratepayers to carry the full cost of Famine relief – with each electoral district responsible for supporting its own poor – increases the pressure on larger farmers to dispense with labourers. Thirdly, making landlords liable for all poor rates on holdings valued at £4 or less tips the scales in favour of evicting smallholders unable to pay rents.

But the consolidation of farms is considered a necessary part of restructuring Irish society.

A separate Poor Law Commission for Ireland is created.

Granard (County Longford) board of guardians requests, unsuccessfully, its own dissolution due to the intolerable burden of relieving the destitute from local rates.

Despite being made scapegoats for their country's social ills by the burgeoning English middle class, Irish landlords share a strong community of interests with British ministers. Lords Lansdowne, Clanricarde and Palmerston are cabinet members and Irish landlords. They are votaries of political economy and favour minimal government intervention.

On the other hand, a high proportion of people on Irish estates are squatters or sub-tenants. Lord John Russell, voicing the general opinion of landed men on their rights, says: 'You might as well propose that a landlord compensate the rabbits for the burrows they have made.'

Unsurprisingly therefore, a second reading of William Sharman Crawford's Bill to give legal effect throughout Ireland to the Ulster custom is refused by 112 votes to twenty-five in the House of Commons.

Patriotic gentlemen such as Lord Cloncurry, William Smith O'Brien and Sir Colman O'Loghlen lament in vain that the principle of securing compensation to tenants for permanent improvements has been neglected in the present session of parliament.[94]

Hospitable Canada

5 JULY 1847

The United States, while generous in sending food to Ireland, is unwilling at this time to become the home of the diseased and the destitute. Congress has virtually closed US ports to such immigrants.

New York and Boston are empowered to require masters of vessels to give a financial guarantee that no passenger will become a burden on the community. Boston also refuses to give ships carrying sick passengers permission to enter the harbour. Irish Catholics are regarded 'with commiseration but also with disgust'.

The despair of emigrants, who, having endured the hardships of an Atlantic crossing in a crowded sailing ship, are ordered to put to sea again, breaks out in violence. The brig *Seraph*, for instance, with 118 cases of fever on board, is turned away from Boston. Her passengers are in such a state of starvation that the British consul provides food supplies. When ordered off to St John, New Brunswick, 'or some other British port', the passengers try to land but are driven back on board.

Another ship, the brig *Mary*, also from Cork, is refused permission to land passengers and ordered to go on to Halifax in Nova Scotia. The passengers riot and cutlasses are drawn before the disturbance is quelled.

As a result of these defensive measures, the fever-stricken are almost invariably landed on the shores of British North America. But thousands of Irish cross into the US, 'notwithstanding the exertions used to prevent their entrance there', writes a New Brunswick emigration officer. In his experience half the survivors of the Canadian epidemic make their way south of the border.

Able-bodied men go first. If they establish themselves in the US, their families will join them; if not, the families remain a permanent charge on Canadian charity.

Meanwhile, nine vessels have left Sligo carrying tenants from the estates of Lord Palmerston, the British Foreign Secretary. The Canadian authorities are enraged when the first ship arrives in St John. The *Eliza Liddell* has brought few men of employable age to the colony, mainly widows with young children and the decrepit who are unfit to work.

George Mountain, Anglican bishop of Montreal, is touched by the plight of children during a visit to Grosse Isle. Among the dozens of waifs, two particularly catch his attention: a dying child, covered with vermin, in one of the tents; and the body of a little boy, who sat down to rest under a tree and died.

Some 453 children are orphaned. Fr Charles-Félix Cazeau, 'priest of the Irish', finds homes for them. While Catholic charities in Montreal and Quebec take charge of the children, priests go on circuit in the province urging parishioners to adopt them. Many orphans adopted by French-Canadian families are magnanimously allowed to retain their Irish surnames.[95]

'Nation of beggars'

12 JULY 1847

Somewhat unreasonably, now that the British administration is feeding three million Irish people, it is accused of reducing us to a nation of beggars.

In Anglo-Irish relations, none the less, compassion and gratitude are in short supply. The poor are not treated with much kindness in Britain either; nevertheless, they have not been allowed to die in their hundreds of thousands.

But the good news is that Famine mortality has fallen to almost zero. The soup-kitchen scheme shows that Britain does possess the administrative and logistical resources to provide massive aid.

The provision of free food is, none the less, contrary to prevailing doctrines on the amelioration of poverty. By the autumn, therefore, relief measures will cease to contravene Whig ideology.

Meanwhile, the relief commissioners estimate that each adult male on lists compiled by local committees has an average of three dependants, including his wife. The person named on the list is supposed to attend the soup kitchen daily, bringing with him a suitable container. Double rations are provided on Saturdays as the kitchens close on Sundays.

The commissioners justify their unpopular decision to provide cooked food by claiming that men have sold uncooked rations and become 'drunk upon the proceedings, leaving their children to starve'.

In the short-term, the soup kitchens tackle the problems of food scarcity and hunger successfully. The long-term nutritional effects of a watery soup diet on an already weakened people is another matter.

Archbishop Slattery of Cashel laments its effect on the national psyche. He writes to Fr Laurence Renehan, president of Maynooth College: 'We are still struggling with famine and fever and, what is more than both, the demoralisation of our people consequent on the system of relief that this incapable government has inflicted on our country. Every feeling of decent spirit and of truth has vanished, and instead there is created for us a cringeing lying population, a Nation of Beggars.

'It would actually make one's blood run cold to be an eyewitness of what we are obliged to submit to, the able-bodied obliged to leave their work and the youth their schools and spend their time congregated about the gate of a soup kitchen, where their scanty rations are doled out, mixed up with all manner of persons good and bad.'

The Quakers agree with Dr Slattery. Their Dublin committee writes to Jacob Harvey, a New York merchant who is helping to co-ordinate the Irish relief operation in the US: 'It is a sad to think how much our country is demoralised. We are a nation of beggars. It is shocking to see nearly half our population subsisting, without labour, on the rations doled out to them daily by the State.'[96]

Loathsome scenes

19 JULY 1847

At Grosse Île the fetid holds are emptied slowly of their human cargoes. The superintendent of the quarantine station is criticised for delaying disembarkation but there are now 2,500 sick on the island. Dr George Douglas and his dwindling staff – four doctors have died of typhus – are overwhelmed by a tidal wave of suffering.

The fever patients endure agonies in the summer heat due to lack of medical attention and care. Fr Bernard McGauran, who has led the first group of priests to the island, records seeing 'in one day thirty-seven lying on the beach, crawling in the mud and dying like fish out of water'. At the same time 'we have thirty-two of these vessels which are like floating hospitals, where death makes frightful inroads, and the sick are crowded in among the more healthy, with the result that all are victims to this terrible illness.'

Fr Bernard O'Reilly, from Galway, adds: 'Vessels come daily crowded with sick and, unless some person through kindness brings us on board, the wretched emigrants are allowed to die in the sight of their clergy, without the supreme consolation of an Irish Catholic, the last rites of his church.'

A medical commission notes the traumatisation of the Irish, 'common sympathies being apparently annihilated by the mental and bodily depression produced by famine and disease.' Dr Douglas says he 'never saw people so indifferent to life; they would continue in the same berth with the dead person until the seamen or captain dragged out the corpse with boat hooks'. Bishop Mountain witnesses 'scenes of loathsomeness, suffering and horror in the holds'.

Ashore, Fr Jean Baptiste Antoine Ferland finds men, women and children huddled together in the hospital sheds. Many who entered without any serious illness, die of typhus caught from their neighbours.

Another French-Canadian priest, Elzéar-Alexandre Taschereau, is filled with courage and consolation by the blessings of the dying.

Stephen de Vere, who is standing by those with whom he crossed the Atlantic, describes the hospital sheds as miserable: 'Many poor families prefer to burrow under heaps of stones near the shore, rather than accept the shelter of the infected sheds.'

When they reach Quebec, de Vere rents a large house to enable emigrants to recover their strength. His 'coffin-ship' report has made a profound impression, being read aloud in the House of Lords, and will lead to reforms.

The Famine refugees are dying at the rate of forty to fifty a day on Grosse Isle. Six men dig trenches in which the corpses are 'stacked like cordwood'. As a final indignity in this world, rats leave the ships to devour the bodies which lie in shallow mass graves eerily reminiscent of potato lazy beds.[97]

Potato yield small

26 JULY 1847

This year's potato yield is good but small. Only about one-sixth of the normal acreage was planted due to seed shortage and loss of confidence. Unfortunately, therefore, Famine conditions are set to continue – *pace* Charles Trevelyan and those ministers determined to disengage from Irish aid.

Although the Temporary Relief Act stipulates that the soup kitchens can remain open until September 30th, the government decides to begin closing them next month. To expedite this process, it decrees that all able-bodied men receiving poor relief are to be made work on the roads as a test of destitution.

Parliament voted £2,250,000 towards the operation of the Relief Act – making the soup kitchens the most generously supported of the government's relief schemes after the public works. Over half this money is provided as a loan to the local relief committees. Not all of it is spent, so the Irish Executive asks if the residue (£500,000) can be reallocated to medical relief. The Treasury refuses on the ground that to do so would only further the 'unhealthy dependence' of the Irish on the British government.

As the size of the harvest becomes apparent, the Relief Commissioners believe the government will have to continue providing financial aid to several Poor Law unions, despite its stated intentions. The need for assistance is highest in the unions with the least resources. Hence the abdication of responsibility in leaving Irish property to pay for Irish poverty.

Westport union being badly in debt, the paupers are in danger of starving. When the guardians abandon their weekly board meeting, the workhouse clerk begs until he obtains provisions from local merchants.

In Ballinrobe union, a rate collector is dismissed for embezzling £720.

Sporadic violence is increasing. A crowd raids a mill in Dunfanaghy, County Donegal. The mob persists despite a bayonet charge by paramilitary police, during which two peasants are killed and others severely wounded. The constabulary retreats, leaving the people in possession of the mill and store. After they flee with their booty, soldiers and policemen scour the countryside and arrest four of the ringleaders.

In Mayo, about 100 men fire shots at big houses outside Castlebar. Calling themselves 'the children of Molly Maguire' – an agrarian secret society – they take a gun and bayonet.

James Watson, agent of the Arthur estate and a member of the Killaloe relief committee, is assassinated in Clare. A greedy farmer and shopkeeper, John Crowe, was motivated by revenge. Fifteen of his cattle were seized in lieu of five years' rent, which he could afford to pay. He declined an offer to buy them back at a shilling a head and, instead, hired 'Puck' Ryan for £5 to murder Watson.[98]

Paupers sent home

2 AUGUST 1847

While the 'surplus population' of Connacht estates is being shipped to Canada, Irish paupers are deported from Liverpool.

The *Liverpool Albion* reports that under new legislation poor emigrants are to be sent back to Ireland. 'About 300 of them had sailed up to Saturday night. All of these embarked with reluctance so marked that, were it not for the passing of the Poor Removal Bill, doubtless we should have had the pleasure of their company and the gratification of contributing to their continued support for many a day.

'Twenty of them refused point blank to quit England upon any terms, and seemed to think that the kind treatment and the excellent fare they had been receiving here were amply sufficient to banish from their minds every vestige of love of fatherland.'

They are arrested and told, 'what they appeared to be ignorant of, that the system of giving outdoor relief, as in England, was now in full operation in their own country; that they had long enough been a burden upon the industrious shopkeepers of Liverpool; and that they must go back that night and be supported in future by Irish landlords. And, accordingly, that very night they set sail, along with others, for Mayo, Roscommon, Cavan, Louth, Dundalk and Drogheda.'

So they lay, the *Nation* comments, 'that human freight, in the night air, on the bare deck, in the skipper's custody, a squalid, steaming mass – a horrid sight, unseen on earth before'.

In Manchester, on the other hand, a surgeon has died after attending to patients in the workhouse, where fever is rife among Irish inmates.

Meanwhile, Major Denis Mahon is clearing his 9,000-acre Roscommon estate of 3,000 tenants. He charters vessels to deport more than 1,000 of them to Canada, at a cost of £2,400.

The first shipload arrives at Grosse Isle. Conditions during the nine-week voyage of the *Virginius* were appalling; 158 of the 476 passengers died at sea; 180 are sick. Those able to come on deck, Dr George Douglas reports, are 'ghastly yellow-looking spectres . . . not more than six or eight were really healthy'.

Douglas adds: 'Since writing the above another plague ship has dropped in, the *Naomi* from Liverpool. This ship sailed on June 15th with 331 passengers, seventy-eight have died on the voyage and 104 are now sick. The filth and dirt in this vessel's hold create such an effluvium as to make it difficult to breathe.' Some of the dead have to be dragged out with boat hooks, since even their own relatives refuse to touch them.

Some £2,500 is sent from Calcutta for Irish Famine relief (£14,000 has already been collected by members of the British garrison, many of whom are Irish-born). A sum of £3,000 is raised in Bombay.[99]

Heroic priests

One priest attending the fever-stricken at Grosse Île has been on his feet for five days.

Fr McGauran, a Sligo man ordained recently in Quebec, caught typhus but recovered and has returned to serve on the quarantine island.

Fr McGauran reports to his archbishop that he has just spent five hours on one of the moored ships administering the sacraments to 100 people. While he and another priest were on the ships, people lay dying in the island hospital without the sacraments.

'I have not taken off my surplice today; they are dying on the rocks and on the beach, where they have been cast by the sailors who simply could not carry them to the hospitals. We buried twenty-eight yesterday, twenty-eight today, and now (two hours past midnight) there are thirty dead whom we will bury tomorrow. I have not gone to bed for five nights.'

The spectacle, he continues, is heart-rending. 'Once these hapless people are struck down by this strange malady, they lose all mental and physical powers and die in the most acute agony. We hardly give anyone Holy Communion because we do not have the time . . . I am not at all afraid of the fever. I have never felt happier than in my actual state. The Master Whom I serve holds me in His all-powerful Hand.' But Fr McGauran's legs are beginning to bother him.

A captain remarks to Fr Taschereau that it would be more humane to send a battery of artillery from Quebec to sink the ships than to let those people die in such an agonising manner. Many who were healthy on reaching port have contracted disease while cooped up with the dying and the dead.

'How can we wish them health,' asks Fr Taschereau, 'when all breathe the foul air of the between-decks, walk on flooring covered with muck; consider the unwholesome food and dirty water they take for their meals. Most of them have for a bed the boards or a few filthy wisps of straw . . . How many more after a month and a half of the crossing are wearing the same clothes and the same shoes they had when they came on board, and which they have not taken off day or night?

'I have seen people whose feet were so stuck to their socks that I could not anoint them.' He observes a child playing with the hand of its dead mother.

Among the helpers willing to enter the fever-ridden holds is Fr Hubert Robson, who declares: 'I will give my life if I must for those unfortunates.' In the Canadian summer heat, he goes down into the holds where, walking ankle-deep in slime, he loads the diseased on his shoulders and carries them to the hospital.

Two Anglican and four Roman Catholic priests, including Fr Robson, lose their lives ministering to the sick and the dying.[100]

Whigs re-elected

16 AUGUST 1847

The general election is an incongruous intrusion in this part of the United Kingdom. Nevertheless, it confirms the Russell administration in office and shifts the balance of power within his party in favour of those who, like the Chancellor Charles Wood, oppose intervention in Ireland. An impending economic crisis in Britain strengthens the 'famine fatigue' syndrome.

The success of the soup kitchen network has shown that Britain possesses the means to feed the starving Irish. But the will is not there. Charles Trevelyan, the Treasury mandarin, is already talking about the Famine being over, even though this year's potato harvest is grossly inadequate.

Lord John Russell is a weak prime minister, full of ill-advised schemes for Ireland's improvement. He is critical of the clearances, which are a by-product of his government's Irish policy.

Despite the enormous supply of free food, the Quakers are still receiving appeals for help. They issue up to £5,000 worth of Indian meal each week, assisted by committees in Cork, Waterford, Clonmel and Limerick.

This operation now relies almost completely on American munificence, Joseph Bewley and Jonathan Pim inform the Irish Relief Committee in New York. 'The solicitations for help are now chiefly on behalf of those who in ordinary times have been far removed from want – small farmers, decent tradesmen and others, who are not quite arrived at the point of complete destitution, entitling them to be placed on the public relief lists, or who would shrink from the exposure of their necessities inseparable from a system of legislative relief.'

In particular, the Quakers wish to support those left most at risk by the Poor Law Amendment Act: Tenant farmers holding 'perhaps from four to five acres of ground, which they have with great difficulty managed to cultivate and sow with grain or green crops, and in so doing exhausted all their little resources.

'These persons are generally refused public assistance as not completely destitute; but the alternative of selling their farms at a ruinous price is such as is not to be resorted to but in the very last extremity; and hence they are willing rather to struggle with starvation for the few months which may elapse ere they can reap the fruit of their labours.'

While the government is coping efficiently with the crisis at present, the Quakers fear renewed starvation when the Temporary Relief Act expires.

The *Nation* lists twenty-seven clergymen who have given their lives attending to Famine-fever victims: eighteen Catholic and nine Protestant (including Dr Traill, rector of Schull).[101]

American dream

23 AUGUST 1847

What would Ireland do without the United States, a New York Quaker asks the Dublin committee. The British colonies cannot take one-quarter of those who must emigrate, Jacob Harvey observes; and except to Canada the passage money is enormously high; emigrants to the US 'not only relieve you from their own wants, but they assist you by their remittances in supporting the poor who remain behind'.

Harvey, a philanthropic exponent of the American Dream, never encourages men of property or clerks to emigrate, 'but when we come to the broad-fisted farmer and mechanic, with a young family, I say make a new home for your children in a country where you will find thousands of your own people, and where starvation is unknown'.

A new US emigration law is working well. He advises against sailing during winter months: 'We receive emigrants with open arms for seven months in the year and this ought to satisfy them.'

Mr Harvey reports that industrious Irish immigrants 'soon get into profitable employment and attend very much to their own affairs. When they get above the world, their ideas of comfort become exalted and they give their children a good education. Many others who come out are too easily satisfied in the cities; the high wages tempt them to remain as hewers of wood and drawers of water.

'They do all the rough work, carrying the hod, paving the streets, digging canals, etc., and care not much for the comforts of life. These are mostly too old to change their habits, and we must look for improvement to their children, who become Americanised as they grow up. The city Irish, I must say, have not the ambition of the Americans to rise above their condition. I speak in the general; but they are affectionate and kind-hearted, generous to their relatives at home and willing to serve each other.'

Mr Harvey wishes more of this class could be induced to go west. 'As farmers, they very soon catch the native spirit and long to become proprietors of land themselves. But so long as there is so much hard labour to be done in the city, which Americans dislike to do, the very poorest emigrants, to whom a dollar-a-day is a fortune, cannot be enticed into the country.'

Harvey's impressions are valuable but limited. Although an energetic fund-raiser, he is a stranger to the stricken Irish countryside. He has little comprehension of the exodus from Ireland, where tens of thousands of Famine refugees are migrating eastwards, mainly to Dublin port.

In contrast with raucous pre-Famine crowds, their silence is striking. As they pass through relatively prosperous towns, citizens are shocked by their appearance but for the most part shun any contact with them. This is largely because of fear of infection, but also from an aversion to the sight of their passivity and degradation.[102]

Quaker warning

30 AUGUST 1847

The soup-kitchen operation is being wound down.

On August 15th, the Treasury ordered that the distribution of rations by public relief committees was to cease in fifty-five Poor Law unions, mainly in the east and midlands. It ended in the remaining unions yesterday, except for the twenty-six poorest unions where assistance may continue until September 30th.

The Catholic chaplain consecrates a quarry near Westport workhouse for use as a mass grave. Bailiffs enter Ballina poorhouse and seize goods in distraint for debt.

The Quakers warn that the coming period is likely to be catastrophic for the poor. Jonathan Pim fears 'the new Poor Law may not be found capable of preventing a severe pressure and grievous suffering in many places.'

He reports the death of a Cork Friend, Abraham Beale: 'The constant anxiety, together with the painful effect on his mind of tales of sorrow beyond his power to relieve, was too much for him.'

The harvest employment is temporary, Joseph Bewley points out, 'and we continue to look forward with considerable apprehension to the approaching period when the demand for labour will be so abridged as to leave without the means of subsistence that large proportion of our rural population, who have been heretofore accustomed to live for a considerable part of the year solely on the produce of their potato ground.

'In dealing with this state of things great difficulties will be experienced; in the first place, to preserve from starvation those who are really destitute, and in the next place to administer the required help in a way as little calculated as possible to foster habits of idleness and dependence on others.'

The *Nation* has accused the Catholic Church of not speaking out against the 'murder' its people. While discharging their local duties 'with a devotion unsurpassed in the annals of martyrdom', the priests should have excoriated the non-interventionist policy of the government, thunders an increasingly agitated John Mitchel.

'Did this gentleman ever read any of the thousand letters of the Catholic priesthood complaining of the murder of their parishioners by starvation?' asks Fr James Fitzpatrick, of Castletownroche. 'The Catholic clergy took every opportunity, publicly and privately, of denouncing the criminal policy of the Whigs.' But by raising their voice against oppression they are accused of inciting the people to crime.

According to the Viceroy, Lord Clarendon: 'The priests are everywhere behaving ill and are bitterly hostile to the government whom they accuse of starving the people, etc., nor is it much to be wondered at for they are in great distress and consequently in bad humour; they must have some cry wherewith to excite the people.'[103]

Crown tenants depart

6 SEPTEMBER 1847

The first batch of Ballykilcline emigrants assembles in the market square of Strokestown, County Roscommon.

They are tenants from a Crown estate who have been on rent strike for twelve years. Their final attempt to seek legal redress has failed. Six months ago – within three weeks of the departure of Major Mahon's ill-fated tenants on the *Virginius* – the leaders of the 'Ballykilcline rebellion', along with the townland's 500 inhabitants, were issued with eviction notices.

The Crown has now offered free passage to New York if they surrender their cabins and holdings. The gradual emptying of Ballykilcline begins. Its people are to be shipped out in five batches, each containing approximately 100 peasants.

After years of resistance, they march to Dublin port like a defeated army. They represent the Famine exodus in microcosm, although better provided for than the mass of unassisted emigrants. On every tree, corner and pump in a fifty-mile radius of Dublin they notice handbills proclaiming that only fools remain in Ireland.

Dublin and Liverpool are the first and last of Europe's great cities that the emigrants will see. About 1,000 Famine refugees a week are pouring into Liverpool – 'the Gateway to the Atlantic' – where the emigrant business has become almost as vicious as the recently-abolished slave trade.

Many arrive in cattle boats. Peasants who have never seen ocean-going ships of sail or steam now observe hundreds in motion at once. Having just left a countryside where the chapel and a few cabins formed the centre of their world, they see gigantic walls of granite and thousands of multistoreyed buildings lining the wharfs.

This uncontrolled rush of humanity breaks off the Mersey waterfront. Nowhere else in the world is the contrast between economic vitality and utter destitution more manifest. On entering the city's streets, the refugees cannot miss the 'want and woe' of their fellow emigrants, or the revulsion of Liverpudlians.

Their *via dolorosa* to the New World continues amid disease, predators and despair. Weaned on a culture of secrecy, the transplanted peasants seek survival in furtiveness.

It is not known if the eight from Ballykilcline who went missing in Liverpool died of fever. Among them was Patrick Culkin, a former schoolmaster marooned with his wife and three children. When the parish relieving officer discovers them in a putrid cellar, Culkin is lying in bed beside his dead wife.

Their eldest daughter is laid out on a table, having died of cholera. On returning to remove the bodies, the officer finds that Culkin has cut the throats of his two younger children and barely failed in taking his own life.[104]

Liverpool experience

13 SEPTEMBER 184

The passage through Liverpool is the most common experience of Famine emigrants. Dr George Douglas, the medical superintendent at Grosse Isle, insists that the filthy slums in which poor emigrants lodged before they embarked were one of the main causes of the ship fever disaster.

The spectacle of the exodus is concentrated in the few square miles of the waterfront where, in a sense, all Irish townlands meet for the first time and witness their common fate.

In Liverpool, the poverty of the emigrants is visible in their malnourished bodies and rags. But their demeanour also distinguishes them from other paupers. The Famine refugees are described as 'passive', 'stunned' and 'mute'.

The authorities, especially the unenviable health and parish relieving officers, are frustrated by the tendency of the sick or starving peasants to hide themselves in cellars and tenements. Up to 27,000 Irish have crept into Liverpool's notorious cellars, in which as many as forty people can be found in dens of twelve by fifteen feet.

The secrecy is due partly to a fear of being sent back; some 15,000 have been returned to Ireland under the Poor Law Removal Act. Speaking Gaelic above a whisper outside the Irish wards also brands the emigrant for both the authorities and the swarms of predators. Ultimately, according to a missionary who has died since of typhus, the fever-stricken seem 'resigned beyond natural resignation'.

Crowds of paupers lining the waterfront are among the first of their countrymen the newcomers see on landing. Begging has become a scourge of the town and, although practised by many others, is associated particularly with the Irish.

The bedraggled hordes fleeing from Ireland provide an irresistible scapegoat for public fears and official impotence, while their brutalised condition confirms sectarian hatreds. The *Liverpool Herald*, a leading Orange newspaper, comments: 'It is remarkable that the lower order of Irish papists are the filthiest beings in the habitable globe, they abound in dirt and vermin and have no care for anything but self-gratification that would degrade the brute creation.'

They are associated with typhus by reason of their rags and otherness, rather than the deadly lice. Ignorant of the nature of the disease, many take the symptoms of deprivation and exposure, the consumption, ophthalmia and diarrhoea which beset the emigrants, as signs of infection and shun contact with the suffering people.

Anticipating the odour of racial prejudice awaiting them in the US, the American consul, Nathaniel Hawthorne, notes of the dock scene: 'The people are as numerous as maggots in cheese; you behold them, disgusting and all moving about, as when you raise a plank or log that has long lain on the ground, and find vivacious bugs and insects beneath it.'[105]

Violent irritation

20 SEPTEMBER 1847

Besides Liverpool, the refugees stream into Britain through Glasgow and the ports of south Wales.

A fever epidemic has broken out in Glasgow, which is swarming with Irish beggars. As in Liverpool, they crowd into such shelter as they can find; one cellar, measuring ten feet by ten, holds eight adults and seventeen children. Great numbers of Irish are landed on the Welsh coast, 'bringing pestilence on their backs, famine in their stomachs'.

Manchester's experience of Famine immigration is typical of industrial towns. It already has a 'little Ireland' slum, the population being one-tenth Irish. The newcomers ramble about the streets 'in droves' seeking shelter.

In Birmingham, the Irish influx has caused such overcrowding that 115 women are found sleeping in three rooms. The Irish are reported to be entering London at the rate of 1,000 a week, mainly by road from the west.

Not only are they detested: any hope that the misery of the destitute might evoke compassion is destroyed by the fear of fever. In York, for instance, when the Irish flock into the city, its citizens refuse to allow any building to be used as a fever hospital. Outside the city, however, live the Hacks, members of the Society of Friends; their eldest son, James Hack Tuke, is to visit Connacht shortly. Mr Hack, snr, a member of the York Board of Guardians, erects a wooden shed in one of his fields which is filled immediately with Irish fever patients.

But the general British reaction is one of violent irritation, epitomised by Thomas Carlyle, who describes the Irishman as 'the sorest evil this country has to strive with. In his rags and laughing savagery, he is there to undertake all work that can be done by mere strength of hand and back – for wages that will purchase him potatoes. He needs only salt for condiment, he lodges to his mind in any pig-hutch or dog-hutch, roosts in outhouses, and wears a suit of tatters . . . There abides he, in his squalor and unreason, in his falsity and drunken violence, as the ready-made nucleus of degradation and disorder.'

Fredrich Engels considers this racial imagery 'one-sided' but otherwise 'perfectly right'. What does such a race want with high wages, he asks. The worst quarters of the large towns are inhabited by Irishmen. 'Filth and drunkenness, too, they have brought with them. The lack of cleanliness, which is not so injurious in the country . . . becomes terrifying and gravely dangerous through its concentration here in the great cities. The Milesian deposits all garbage and filth before his house door here, as he was accustomed to do at home, and so accumulates the pools and dirt-heaps which disfigure the working-people's quarters and poison the air. He builds a pigsty against the house wall as he did at home, and if he is prevented from doing this, he lets the pig sleep in the room with himself . . . '[106]

Soup distribution ends

27 SEPTEMBER 1847

The distribution from government soup kitchens is to cease at the end of this month without reference to the grossly inadequate supply of potatoes. With an economic slump in Britain, middle-class opinion now agrees with the Chancellor of the Exchequer, Charles Wood, that the Irish must rely on their own inadequate resources.

For Charles Trevelyan, his right-hand man in the Treasury, 'the change from an idle, barbarous isolated potato cultivation to corn cultivation, which frees industry and binds together employer and employee in mutually beneficial relations . . . requires capital and a new class of men.'

Potato cultivators and improvident landlords are seen as barriers to progress.

Lord Clarendon, too, considers the blight has initiated a social revolution which must be consolidated: 'In the next two years there will be a grand struggle and the government of Ireland will be a painful thankless task, but I am convinced that the failure of the potatoes and the establishment of the Poor Law will eventually be the salvation of the country – the first will prevent the land being used as it hitherto has been.'

Even though the Irish Poor Law administration is already in crisis, the British government forces it to assume responsibility for providing relief. The starving are to be left to the mercy of a Poor Law system maintained by whatever can be extracted from landlords and stronger farmers.

Relief Commission operations are to be wound up, Trevelyan informs Sir John Burgoyne: 'The duties we lay down have been imposed by the Legislature on the Poor Law Commissioners and the Boards of Guardians.'

While regulations to protect the paupers are flouted, misery and chaos prevail in the workhouses. Guardians routinely abuse their position by awarding themselves lucrative supply contracts, which they fill with substandard materials to the detriment of the powerless inmates. Ratepayers are becoming cynical, blind to anything which might increase their burdens.

Wood warns Trevelyan to 'look sharp after the rates', amid reports that landlords are seizing corn for rent, in advance of rate collectors.

Britain is not abdicating its responsibility totally, however. The twenty-two poorest unions on the western seaboard will continue to receive assistance. But as far as possible, the money distributed is to be drawn from the funds of the British Relief Asociation rather than the imperial Treasury.

Trevelyan takes his family for a fortnight's holiday to France, 'after two years of such continuous hard work as I have never had in my life'.[107]

Famine fatigue

4 OCTOBER 1847

A second Queen's Letter fails to elicit many subscriptions for Ireland. An earlier letter from Queen Victoria read in all Church of England churches, coupled with a day of 'Fast and Humiliation' last March, raised almost £172,000 for the destitute Irish. (The emphasis on atonement reinforced providentialist interpretations of the Famine.) But now public opinion has turned against assisting Ireland and only £30,000 is donated.

Chancellor Wood tells Lord Clarendon that the editor of the *Times* received sixty-two letters by one post from clergymen who objected to making a collection. Several refused to collect and Wood's preacher in Whitehall 'took the opportunity of pointing out the ingratitude of the Irish'.

The second appeal arouses a vitriolic debate in the columns of the *Times*. One protagonist asks: 'Why should the United Kingdom pay for the extravagance of Ireland?' An Anglican minister says that giving any more money to Ireland would be 'about as ineffectual as to throw a sackful of gold into one of their plentiful bogs'. The *Times* is against 'begging for Ireland' and suggests that any money raised by the queen's letter should be given to the English poor.

Burgoyne, the Relief Commissioner, is compelled to point out that in Ireland 'absolute famine still stares whole communities in the face'.

Lord John Russell, who presides over a divided cabinet, feels caught between resentment on both sides of the Irish Sea: British opinion thinks too much has been done for Ireland, while the Irish 'seem always to act in the manner most opposite to that which is usual in other countries. The expenditure of £10 million to save the people from starving has thus raised a bitter spirit of hostility.'

The government has remitted half the money loaned for relief. Wood is convinced that if further concessions are made Irish taxpayers will never again take repayments seriously. Not for the first and perhaps last time, Russell allows his better instincts to be overruled by the parsimonious Treasury.

He writes lamely to Clarendon, who has softened somewhat since his appointment as Lord Lieutenant: 'I fear you have a most troublesome winter ahead of you . . . and here we have no money.'

In Ireland, not even the strength of the British army can wring rates from places where nothing is left to seize. Lord Sligo warns: 'Public funds must feed our poor or they must die, and how are these funds to be produced? Not in Sligo, for a stone is not bread.'

Increasingly, hard-pressed landlords solve their financial difficulties by evicting smallholders.

Henry Grattan MP, powerless because of the abolition of his father's parliament, remarks that the Lord Lieutenant has no power and Downing Street no heart.[108]

Prospect 'terrifying'

11 OCTOBER 1847

As winter approaches, the Chief Secretary, Sir William Somerville, finds the prospect of providing relief through the machinery of the Poor Law 'terrifying'. Poor Law Commissioner Twistleton anticipates a continuation of deaths from starvation for which he will be held responsible. Crowds of vagrants roam the countryside.

In the distressed western and southern unions, the Poor Law officers paint an ominous picture. The condition of the people is described as 'wretched' and 'debilitated', and worse than last year.

In the Castlebar union, the vice-guardians refer to the applicants for relief as 'a wretched mass of human misery'; they are admitted to the workhouse although it is already full.

In Swinford, nine properties are being administered by the Court of Chancery. 'Out of 60–70 names returned as ratepayers, 50–60 are non-resident,' reports Captain Delves Broughton, a Poor Law inspector. 'The tenantry are proportionately neglected, or I might say abandoned, for in few instances is the agent resident either and, in some cases, no one but a driver is left as the representative of a proprietor.' A driver drives away cattle seized for rent or rates and forces evicted people out of the ruins of their homes. During the past week, only £25 out of a rate of £2,600 has been collected in Swinford.

While the guardians are assembled in the board room of Rathkeale workhouse, 3,000 peasants from Glin, Shanagolden, Pallaskenry and Askeaton surround the institution and demand assistance from the master. The crowd attempts to demolish the poorhouse and, according to the *Limerick Chronicle*, 'rioted on the military'.

Regardless of increased distress as the harvest work draws to a close, the government and the Poor Law Commissioners refuse to permit outdoor relief until it is absolutely necessary. A circular from the commissioners informs boards of guardians that 'the evil which is to be most guarded against is the necessity of granting outdoor relief to able-bodied men'.

The 'workhouse test' is employed as proof of destitution. If additional accommodation is not possible, the guardians are to discharge the old and infirm paupers already in the workhouse to make way for able-bodied applicants.

The Rathkeale guardians, remembering the recent riot, resign in protest against the policy of making the most vulnerable categories of paupers leave the shelter of the workhouses.

When extra poorhouse accommodation becomes available in Tipperary, 600 men are offered admission; on refusing it, they are struck off the relief lists. While outdoor relief costs less, the problem is one of scale; for every five people applying to enter the dreaded workhouse, fifty want outdoor relief.[109]

Evictions increasing

18 OCTOBER 1847

Clearances are mushrooming under the spur of the Gregory Clause, which precludes anybody holding more than a quarter acre of land from receiving public relief. In the Golden Vale of Tipperary, vast numbers of smallholders are surrendering their farms to qualify for assistance. The main incentive for landlords to evict tenants is to avoid liability for poor rates on all holdings valued at £4 and under.

Many landowners and their agents now seize the opportunity provided by the Famine to impose order on estate management.

When a family enter the poorhouse their cabin is generally pulled down, thus making them permanent paupers. But the system ensures that the focus of the guardians is on the bottom line of the ledger rather than humanity. Thus a father is threatened with prosecution for leaving Clogheen (County Tipperary) workhouse to visit his children in the adjacent fever hospital.

Yet dispensary medical officers minister to the fever-stricken in their ill-ventilated cabins. In single-room homes fever patients are placed at one end of the dwelling, while the healthy try to ward off infection at the other. In larger houses, the practice is to isolate the infected in a room by blocking the door with sods. A hole is made in the rear wall, through which the doctor scrambles. Not surprisingly, forty-eight doctors have died in Munster this year.

The *Cork Examiner* reports food riots in Bantry: 'The withdrawal of rations, coupled with the frightful prospect of an approaching winter, have blighted all hopes of existence and goaded the enraged multitude to desperation. The wretched and famished inhabitants of the neighbouring parishes proceeded to town, and from thence to the workhouse, where they demanded admission and were refused.'

They are dispersed by a large party of military and police. Some of the people pluck turnips and eat them while retreating.

A English clergyman, Sidney Osborne, observes mealtime in a west of Ireland poorhouse: 'It was quite a complete scramble; the parties bringing in the food – men – had short thick sticks, which they used very freely and I thought brutally, to protect the tons of stirabout from the rush made for them by these hungry women.'

William Forster writes to his wife from Galway: 'It was enough to have broken the stoutest heart to have seen the poor little children in the workhouse yesterday – their flesh hanging so loose from their bones, that the physician took it in his hand and wrapped it round their legs.'

A coastguard officer points out indignantly that two-thirds of the people of Connemara are destitute; many ratepayers have become paupers, yet 'collectors, aided by police, are out daily, seizing wearing apparel and tools even'.[110]

Right to life asserted

The Catholic bishops speak out against Britain's Irish policy. Finally overcoming their timidity and divisions, they assert the supremacy of the right to life over the rights of property.

In common with the Catholic Church throughout post-Napoleonic Europe, the Irish church is anti-revolutionary and in general its clergy exercise a moderating influence on their flocks. Yet two of the leading prelates – Murray of Dublin and MacHale of Tuam, quite different men – were marked by the rising of 1798.

Fifty years ago, Daniel Murray narrowly escaped being slaughtered with his congregation in Arklow by the Antrim militia. As a child, John MacHale was aware that his parish priest had been hanged in Castlebar for harbouring French officers.

In an extraordinary submission to Lord Clarendon, the hierarchy now rejects the view propounded by the *Times* that the Famine was caused by the 'innate indolence' of the Irish people. The real causes are the laws which deprive the bulk of the people of the right to property and to the fruits of their labour. In Ireland, laws sanctioning injustice are enforced 'with reckless and unrelenting vigour'; in those conditions, the failure of the potato precipitated a catastrophe.

While sharing the widespread fear that 'mere gratuitous relief' has a demoralising tendency, the bishops' memorial shows no trace of a providentialist explanation of the Famine as God's retributive justice. Demanding a fair arrangement between landlords and tenants, it reminds Clarendon that 'large tracts of land capable of cultivation are now lying waste', that the seas are teeming with fish, and that the country abounds in mineral wealth.

Requesting productive employment, the bishops consider the government relief measures wholly inadequate. The workhouses are overcrowded, fever-ridden and capriciously managed. The choice facing the people is either to starve if they do not enter them, or die of contagious disease if they do.

The bishops' call for special government intervention is out of line with established economic thought. They go beyond the strict bounds of 'religion' to criticise the existing order and express principles of social justice:

'The sacred and indefeasible rights of life are forgotten amidst the incessant reclamations of the subordinate rights of property . . . Hallowed as are the rights of property, those of life are still more sacred, and rank as such in every well-regulated scale that adjusts the relative possessions of man; and if this scale had not been frequently reversed we should not have so often witnessed in those heart-rending scenes of the evictions of tenantry, "the oppressions that are done under the sun, the tears of the innocent having no comforter and, unable to resist violence, being destitute of help from any".'[111]

'Awful condition' outlined

1 NOVEMBER 1847

Lord Clarendon meets a bishops' delegation which lays 'at the foot of the throne the starving and awful condition' of Ireland. The lord lieutenant, believing Archbishop MacHale is the principal author of the episcopal statement, finds him surprisingly reasonable. Encouraged, Clarendon now writes to MacHale expressing concern at rural disturbances and clerical involvement.

This formidable archbishop, gratified that for the first time a government has sought his advice, replies outlining the situation in the west. The Poor Law is utterly inadequate. As evictions intensify the human misery, 'the struggling people are burdened with the support of these outcasts from their homes'. Men enraged by hunger and despair threaten the 'derangement of society', he concludes.

Fear of social disorder is a constant concern of the clergy 'anxious to preserve the souls of their flock from crime'. The increase in evictions, coming on top of hunger and disease, has provoked a number of murders and attempted murders of landlords and agents.

In Ennistymon, County Clare, a priest expects infractions of the law from people who say they would prefer to be shot by the military 'than die the cruel death of starvation'.

Alarmed at the prospect of a peasants' revolt, Clarendon impresses on the cabinet that Ireland needs help urgently: 'It is impossible that this country can get through the next eight months without aid in some shape or other from England. Irish ingratitude and the poverty of England may be urged . . . but none of these reasons will be valid against helpless starvation or servile war.'

James Fintan Lalor convenes a meeting of farmers in Holycross, County Tipperary, to form a tenant league. A considerable number of the 4,000 present appear to be comfortable farmers.

Lalor says their principal object is to establish in Tipperary 'the tenant-right of Ulster', which he defines as security of tenure so long as the tenant pays a fair rent.

The chairman, Michael Doheny, saw three cabins levelled this week. The notion is being promulgated among landlords that small farmers should be got rid of. Will the people submit tamely to the destruction or deportation of this class, he asks. Doheny urges constitutional rather than violent action. He advises payment of rent 'where you are able but . . . not to starve for the sake of meeting any demand'. He refutes the argument that parliament has no power to interfere with the rights of property.

Meanwhile, 'midnight legislators' are organising sporadic resistance to the payment of rents and poor rates. Near Mullinahone, between sixty and 100 armed men imprison two bailiffs while corn seized in lieu of rent is carried off. Elsewhere in County Tipperary, constables protecting a rate collector fix bayonets to keep the people at bay.[112]

'As bad as slave trade'

8 NOVEMBER 1847

Famine refugees continue to cross the Atlantic even though it is perilously late in the season. Many of the emigrants flee in a mood of despair, anxiety, even hysteria, being willing to risk an autumn or winter sailing in their determination to leave Ireland.

The dramatically increased volume of traffic is too great a temptation for agents to resist extending the season, leading to more turbulent crossings and exposing already weakened emigrants to the North American winter.

The *Lord Ashburton* is the last vessel to be inspected at Grosse Isle during the 1847 navigation season. Its condition is 'a disgrace to the home authorities,' says the *Quebec Gazette*: 107 passengers died during the crossing and another sixty are ill. Two other ships chartered by Lord Palmerston unload their human cargoes – tenants 'riddled with disease' from his Sligo estates – in Saint John, New Brunswick, as the St Lawrence is closed by ice.

The citizens of Saint John declare they cannot support those emigrants, and offer them free passage and food as an incentive to return to Ireland. The city council censures Palmerston, one of Her Majesty's ministers, for having 'exposed such a numerous and distressed portion of his tenantry to the severity and privations of a New Brunswick winter . . . unprovided with the common means of support, with broken-down constitutions and almost in a state of nudity'.

Saint John is filled with 'swarms of wretched beings going about the streets imploring every passer-by, women and children in the snow, without shoes or stockings and scarcely anything on'. They are more like ghosts than human beings.

A member of the Legislative Council asserts, in a letter to the British Colonial Secretary, Earl Grey, that conditions aboard the ships bringing the destitute Irish to Canada are 'as bad as the slave trade'.

The *Roscius* arrives at Staten Island after a crossing of forty-four days with the first batch of Ballykilcline exiles. Although she reports no losses at sea, the *Roscius* lands only forty-three Crown emigrants in New York, leaving sixty-eight men, women and children missing somewhere between Strokestown and Staten Island.

The immigrant slum is a profound psychological shock. Even before the Famine hordes arrived, child mortality reached hideous levels in the Irish areas of Boston and New York. Children in the Irish districts of Boston seem 'literally born to die'.

In New York, the old men cadging drinks in the shebeens of the Sixth Ward, or confined in the lunatic asylum on Blackwell's Island, or dying in the Bellevue wards are heading for the Potter's Field pauper cemetery.[113]

Mahon assassination

15 NOVEMBER 1847

Denis Mahon is shot dead on his way home from a meeting of Roscommon board of guardians. His assassination, one of a half-dozen murders or attempted murders of landlords or their agents this autumn, alarms the gentry.

The sharp reaction by press, peers and parliament hardens opinion against further expenditure on Ireland. A local priest is accused of having incited the assassins. Sectarian tensions are inflamed and the Catholic priesthood replaces Irish landlords as scapegoats.

Lord Farnham claims in the House of Lords that the parish priest of Strokestown, Michael McDermott, had declared at Mass on the Sunday before the murder that 'Major Mahon is worse that Cromwell and yet he lives'. The allegation of Farnham, a leading Orangeman, causes a sensation.

Lord Palmerston, the Foreign Secretary, avers that the best way to stop the assassination of landlords is to hang the local priest. The *Times* announces the formation of a combination, whose members swear 'that for the life of every Protestant . . . we will take the life of the parish priest where the deed was committed'.

The assassination of Mahon occurs against a background of rent strike, clearances, forced emigration and coffin ships.

The major had clashed at meetings of the Strokestown relief committee with Fr McDermott, who accused him of amusing himself in London while his tenants starved. Mahon retorted that 'whatever I did with regard to my property I conceived rested with myself, and desired the reverend gentleman not to presume to meddle in my private affairs.'

Like other landlords with congested estates, Mahon turned to a land agent. He employed his cousin John Ross Mahon, of the Dublin firm of Guinness and Mahon [the future bankers]. The major was advised to clear his estate of two-thirds of its population: 'If you do not there is no prospect of your getting any rent for years . . . '

He was informed that the cost of emigration, while considerable, would be half that of maintaining paupers in Roscommon workhouse. This political economy resulted in the coffin-ship disaster which ignited murderous passions in Strokestown.

Bonfires burn for miles around on the night of the crime.

Father McDermott denies indignantly that he denounced Mahon from any altar. He goes on to assert, however, that the 'sole cause' of the shooting was 'the infamous and inhuman cruelties which were wantonly and unnecessarily exercised against a tenantry, whose feelings were already wound up to woeful and vengeful exasperation by the loss of their exiled relatives, as well as by hunger and pestilence'.

Bishop George Browne of Elphin affirms that he can find no evidence against the priest. He publishes a list of 3,006 tenants dispossessed by Mahon's agent, most of whom are now dead.[114]

Church blamed

22 NOVEMBER 1847

Lord Clarendon shuts himself up in the viceregal lodge after the Mahon murder. He renews his calls to the prime minister for a special powers act.

Russell, who still hopes to integrate Catholic Ireland into the Union, replies: 'It is quite true that landlords in England would not be shot like hares and partridges. But neither does any landlord in England turn out fifty persons at once, and burn their houses over their heads, giving them no provision for the future. The murders are atrocious, so are the ejectments.'

But the prime minister encourages Lord Shrewsbury, an English Catholic peer, to comment publicly on the crisis. Shrewsbury, while accepting the allegations against Fr McDermott, contends (in a letter written by his eccentric chaplain to the *Morning Chronicle*) that the British public sees the church as 'an accessory to crime'; responsibility for the Famine deaths, which MacHale and many Irish clerics blame on government incompetence, should be imputed to the 'unerring, though inscrutable, designs of God'; the Irish are to blame, too, 'for God's visitation was grievously aggravated by their ingratitude [towards] . . . England'.

From Kinsale, Daniel Murphy, vicar forane to the bishop of Cork, sums up the feelings of the Irish Catholic clergy: 'The unhappy Shrewsbury has done us all great harm and it is quite clear that he is playing the game of the government for our enslavement and that his letter will be submitted, if it has not already been done, to the Holy See as a proof of our rebellious propensities and the necessity of government control over the Irish priesthood.'

'I know not what the English mean to do with us,' remarks Professor James Cooke, of St John's College, Waterford. 'The papers and parliamentary speeches last year held up the landlords to the nation's contempt and execration. This last session they have turned on the priests with the most unaccountable fury; now they attack priests and people together.'

All occupants of the townland of Doorty, where Major Mahon was shot, have been evicted. Three murder suspects – including James Hasty, a shebeen-keeper – are in the Strokestown Bridewell. Informers emerge from an adjoining townland.

The tenants of Cornashina come twice before the agents Guinness and Mahon, promising to make up their arrears and begging to be left on their holdings. They are persuaded to give evidence when told: 'Prosecute to conviction the murderer of Major Mahon and you shall have your farms.'

Hasty is hanged in Roscommon before a crowd of 4,000, confessing his guilt and denouncing 'that accursed system of Molly Maguirism'.

A second man is executed and others are transported. Fr McDermott's name does not feature at the trial, Clarendon having tried in vain to gain evidence of his involvement.[115]

Starvation returns

29 NOVEMBER 1847

As death from starvation returns, the Poor Law Commissioners begin to sanction outdoor relief.

Initially, able-bodied paupers in receipt of outdoor relief are expected to work at least eight hours a day. The commissioners lay down guidelines for this type of labour: 'It should be as repulsive as possible consistent with humanity, that is, that paupers would rather do the work than starve, but that they should rather employ themselves in doing any other kind of work elsewhere, and that it would not interfere with private enterprise or be a kind of work which otherwise would necessarily be performed by independent labourers.'

With another harsh winter in prospect, stone-breaking represents a cruel test of destitution for the poor, whose clothes are increasingly ragged or long since pawned. A third consecutive year of Famine is devastating for them.

After intense British lobbying in Rome, Cardinal Fransoni, secretary of the Congregation of Propaganda, sends a sharp letter to the Irish archbishops seeking information about press reports that the clergy approved of murders.

Bishop Edward Maginn of Derry asserts that 'no clergyman has transgressed the bounds of Christian duty, which makes it incumbent on every follower of the Redeemer to stand by the oppressed'.

The elderly bishop of Kilmacduagh and Kilfenora, Dr Edmund French, describes conditions to the rector of the Irish College in Rome, Dr Paul Cullen: 'The yellings of the poor, on the roads, in the streets of our towns, at all our houses . . . the heart-rending scenes in the houses of the poor, lying sick of fever, starvation, of inanition and want are the daily prospects of our clergy . . . In one parish alone there were twenty-one deaths of heads of families in four days . . . they all died with the utmost resignation to the will of God, blessing the priest for a very small temporary help. These are the scenes witnessed by our clergy in the south and west of Ireland, and alas if we dare describe these afflictions of our people and our own agonies at their heart-rending sufferings we are stamped by our enemies of this English press and the leading Members of Parliament as surplissed [sic] ruffians and instigators of the murder of the landed gentry and the exterminators of the people.'

Archbishop Michael Slattery tells Cullen: 'The Catholic clergy being the only persons to stand forward against the oppression of the people, the landlords availed themselves of the national bigotry of England to raise the cry of murder against them to turn away public attention from the numberless murders caused by themselves. Hence the calumnies sanctioned by the government to forward their own purposes of blackening us in the eyes of Europe and even of Rome, thereby to destroy the liberty of our church.'[116]

Vicious circle

Tightening hunger, pitiless evictions and growing violence form a vicious circle.

Three families – twenty-three people – are removed from the property of J.M. Walsh, a Tipperary magistrate. The occupant of one cabin is so ill that the sheriff hesitates to carry out his orders. But Mr Walsh is inexorable. The sick man is placed in a piggery while his house is levelled. The roof of the outhouse is then removed. The man remains in the open air for two days until death puts an end to his sufferings.

In Kilmastulla, forty-seven people are evicted. They squat in dykes and glens, 'burrowing in the earth for shelter, victims to every inclemency of the weather.'

In 'consolidation clearances' in Leitrim, a detachment of military from Mohill and fifty policemen assist in dispossessing fifty-five men, women and children. Ten dwellings are burned to the ground. The landlord refuses to accept rent from any tenant holding under twenty acres.

The *Wexford Independent* reports that some landlords are taking advantage of the helpless condition of their tenants by evicting them.

In west Clare, 800 families have no means of support 'except by second digging the potato fields for the purpose of collecting a scanty meal, at which work they may be seen engaged in groups of one to two hundred'. Kilrush workhouse is attacked by 600 hungry people refused admission; they are driven away by military and police with fixed bayonets.

In east Clare, magistrates apply for more police in Tulla and for a barracks in Feakle. Constables remove a placard announcing a meeting at Meelick Pike 'for the purpose of demanding relief or employ', and signed 'your true and loyal brethren until death'.

Famine has returned to Kilfenora, where two people have died of starvation and great numbers are subsisting on cabbages and turnips.

Fever is reported from Tullamore, King's County, where destitution has caused several deaths. The bad food – diseased turnips and weeds – on which the poor subsist is the chief cause of the increased sickness.

Bands of armed men prowl the Tipperary countryside at night, while 'an organised body of conspirators has suddenly sprung into existence' in

County Sligo. Bailiffs are attacked in south Armagh; a would-be informer is murdered in Tipperary; a steward is shot dead in Scarriff. In Cappamore, County Limerick, four men stone a rich farmer and money-lender to death.

The *Nation* is appalled at the growing number of cruel murders. But a new Irish Coercion Bill is no remedy: 'Like all injustice, it will widen the circle of sympathy with the crime it is provided to arrest.'

A special commission is to try prisoners in Limerick, Clare, Tipperary and Roscommon – where up to 700 families have been evicted.[117]

Quakers withdraw

13 DECEMBER 1847

The charitable organisations begin to wind down their activities.

But the General Central Relief Committee, formed in Dublin last December, warns that 'in some respects the condition of the peasantry is this year more lamentable than it was during the past season'.

The Quakers decide to withdraw from providing direct relief. They are exhausted after their life-saving efforts, especially last spring when the government ordered the closure of the public works before the soup kitchens were in operation. The Friends, with their intimate knowledge of the west and south, realise that the Poor Law is incapable of relieving the starving masses in the remote parts of Ireland, where no workhouse exists for up to fifty miles. They will still provide aid in the form of farm implements, seeds and fishing tackle.

The British Relief Association is feeding 200,000 schoolchildren daily throughout the distressed Poor Law unions. The inspector of the Skibbereen union reports: 'You have no idea of the great good the British Association bounty is doing to this union: hundreds of lives have been saved by it, and were it not for this the scenes of last year would have been witnessed in Skibbereen again.'

The Irish church, through its overseas network, continues to generate a substantial flow of relief money from all over the Catholic world.

The English Quaker philanthropist, James Hack Tuke, witnesses the eviction of six or seven hundred people in Erris, County Mayo. He finds large families living in 'human burrows'; they are 'quiet harmless persons, terrified of strangers'.

The barony's population last year was estimated at 28,000; 2,000 have emigrated and 6,000 died of starvation, dysentery and fever; of the 20,000 left, 10,000 are on the verge of starvation: '10,000 people within 48 hours' journey of the metropolis of the world, living, or rather starving, upon turnip-tops, sand-eels and seaweed, a diet which no one in England would consider fit for the meanest animal.'

A crowd of almost naked, perishing creatures gathers in Belmullet. They have no homes, no shelter, no land, no food. They sleep in the streets and beg during the day from neighbours scarcely richer than themselves. The innkeeper informs Mr Tuke that six people died in the last few nights. 'And I am sure that several I saw there are now beyond the reach of earthly calamity. The ghastly smile which momentarily played on the countenances of these living skeletons, at the prospect of a little temporary relief, I cannot easily forget. It rendered still more painful the expression of intense anxiety and bitter misery which was exhibited in their livid and death-set features.'

The *Galway Mercury* reports that several starving peasants have been jailed for ten days for rooting tillage in search of potatoes. Thousands are famishing from cold and hunger in Galway union. The overcrowded workhouse has to refuse admission to 300 'wailing applicants'.[118]

Death from exposure

20 DECEMBER 1847

As the year draws to a close the poor face a new threat besides famine and fever – death through exposure. The homes of evicted tenants are levelled to prevent them returning. They huddle in scailps – made by placing their cabin roofs on ditches – there to perish not only of hunger but also from cold.

'How I wish the real sufferings of the people could reach the ears of the rich of this life,' writes a priest from Clifden. But the satiated never understand the emaciated. The destitute starve in one world, the landowning classes inhabit another.

James Maher, a parish priest in Queen's County and uncle of Paul Cullen, rector of the Irish College in Rome, describes the Famine deaths as a 'hecatomb' or holocaust. If priests raise their voice against oppression they run the risk of being accused of incitement to murder. Denouncing the sixteen ounces of food doled out to the paupers in Carlow workhouse, Fr Maher comments: 'Talk indeed of a conspiracy against life! Here we have it . . . '

The inmates of Sligo poorhouse are 'actually beginning to starve,' a Poor Law inspector reports.

Bishop John Ryan of Limerick, while condemning agrarian violence, denounces the upper classes for being 'cold and callous to the voice of humanity . . . untouched by the cries of famine and pestilence, the wailings of hunger, the lamentations of women and children'.

Sir Vere de Vere, of Curraghchase, is an honourable exception. He has reduced the rents of his tenantry; he plans to provide employment for the labourers on his estate; and, 'under the directions of Miss Vere, work suited to them will be furnished to the labourers' wives'.

The labourers are worse off than last year, according to the *Tipperary Vindicator*. Hundreds of families in the county are now reduced to living on one meal of turnips a day. 'At the market cross of Nenagh, from one to two hundred men may be seen every morning in the vain hope of getting a day's work.' After standing sometimes for hours in the wet and cold, they are compelled to return to their homes to hear the cries of famishing children. In Templemore, however, a humane farmer gives three acres of turnips to his neighbours.

The parish priest of Duagh, County Kerry, informs Tralee guardians that there are 13,500 destitute people in his district.

Fr Thomas Walsh, of Rosmuc, says his parishioners are like spectres without hair, the result of fever, or clothes except for a few flannels in awful weather. Galway city is swamped by a tide of evicted cottier paupers from Connemara. Unable to gain admission to the workhouse, they throng the doors of the townspeople, demanding a morsel of food.

Shortly before Christmas, three villages are reduced to ruins in the Mullet Peninsula. The evicted families implore the landlord's 'drivers' to allow them to remain a short while 'as it was so near the time of festival but they would not . . . '[119]

500,000 dead

Nearly 500,000 people have died of starvation and disease – mainly fever, dysentery and smallpox. One should add so far, because this Famine is far from over.

John Mitchel foresees further 'tremendous destruction' of human life unless radical steps are taken. He contends 'that Ireland has wealth enough in her hands to support her own people if she will but use it'. Mitchel's revolutionary views are considered impracticable by most of the Young Irelanders, however, and he resigns from the *Nation*.

At a lecture to the Confederate club in Newry, County Down, his friend John Martin asserts that Irish agriculture is capable of producing food for a population of twenty million.

More than 100,000 Famine refugees fled to British North America this year. At least 20,000 of them perished on the coffin ships, at Grosse Île, and in the fever hospitals and emigrant sheds of Canadian cities.

Irish immigrants turned Liverpool for a time into a 'city of the plague', according to the medical officer's report. Up to 60,000 contracted fever and 40,000 dysentery and diarrhoea. Nearly 7,500 died, more than half of them in predominantly Irish wards. Priests picked up lice when they visited cellars to give the last rites and during the year ten died. One Unitarian minister also died of typhus, along with more than thirty medical staff.

The Famine has claimed the lives of about seventy-five Catholic priests: almost forty in Ireland; twenty-five in Britain; thirteen in Canada, including the first bishop of Toronto, Michael Power.

Captain Wynne reports from Carrick-on-Shannon, County Leitrim, where he is now employed as a Poor Law inspector: 'I fear the extent of destitution in this union has never been fairly represented, it is perfectly frightful; accustomed as I am to scenes of misery in the western counties, I have never met with so extensive and hopeless destitution.'

In one area of west Waterford, 200 constables assist rate collectors 'to force from the poor the means of relief for the poor.' Relentless rate collecting has produced £1 million this year to administer the Irish Poor Law.

The Coercion Bill receives royal assent – the 35th coercion measure enacted for Ireland since the Union. 'The Famine may murder undisturbed,' comments the *Nation*. This is our condition at the close of 1847: 'A country to which its inexorable government awards punishment, but refuses protection.'

Lord Clarendon feels as if he 'was at the head of a Provisional government of a half-conquered country'.

So with 15,000 extra troops in the country, workhouses enlarged to take 150,000 additional inmates, people dying of starvation in the west and fever still raging, Ireland wretched as never before passes from Black '47 into 1848.[120]

Epilogue

THE FAMINE, 1848–50

More than half a million excess deaths occurred during the remaining Famine years, 1848–50. Relatively few died of literal starvation: hunger-induced infectious diseases caused most of the damage. While Britain declared the Famine was over in 1848, 1.5 million Irish people depended on the Poor Law for existence, despite the harsh regulations governing the provision of relief; three-quarters of the destitute were on outdoor relief; over 40 per cent of the workhouse inmates were children, many of whom were orphaned or abandoned. Desperate people clamoured for admission to pestilential poorhouses – known as 'slaughter asylums' – which guardians no longer inspected for fear of infection. Mass graves filled pauper cemeteries.[1]

In one week at the beginning of 1848, 1,460 workhouse inmates died. Captain Arthur Kennedy, the Poor Law inspector in Kilrush union, attributed the high level of mortality in west Clare to people delaying entry to the poorhouse until 'their health and constitution are broken down beyond repair'. He informed the Poor Law commissioners: 'Their misery and utter helplessness baffles description. The parents of a large family often displaying hardly the sagacity of an animal'.[2]

Key members of the Whig administration believed that, to transform Ireland from a subsistence to a wage-earning economy, it was necessary to consolidate smallholdings by removing a large portion of the population. London saw the crisis as a means of ridding Ireland of its less viable holdings and less competent proprietors. After 1847 the Poor Law was used increasingly to encourage not only paupers but also small ratepayers to emigrate.

The Poor Law Amendment Act, designed to hold ratepayers responsible for the welfare of the destitute, made it in the interests of landlords to get rid of them. Killarney board of guardians observed that the Gregory quarter-acre clause had introduced a 'spirit of ejectment' into the country.

161

In February 1848, a Waterford newspaper traced 'much of the pauperism by which the country is at present overrun' to the clause.[3]

While starvation and disease loosened the grip of smallholders on their land, the mounting burden of poor rates and arrears of rent propelled many landlords into a frenzy of destruction. Probably more than half a million people were driven off the land as proprietors and strong farmers seized the opportunity to evict demoralised smallholders, cottiers and labourers.[4]

By October the Marquis of Sligo, who had hitherto shown leniency to his tenants, said he was 'under the necessity of ejecting or being ejected'. 'The landlords are *prevented* from aiding or tolerating poor tenants,' the Galway proprietor Lord Clanricarde declared. 'They are compelled to hunt out all such, to save their property from the £4 clause.'[5]

In Clare the Famine unmasked the paternalism of Crofton Vandeleur, who between November 1847 and July 1850 removed over 1,000 people from his estate in what one Select Committee report described as a 'wholesale system of eviction and house levelling'.[6]

Captain Kennedy said in April 1848 that deceit and small sums of money were used to bring about acquiescence: 'the wretched and half-witted occupiers are too often deluded by the specious promises of under-agents and bailiffs, and induced to throw down their own cabins for a few shillings and an assurance of outdoor relief'. Many of the evicted 'betake themselves to the ditches or the shelter of some bank, and there exist like animals till starvation or the inclemency of the weather drives them to the workhouse. There were three cartloads of these creatures, who could not walk, brought for admission yesterday, some in fever, some suffering from dysentery, and all from want of food.'

In the tense circumstances of July 1848, Lord Clarendon informed Sir George Grey that 4,000 people had been evicted and 900 houses levelled in Kilrush union since the previous November; 'the misery has been beyond description but the law has not been violated!'; the lord lieutenant asked the home secretary to suppress the facts because 'the case is too shocking for publication if it can be avoided'.[7]

Fr James Browne, of Ballintubber, lamented: 'My fine virtuous, holy people have been starved to death. The landlords of all sects and creeds have conspired for their destruction – the Catholic landlords the most cruelly disposed.'

James Dwyer, parish priest of Lackagh, Claregalway, saw the evicted 'dying on the roadside or under bridges or in sheds where a few sticks are erected for their reception, to be visited by myself who am doomed frequently to crawl *on my knees* into the abode of death'.

In south Ulster, 'the landlords exterminate right and left'. Fr Thomas Brady, of Drung parish, reported fifty farms vacant, with '200 human beings sent adrift in an inclement weather to beg or die . . . wishing for the happy release of death'. It was hard to teach patience, said Fr Philip Foy, of Shercock, 'to a man who sees his father and mother or wife and children driven from the houses of their ancestors to the bogs and ditches to starvation and death'.[8]

British officials and Irish landlords insulated themselves mentally against the inhumanity of mass evictions by taking the view that clearances were essential to economic progress. The dispossessed paid the cost of this brutal social engineering.

Charles Trevelyan's apologia *The Irish Crisis*, published in January 1848, described the Famine as 'a direct stroke of an all-wise and all-merciful Providence'. He laid down the principle on which British policy henceforth rested: 'There is only one way in which the relief of the destitute ever has been or ever will be conducted consistently with the general welfare, and that is by making it a local charge.'

Lord Palmerston considered 'it is useless to disguise the truth that any great improvement in the social system of Ireland must be founded upon an extensive change in the present state of agrarian occupation, and that this change necessarily implies a long, continued and systematic ejectment of smallholders and of squatting cottiers.[9]

The gap between how the Famine was perceived in London and Dublin widened. Edward Twistleton, the Chief Poor Law Commissioner, reminded Trevelyan: 'It is wished that the Irish should not come upon the national [UK] finances for the relief of their destitute. It is also wished that deaths from starvation should not take place. But these wishes are as unreasonable as if you ask us to make beer without malt, or to fly without wings.'[10]

When Twistleton requested financial assistance for distressed unions, Trevelyan refused, declaring in September 1848:

> I do not know how farms are to be consolidated if small farmers do not emigrate, and by acting for the purpose of keeping them at home we should be defaulting at our own object. We must not complain of what we really want to obtain. If small farmers go, and their landlords are reduced to sell portions of their estates to persons who will invest capital, we shall at last arrive at something like a satisfactory settlement of the country. [11]

The Chancellor, Sir Charles Wood, believed that if rate collection was enforced 'the pressure will lead to some emigrating . . . what we really want to obtain is a clearance of small farmers'. The Prime Minister, Lord John Russell, who was sick during much of 1848, summed up lamely: 'It is better that some should sink, than that they should drag others down to sink with them'.[12]

In July the blight returned and the potato crop was destroyed by the end of the month. The renewed failure broke the will of many farmers who had weathered earlier blights to remain in Ireland. It helped to produce the tidal wave of emigration, which crested at 245,000 departures in 1851 and did not subside to pre-Famine levels until 1855.[13]

'Scarcely a day passes in which strangers are not observed wending their way towards the sea ports of Drogheda or Dublin,' the *Meath Herald* noted in October 1848. They preferred the risk of emigrating in the winter season to remaining with no better prospect than the poorhouse. A landlord travelling through west Cork a year later was struck by the number of farms lying waste, their cabins derelict, and by the large parties of emigrants heading for the ports.[14]

Jeremiah O'Donovan Rossa recalled his family's departure for the United States. 'The cry of the weeping and wailing of that day rings in my ears still. That time it was a cry heard every day at every crossroad in Ireland. I stood at Renascreena Cross till this cry of the emigrant party went beyond my hearing. Then, I kept walking backward toward Skibbereen, looking at them till they sank from my view over Mauleyregan Hill.'[15]

Just before Christmas 1848, the sheriff visited Ballinrobe, County Mayo, with horse and foot soldiers and a posse of well-paid men, to evict forty-eight families and tumble houses. Those starving people, Fr Edward Waldron reported, 'are wandering about as there was no room for them in the workhouse and if you were to see where some of them slept at night. I can only say that it was not fit for pigs. Man made to God's image and likeness to be thus treated by fellow man, the same by nature but that birth and fortune has made a distinction.'[16]

POOR LAW

As the Poor Law administration broke down in many western unions, elected guardians were replaced by paid officers, such as Captain Edmond Wynne. Formerly a Board of Works inspector in Clare, he was appointed temporary inspector of the Carrick-on-Shannon union, where 1,900 people were crammed into the poorhouse, sheds and auxiliary buildings.

His workload included the supervision of food distribution to school-children and providing emergency shelter for evicted families.

Wynne, who was no philanthropist, observed that many townlands in the Boyle union 'exhibit strong marks of the march of the enemy, in the multitude of ruined cottages or cabins, the absence of every description of cattle, and the neglected state of the land'.[17]

In March 1848 mortality in the Tipperary Poor Law union reached eighty a week, due to the consumption of inadequately cooked Indian meal by people in already weak health. Archbishop Slattery found Cashel 'one vast poorhouse' as late as 1851.[18]

Between Scarriff and Toomgraney there were eight auxiliary workhouses where the average mortality was ten people a day. 'They were crammed to suffocation – four in fever in each bed. The healthy man is compelled to sleep with the fever patient, and the beds are literally heaps of manure'; there was no medicine and in one house the parish priest found a putrefying corpse in a room with patients.[19]

The parish priest of Ballingarry, County Limerick, Michael Fitzgerald, asserted on 25 March 1848:

> The able-bodied, or those who were such before hunger and misery had made them stooping, feeble, ghastly scarecrows, are receiving at present outdoor relief at the same rate as the others. But all males between sixteen and sixty are required in return for these fifteen-sixteenths of a penny to spend eight hours breaking stones in the open air. Most of these are in rags, as may be supposed, all of them emaciated and enfeebled by penny-a-day, dirt, cold and misery. This test, as it is called, was introduced in the middle of January. What a fine thing it must be to be a partaker of all the blessings of the British constitution – a poor man can obtain fifteen-sixteenths of a penny on the easy condition of breaking stones for only eight hours on a bleak hillside with his miserable clothing searched by the frost blast, or drenched in the sleet of January; that some must fall victims to a test of this description is inevitable. The transition from the bleak hillside of Knockfierna to the coffinless grave in the churchyard of Ballingarry, is a transition as common and indeed natural that it attracts no attention and excites no sensation.[20]

In April, the working day for able-bodied paupers on outdoor relief was increased to ten hours. Fr James Maher – uncle of Dr Paul Cullen – commented: 'To work poor men ten hours every day before they touch food is, to my judgment, incomparably more cruel and wicked than to overwork a well-fed horse for twelve hours.' From June a coffin was conceded to those who died while in receipt of outdoor relief.[21]

When the Poor Law system teetered on the brink of collapse in 1849, the Rate-in-Aid Act introduced to assist bankrupt western unions still confined the burden of providing relief to Ireland, not the United Kingdom. With the debts of the unions at £500,000, Twistleton resigned. 'He thinks that the destitution here is so horrible' – Clarendon explained to Russell – 'and the indifference of the House of Commons to it so manifest, that he is an unfit agent of a policy that must be one of extermination.'

The lord lieutenant was regarded as an alarmist by the cabinet. While increasingly critical of the prime minister for having lost authority, Clarendon blamed Wood, Grey and Trevelyan: 'C. Wood, backed by Grey, and relying upon arguments (or rather Trevelyanisms) that are no more applicable to Ireland than to Loo Choo, affirmed that the right thing to do was to do nothing – they have prevailed and you see what a fix we are in.'

He urged Russell in April 1849: 'Surely this is a state of things to justify you asking the House of Commons for an advance, for I don't think there is another legislature in Europe that would disregard such suffering as now exists in the west of Ireland, or coldly persist in a policy of extermination.' Instead, Trevelyan offered the Quakers £100 to restart direct aid. They declined, pointing out the support that Ireland needed was 'far beyond the reach of private exertion, the government alone could raise the funds and carry out the measures necessary in many districts to save the lives of the people'.[22]

The cabinet secretary, Charles Greville, recorded in his diary on 9 February 1849 that, while the Irish people died of hunger, the government did not know what to do. It had no plan and there was nothing but disagreement among the ministers. Wood had all along set his face against giving or lending money, and thought 'the misery and distress should run their course'.[23]

Paralysis and hard-heartedness presided over 'the operation of natural causes'.

The Asiatic cholera pandemic of 1848–9 added to the physical and mental agony. In the early months of 1849, mortality again reached about 2,700 a week. Suffering in the west of the country approached 1846–7 levels. A report from the unions of Ballina, Ballinasloe, Ballinrobe, Castlebar and Tuam in June described the peasantry as having 'famine unmistakably marked on their brows'. In the same month, alleged cannibalism was reported from Clifden.[24]

After 1849, the impact of potato blight was severest in Clare, Kerry and Tipperary. Kilrush began to attract notoriety similar to Skibbereen; nearly 7,000 'helpless, hopeless people' were evicted in the union between August 1848 and January 1849. A select committee inquiry into the administration of Kilrush union concluded that a neglect of public duty 'has occasioned a state of things disgraceful to a civilised age and country, for which some authority ought to be held responsible, and would long since have been held responsible had these things occurred in any union in England'.[25]

Captain Kennedy recalled many years later: '. . . that there were days in that western county when I came back from some scene of eviction so maddened by the sights of hunger and misery I had seen in the day's work that I felt disposed to take the gun from behind my door and shoot the first landlord I met.'

Only in Mayo were evictions, relative to population, almost as numerous as those in Clare. More than 26,000 Mayo tenants were dispossessed between 1849 and 1854. Lord Lucan, one of the exterminating landlords, demolished over 300 cabins and evicted 2,000 people in the parish of Ballinrobe during 1846–9. The depopulated holdings, on being consolidated, were stocked by Lucan himself or leased as ranches to wealthy graziers.

The clearances continued under the Encumbered Estates Act. 'In the revolution of property changes,' the *Roscommon Journal* observed in 1854, 'the new purchaser accelerates the departure of the aborigines of the country, by which he seems to imagine he has not only rid himself of their burden but enhanced the value of his property.'

The *Times* found that 'the rigorous administration of the Poor Law is destroying small holdings, reducing needy proprietors to utter insolvency, compelling them to surrender their estates into better hands, instigating an emigration far beyond any which a government could undertake, and so leaving the soil of Ireland open to industrial enterprise and the introduction of new capital . . . We see Ireland depopulated, her villages razed to the ground, her landlords bankrupt – in a word, we see the hideous chasm prepared for the foundation of a future prosperity.' It added hopefully: 'In a few years more, a Celtic Irishman will be be as rare in Connemara as is the Red Indian on the shores of Manhattan.'[26]

Lord Clarendon exulted: 'Priests and patriots howl over the Exodus but the departure of thousands of papist Celts must be a blessing to the country they quit.'[27]

Evictions peaked at 20,000 families – over 100,000 children, women and men – in 1850. In 1847 there were almost 730,000 farms in Ireland; by 1851 the number had fallen to 570,000.[28]

The dispossessed thronged the roads and towns, begging and hoping for a night's shelter in the next poorhouse. As the fabric of society unravelled, kinship support and the traditional sharing with strangers also collapsed. Even 'the bonds of domestic affection were loosening under the pressure of want,' one relief worker testified; 'the parents have become hardened to such a degree, by a long continuance of extreme distress and starvation, that they are often not to be trusted with the food intended for their children.'[29]

The historian Richard Robert Madden witnessed a Darwinian scene outside Kilrush workhouse in February 1851, when 1,000 sought admission and the instinct of self-preservation dominated. Low-backed cars, from which the horses had been removed, were ranged along the front wall of the building. The cars were occupied by the old and the young, the majority too emaciated or diseased to even sit upright. Those unable to procure transport had crawled to the poorhouse. The courtyard was thronged with a dense mass of misery, 'clamouring and pressing forward, the less weak thrusting aside the more infirm, the young hustling the old, the women pulling back the children, larger children pushing back the smaller, uttering confused cries of pain, impatience, anger and despair'.[30]

The Famine swept away whole families, townlands and villages, changing the countryside forever. Among its bitter legacies was the reaction to evangelical missions, which saw the catastrophe as a providential opportunity. The stigma of souperism lived on in Irish folk memory, casting a shadow over the relief work of the Church of Ireland and the Protestant clergy, several of whom died of famine-related disease.

The evictions were condemned in unprecedented terms by the Catholic bishops at the Synod of Thurles, called by Paul Cullen on his return from Rome in 1850:

> We behold our poor not only crushed and overwhelmed by the awful visitation of Heaven, but frequently the victims of the most ruthless oppression that ever disgraced the annals of humanity . . . The desolating track of the exterminator is to be traced in too many parts of the country – in those levelled cottages and roofless abodes where so many virtuous and industrious families have been torn by brute force, without distinction of age or sex, sickness or health, and flung upon the highway to perish in the extremity of want.[31]

THE 1848 RISING

James Fintan Lalor's tenant right movement made little headway in the conditions of 1847–8. The moderate majority within the Irish Confederation still accepted the judgment of Gavan Duffy and Smith O'Brien, who decried class conflict and insisted upon adhering to constitutional agitation alone. Disgusted at the Confederations's failure to support Lalor's agrarian campaign in the face of social dissolution, John Mitchel withdrew and started his own newspaper. But few listened to the *United Irishman's* message until the Paris revolution later in February 1848.

The fever of revolution which swept across Europe gave new hope to the divided and dispirited repeal movement. The sudden collapse of established regimes led Irish nationalists to believe that repeal could be won with similar ease. The thinkers and dreamers of Young Ireland were particularly heartened by events in France, where Louis Philippe was overthrown in an almost bloodless revolution and a poet, Alphonse de Lamartine, installed as head of the provisional government of the Second Republic.

With France as a model, it appeared as if the armed yet peaceful peoples of Europe were to be led to victory not by men of action, but by poets, reformers and workers. Fearful of attack by revolutionary France, fearful of social revolution by domestic Chartists, and fearful of nationalist revolution in Ireland, Britain would repeal the Act of Union. The *Nation* became almost as inflammatory as Mitchel's *United Irishman*, with Duffy starting one leading article: 'Ireland's opportunity, thank God and France, has come at last. Its challenge rings in our ears like a call to battle.'[32]

As revolutions broke out on the Continent, raising unrealistic expectations in Famine-ravaged Ireland, Lord Clarendon's anxiety increased. The 'lower orders' were excited in Dublin, he reported to Russell, 'and say now that the French have got their liberties, they will come and help us to get repale [sic]'. The disaffection was 'shared and promoted by the Young Priests everywhere and by the old ones in many districts'.[33]

Initially, several priests were caught up in the fervour. In Waterford, Fr Nicholas Coughlan declared the contract between people and government was broken:

> England's treatment of us for the past two years would abundantly prove that there is *practically* no government in this kingdom and, therefore, in conscience no allegiance is further due . . . In allegiance there is a contract and should either party fail to supply the due

conditions, then it falls to the ground . . . it is pretty clear that *one* of the contracting parties was found wanting. The unworthy deaths of some 800,000 honest men attest it . . . And as to this heavy scourge coming from holy Providence, I believe none of it; I rather believe it comes *from beyond the (Irish) channel.*

In private others expressed similar opinions. Fr Laurence Forde informed Dr Cullen that 'people talk of barricades and street fighting that before would shudder at the thought of it. I have no hesitation in saying that in case of outbreak, the Clergy will be with the people to a man.'

'One of the signs of the times is the bold position now being taken by so many of the Catholic clergy,' the *Limerick Reporter* asserted. 'They will no longer continue peace-preservers for England to the wholesale famine slaughter of their flocks.'

Archbishop Murray, who remembered the repression which followed the 1798 rising, expressed alarm to Cullen in April:

> What I always dreaded has occurred. A section of the Repealers are arming themselves openly, and proclaiming their intention of availing themselves of the first favourable moment to come into hostile collision with the Authorities of the State, except the Repeal of the Union be at once granted. Government is making corresponding preparations to meet the threat; and God grant that our island, which has lately opened its bosom so frequently to give an untimely grave to its perishing children, may not soon, through the rashness of its fiery Patriots, have to endure a still more grievous calamity in the horrors of Civil War.[34]

It quickly became clear, however, that the French Republic, valuing good relations with Britain, would not openly support Irish nationalism. Smith O'Brien, Thomas Francis Meagher and others presented a fraternal address of the Irish Confederation to Alphonse de Lamartine; his reply was non-commital. The most significant outcome of the Paris mission was the tricolour of green, white and orange brought back to Dublin by Meagher and presented to the Irish people as a symbol of 'new life'.

A show of strength by the British state prevented a conspiracy between Irish Confederates and English Chartists from ripening. Ultimately, the state always held the initiative over its confused, if potentially formidable, opponents. The principal thrust of the Chartist and Confederate movements was constitutional mass action, but neither ruled out the possible necessity of force.[35]

Irish nationalists were thus thrown back on their own resources. They were rescued from their divisions, if not their rhetoric, by a government decision to prosecute three of the leading members on charges of sedition: Mitchel for newspaper articles, O'Brien and Meagher for inflammatory speeches.

In May the prosecutions of O'Brien and Meagher failed and the prisoners were discharged amidst nationalist jubilation. After this setback, the authorites went to great lengths to pack the jury in the case of Mitchel, who was tried ten days later under the recently passed Treason-Felony Act. He was convicted and sentenced to fourteen years' transportation.

The severity of his sentence, together with the flagrant packing of the jury, aroused a wave of sympathy among nationalist factions. Unity talks resulted in the identities of the Repeal Association and the Irish Confederation being subsumed into the short-lived Irish League. Attention focused not on a reunited repeal movement, however, but on extending the network of Confederate clubs. While the more militant Young Irelanders looked to the clubs as forming the nucleus of a national guard, they never numbered more than seventy, with a membership of perhaps 20,000 concentrated in the towns. Arms were in short supply and, unsurprisingly, organisation in the countryside was virtually non-existent.

The Irish clergy abandoned any ideas of revolution after the Archbishop of Paris was shot dead at the barricades on 25 June. Denys-Auguste Affré died while attempting to mediate during a workers' revolution. In Rome the liberal epoch ended when 'red' republicans encroached on Pius IX's temporal possessions. The death of Affré, who had organised Famine relief and been supportive of the February revolution, shocked many in Ireland.

But the shooting was a godsend to Clarendon. He wrote gleefully that 'the priests have taken alarm at the death of the Archbishop of Paris who, poor man, never did a better thing in his life than getting himself murdered'. The lord lieutenant pressed home the counter-revolutionary message by manipulating sections of the press.[36]

In the end, the Young Irelanders became the prisoners of their bold talk of action. By calling on the people to arm themselves, the Confederate leaders gave the impression that they meant business, sooner rather than later. They drifted half-heartedly towards insurrection. They were helped along this path by the belief that the preservation of self-respect, their own and that of a famishing people, required action. This attitude was strengthened in July, when the government suspended habeas corpus, arrested newspaper editors, and declared illegal the holding of arms in Dublin and certain other counties.

The abortive rising took place in County Tipperary without the knowledge or support of the vast majority of the Irish people, who lacked the energy and will to challenge British rule. It ended in a skirmish with police at Farrenrory near The Commons, above Ballingarry, on 29 July in which two peasants were killed. According to resident magistrates, popular sentiment in Munster regretted its failure and was irritated by clerical opposition to the rebels.[37]

O'Brien, the reluctant leader of the insurgents, blamed clerial interference for his ignominious defeat, but admitted in retrospect to having 'totally miscalculated the energies of the Irish people'. Fr Philip FitzGerald, the Ballingarry priest, considered O'Brien's failure to feed his ragged army 'gave a death-blow to the entire movement'.

Fr John Kenyon, the most extreme nationalist among the clergy, also declined to join O'Brien's insurrection. He had submitted to his bishop a short time before, promising in effect to withdraw from the movement. Duffy would comment: 'It was but three weeks since he had been a party to transactions for which he and his comrades were liable to be hanged. There were missionaries in New York committing treason with his consent and concurrence, and he made this new and conflicting compact without communicating a tittle of it to the men with whom he was acting.' According to Michael Doheny, who was close to him in temperament, the fire-eating parish priest of Templederry retired from politics in June in protest at the reconciliation with the O'Connellites.[38]

The clergy played an important role in confining the rising to a tiny proportion of the people. The indecisive behaviour of the leaders, as they marched from one town to another, added to their conviction that the venture was hopeless. Their intervention prevented a massacre, Professor Kerr has concluded, and 'why they turned aside at the last moment had much to do with the deteriorating situation in Italy and France, culminating in the death of Archbishop Affré'. They decided to either stand aloof or prevent their people from taking part in an ill-prepared insurrection.[39]

Ultimately, it was doomed to failure because of the government's decisive action and the inept attempt to mobilise a countryside debilitated by hunger. By August there were 35,000 troops in Ireland, with naval support off the southern coast. Britain was determined to hold Ireland, if not to feed her.

After the collapse of the rising ridicule replaced fear in official circles. More ominously, as the stench of rotting stalks recurred, the British press turned a face of brass towards Irish misery. Russell warned Clarendon: 'The course of English benevolence is frozen by insult, calumny and rebellion.'

As revolution, the rising was a pathetic farce; as revolutionary theatre, however, it was a gesture against death and despair, evictions and emigration. Its political effects were profound and far-reaching. While some of these were slow to mature, others manifested themselves quickly. It re-established republican links to the United Irishmen; Lalor and Mitchel brought the issue of landownership into the political arena, albiet too late to help Tone's 'men of no property', most of whom lay in Famine graves or were sailing away to America.[40]

Moreover, the dispersal of the Young Irelanders gave them authority to interpret emigration as exile. Many, including John Blake Dillon and Michael Doheny, evaded capture and escaped to the United States. James Stephens and John O'Mahony, later co-founders of the Fenian movement, fled to Paris.

Four of the captured rebels, O'Brien, Meagher, Terence Bellew MacManus and Patrick O'Donohue, were convicted of high treason and sentenced to death. The state prisoners ennobled their attempted rising by refusing to ask for pardons. The government, wishing to avoid creating martyrs, passed a measure commuting their sentences to transportation for life.

They joined Mitchel and others in Van Diemen's Land. MacManus, Meagher and Mitchel received heroes' welcomes when they arrived in California after escaping in the early 1850s.

Their rhetoric politicised the Famine experience. In the New World, it inspired embittered and impoverished Irish-Americans to seek freedom for Ireland and 'revenge for Skibbereen'. Mitchel's *Jail Journal* became the bible of Irish nationalism. Having witnessed 'scenes that might have driven a wise man mad', he burned into the Irish popular imagination the notion that the Famine had been contrived by England.[41]

In Tasmania, O'Brien brooded on the returns of the 1851 census. He held the British government responsible for the 'premature extinction' of one million Irish people. If a barbarous conqueror had destroyed this number of human beings he would deserve the execration of humankind. O'Brien continued:

> If a ruthless tyrant had driven from their homes into exile a million of his fellow men by his cruelty or oppression, he would justly deserve to be visited with a doom similar to that which divine vengeance inflicted upon Pharoah . . . Yet Englishmen and their rulers calmly contemplate without self-reproach the havoc which they have permitted, if they have not caused it – nay some of their leading

statesmen deem it a subject of congratulation that so large a proportion of its inhabitants has been removed from a country which they considered overpeopled and hostile.

He estimated that a year's warfare would cost England far more than would have been sufficient to provide for the Famine victims. The British government did supply £9.5 million towards various relief programmes (over half of which was given as a loan). This was a considerable figure – multiply by fifty for today's equivalent – even if, by comparison, nearly £70 million was spent on the Crimean war of 1854–5.[42]

THE EXODUS

No fewer than 2.1 million adults and children fled from Ireland between 1845 and 1855. This amounted to about a quarter of Ireland's highest recorded population of 8,175,000 in 1841. (In the century prior to the Famine the Irish population quadrupled; in the century following it was halved.) Almost 1.5 million sailed to the United States; another 340,000 embarked for British North America; 200,000–300,000 settled in Britain; several thousand went to Australia and elsewhere. A significant proportion would have departed even if there had been no Famine, as the emigrant stream had been swelling in the decade before 1845.

The Famine transformed Irish attitudes to emigration, however. Beforehand, there was a reluctance to leave Ireland. Henceforth, not even the lingering nightmare of the coffin ships impeded the exodus. Neither death nor discomfort could staunch the flow out of Ireland.[43]

About 75 per cent of Famine emigration to the New World settled in the United States. The poorest sailed to Canada because of the lower fares. Voyages to the US were much less dangerous due to stricter regulation of passengers ships. But Canada spent five times as much upon relief as the US, on account of the American refusal to accept immigrants with 'ship fever'.[44]

The overwhelming majority of Famine emigrants were drawn from the humblest classes of Irish society; they tended to be Catholic, Irish-speaking and illiterate. Three areas stand out as having experienced high rates of emigration: south Ulster, north Connacht and the midlands. Destitution did not, however, act as a brake on emigration. Four of the five counties with the highest rates of excess mortality (Leitrim, Mayo, Roscommon and Sligo) also ranked among the counties with the heaviest rates of emigration.[45]

The exodus of the late 1840s was characterised by a desperation to escape, even though it involved adversity and degradation.

During 1847–8, according to the Liverpool police, 'there were frequently from 600 to 800 deck passengers on board of one steamer at a time, arriving from the ports of Dublin, Drogheda, Dundalk and Sligo, crowded together on deck, mixed among the cattle and besmeared with their dung, clothed in rags and saturated with wet.' Those unable to embark on Atlantic sailing vessels 'escaped' into Victorian Britain's teeming slums. Professor Neal estimates the number of deaths from famine-related disease in British cities, notably Liverpool and Glasgow, at 10,000–15,000.[46]

The latest Canadian research puts the number of deaths among emigrants arriving through Quebec in 1847 at 17,477. Of the 98,649 emigrants, mostly Irish, who sailed for Quebec, 5,293 perished on board ship, either during the crossing or in quarantine, and 3,452 while detained on Grosse Isle; the remaining deaths occurred at hospital in Quebec city, 1,041; at hospital in Montreal, 3,579; in Saint-Jean, 71; in Lachine, 130; at the emigrant hospital in Toronto, 863; and other towns in Upper Canada (Ontario), 3,048.[47]

Emigration to New Brunswick followed the same calamitous course on a smaller scale. One-seventh of the 16,000 Irish immigrants who passed through Partridge Island and Middle Island quarantine stations died before the year was out. The cumulative effect of federal and state legislation in the spring of 1847 had been to turn the worst of the emigration northwards; and, although the season was among the worst experienced by the United States, New York and Boston avoided the epidemics of Quebec and Montreal.[48]

Black '47 was the most disastrous year of the exodus, with the mortality rate among Irish emigrants to British North America reaching 17 per cent. It fell to 1 per cent the following year.[49]

Stephen de Vere's exposé of coffin-ship conditions helped to reform the transatlantic passenger trade. Such was his admiration for the patience of the Irish poor, which he attributed to their faith, that he became a Catholic later in 1847.

The blight also struck the German countryside, where the potato formed a dietary staple, but there was no mass starvation compared with Ireland. Furthermore, out of a German population of 36 million, only 250,000 emigrated to North America. They generally arrived in good health and were welcomed as useful settlers, while the Irish reached Grosse Isle 'in too many instances only to find a grave'.[50]

The 'American letter', too, contributed significantly to the exodus. By 1849, the chairman of the Emigration Commissioners was marvelling at the rapidity with which the chains of human movement had been forged: 'Emigration begets emigration; almost the whole of the Irish emigration last year, certainly more than three-quarters of it, was paid for by the money sent home from America.'[51]

One Mary McCarthy wrote from New York in 1850, urging her father to bring the family out: 'I must only say that this is a good place and A good Country for if one place does not Suit A man he can go to Another and very easy please himself . . . ' While there were still 'Dangers upon Dangers attending Comeing here', the first two or three days of the voyage would be the worst. She offered detailed advice about preparing for the voyage: her mother was to bring 'all her bed Close', a 'Kittle' and oven with 'handles to them'; her father should provide whiskey for the ship's cook and 'Some Sailors that you may think would do you any good to give them a Glass once in a time'. Her father was to 'Take Courage and be Determined and bold' but to mind his temper, since 'the Mildest Man has the best chance on board'.

The sooner they cleared away 'from that place' the better. 'Come you all Together Couragiously and bid adiu to that lovely place the land of your Birth, that place where the young and old joined Together in one Common Union, both night and day Engaged in Innocent Amusement'.[52]

None the less, the most poignant scene observed by the Fenian propagandist, O'Donovan Rossa, in the US was 'the old father or mother brought over from Ireland by their children. See them coming from Mass of a Sunday morning, looking so sad and lonely; no one to speak to; no one around they know; strangers in a strange land . . . '

Although 95 per cent of Famine emigrants survived the crossing with ingenuity and determination, their lifespan was often short. Reaching North America did not end their nightmare; sectarian bigotry and fear of disease inflamed anti-Irish prejudice. Nativism, poverty and the need for cohesion decreed that they settled initially in shantytowns in the east. While many remained in essentially Irish surroundings, those drawn outward by the lure of wages would eventually make up the main flow of immigrants, completing the transformation from Irish peasant to American worker.

The overcrowded and insanitary housing conditions contributed to severe social problems and a high mortality rate. Bishop Hughes of New York compared Irish ghettos to the hovels from which most of their inhabitants had been transplanted. Irish immigrants made up 87 per cent of that city's unskilled labour-force by 1855.

In general, the Famine Irish experience in the New World was one of poverty and hardship or, at best, gradual improvement. The average emigrant, one exile wrote, 'toils on, year after year, under a burning sun in summer and intense cold in winter, to earn a miserable subsistence, and is not so happy in his position as he would be in his own country with a single acre to raise potatoes for himself and family'. The heads of families often succumbed to disease, overwork or industrial accidents. They entered the American work-force at the bottom, competing only with free blacks, frequently encountering 'No Irish Need Apply' notices.[53]

Robert Scally summed up eloquently:

> Flanked by the scenes of Skibbereen and Grosse Isle at either end of the voyage, the 'coffin ship' stands as the centre panel of the Famine triptych, depicting bondage and fever in the steerage, wailing children and mothers' pleas from the darkness below decks, heartless captains and brutal crews, shipwreck, pestilence and burial at sea. In its own smaller scale, the memory of the emigrant steerage has long been held, like the slaves' 'middle passage' and the trains of the Holocaust, as an icon of Ireland's oppression.

While the mortality of the emigrant voyage cannot be compared in magnitude to the atrocities of slavery and genocide, Scally added, the incidence during the Famine emigration of death and suffering at sea and shortly after landing was appalling enough to stun its witnesses, revolt humanitarians, and alienate Irish nationalists on both sides of the Atlantic.[54]

The response by the powerful to a natural disaster, the Irish theologian Enda McDonagh concluded, 'was a gross human failure, if expressed more in ignoring, denying and inefficiency than in brutal intent and effective execution'. [55]

THE AFTERMATH

Bishop John Joseph Lynch of Toronto declared in 1864: 'An emigration of the poor people of any country, without means, without protection, without leaders, such as that which has taken place from Ireland for several years, is unparalleled in the annals of history.'[56]

In a circular to the Irish bishops, Dr Lynch spoke of the hard struggle by Famine immigrants to win acceptance. More Irish blood had been spilled in the American Civil War than in a recent Polish uprising against the tsar, he wrote, 'and more lives lost in swamps, making railroads, digging canals, by steamboat explosions, and from bad whiskey – forced upon Irish labourers by task-masters desirous of exacting the greatest amount of work from them in their excited condition – than would make up the population of a considerable state'.

Unlike the Germans and other nationalities, most Irish emigrants continued to arrive 'absolutely penniless'. They were obliged to look for the cheapest lodgings in the cities. The hospitals, the poorhouses and the jails in the US, and to a great extent in Canada, had more than their proportion of Irish inmates. Immorality and indifferentism – 'poverty generates crime' – prevailed to an alarming extent among Irish-Americans, Lynch reported. The 'rowdies' of several cities were the uneducated children of Irish parents.

Many of the young Irish women arriving in New York and other ports fell 'into the thousand snares which profligate cities throw in their way. We are informed by the acting parish priest of Montreal that that city was comparatively chaste until 1852–3, when numerous bands of girls were brought from the poorhouses of Ireland and distributed through the cities. They were exposed in public places to be hired, as slaves are in many parts of the South.'

Lynch continued: 'The workhouse system of Ireland is most degrading and immoral in its tendency, if the tree could be judged by its fruits. It is humiliating indeed to see numbers of poor Irish girls, innocent and guileless, sitting round in those large depots in seaport cities waiting to be hired.' Being ignorant of house work, they soon lost their jobs. 'An Irish girl gives up all hope of ever getting honourably settled in life, even after an involuntary fall . . . Hence Irish girls look upon themselves as so degraded and despised that, in their despair, they rush headlong to destruction.'

The fate of many children was also deplorable. 'Numbers of them soon lose their parents, through disease brought on by poverty, a long sea voyage and new modes of living.' An agent for a child protection society informed Lynch that, in the decade after the Famine, he took from New York alone 10,000 children annually.

The bishop met a batch on their way to Wisconsin 'to be given to non-Catholic farmers'. After exhorting them to keep the faith and pray, he shed a tear 'as the cars started with this noble band of children over the Suspension Bridge, New York'. He calculated that if all the descendants of Irish immigrants had preserved the faith, 'the number of Catholics in America would be double what it is at present'.

Lynch considered his exposé of the evils of 'forced, unprepared and excessive emigration' divinely inspired. After it was leaked to the press, he assured Archbishop Cullen of Dublin that his circular had not been intended for publication as 'it would be the cause of too much jubilation and misrepresentation by the enemies of our faith'.[57]

The defections from the church were mainly among second-generation Irish-Americans, Lynch explained. 'A vast number of the youth have been absorbed into the pores of this society, through the medium of common schools, mixed marriages, hiring with Protestant employers, the great scarcity of priests to attend to their spiritual wants, and innumerable injurious associations with the Protestant and infidel element of the country.'

In a letter to Cardinal Alessandro Barnabo, Lynch said he did not think the American church gained in numbers what the Irish church had lost. Much more would be achieved if the Irish had emigrated with some means 'to settle themselves on farms, to follow their old occupations, and to take care of their children'. While England might rejoice at the exodus, it was accumulating enemies 'on this side of the Atlantic'.[58]

Lynch, who became the first Catholic archbishop of Toronto, asked Rome:

> Is the destruction of the tens of thousands Irish both body and soul, brought about by unjust laws and the oppression of the poor that cries to Heaven for vengeance, to be looked on as a casualty that needs not be heeded? . . . If the subjects of the Papal States were seen flying in rags and misery from their fertile country as the Irish are from their shores, and flying to a country engaged in the most cruel war, Our Holy Father and His Government would be held up, especially by the Protestant press, to the execration of the whole world.

Dr Lynch wrote at a time of renewed harvest failure and mass emigration. He urged the Irish bishops, clergy and friends of the Catholic poor to devise 'means for averting the temporal and spiritual loss of thousands of their fellow-countrymen, who are aimlessly rushing across the Atlantic'.

Irish associations in the US and Canada, with an estimated one million members, were animated by one wish – 'to see the miserable condition of the Irish improved, as they are ashamed of the taunts which the people of other nations indulge in at their expense'. Lynch concluded his letter by suggesting the formation of an O'Connellite movement supported by the exiles – 'in the well-grounded hope that England, in her wisdom, will see the necessity of doing justice to Ireland, when her cause is backed up by such a powerful combination'.

Commenting in the *Irish People*, Charles Kickham claimed Lynch's sentiments were the 'principles of Fenianism'. But the inauguration of the National Association of Ireland took place in Dublin on 29 December 1864 with a keynote address by Dr Cullen. While this constitutional alternative to Fenianism never achieved popularity, it ushered in the era of Gladstonian reform.

Notes

INTRODUCTION

1 Peter Gray, 'Famine Relief Policy in Comparative Perspective: Ireland, Scotland and North-western Europe, 1845–1849' in *Éire-Ireland* (Spring, 1997), pp 87, 90, 103–4, 107

2 Quoted in Donal A. Kerr, '*A Nation of Beggars'?: Priests, People and Politics in Famine Ireland, 1846–1852* (Clarendon Press, Oxford, 1994), p. 62.

3 Christine Kinealy, 'Beyond Revisionism: reassessing the Great Irish Famine' in *History Ireland* (Winter, 1995); Kinealy, *A Death-Dealing Famine: The Great Hunger in Ireland* (London, Chicago, 1997), pp 74–60; Thomas P. O'Neill, 'The Organisation and Administration of Relief' in R.D. Edwards and T.D. Williams (eds.), *The Great Famine* (Dublin, 1994 edn.), p. 228; Joe Lee, 'The Famine as History' in Cormac Ó Gráda (ed.), *Famine 150: Commemorative Lecture Series* (Teagasc/UCD, 1997), p. 167; Lee, 'Sins of the Famine' in *Tablet*, 28 June 1997; Cecil Woodham-Smith, *The Reason Why* (London, 1958), p. 126

4 Kinealy, *Death-Dealing Famine*, pp 114, 82

5 *Journal de Quebec*, 17 June 1847; Donal Kerr, *The Catholic Church and the Famine* (Dublin, 1996), p. 90

6 *Nation*, 23 Oct. 1847

7 Edward Laxton, *The Famine Ships: The Irish Exodus to America, 1846–51* (London, 1996), pp 49–50

8 James S. Donnelly, Jr., '"Irish property must pay for Irish poverty": British public opinion and the Great Irish Famine' in Chris Morash and Richard Hayes (eds.), *Fearful Realities* (Dublin, 1996), pp 72–3; Cecil Woodham-Smith, *The Great Hunger* (New York, 1989 edn.), p. 317

9 Tom Hayden (ed.), *Irish Hunger: Personal Reflections on the Legacy of the Famine* (Dublin, 1997), p. 130; Peter Gray, 'Ideology and the Famine' in Cathal Póirtéir (ed.), *The Great Irish Famine* (Dublin, 1995), pp 92, 103; Ó Gráda, "The Great Famine and other famines" in *Ireland's Famine: Commemoration and Awareness* (Famine Commemoration Committee), p. 51

10 Peter Gray, *Famine, Land and Politics: British Government and Irish Society, 1843–1850* (Irish Academic Press, 1998), pp 327, 331–2

11 Cormac Ó Gráda, *Ireland Before and After the Famine* (Manchester, 1993), p. 104

FAMINE DIARY

1   *Nation*, 13 Sept. 1845; O'Neill, 'Administration of relief' in Edwards/Williams (eds.), *Great Famine*, p. 210; Woodham-Smith, *Great Hunger*, p. 40

2   *Freeman's Journal*, 17, 19 Sept. 1845

3   *Nation*, 28 Sept. 1845; *Annual Register, 1845*, Chronicle pp 150–1

4   *Nation*, 4 Oct. 1845; *Freeman's Journal*, 1–6 Oct. 1845

5   *Freeman's Journal*, 11–14 Oct. 1845

6   *Freeman's Journal*, 18 Oct. 1845; D. Thomson and M McGusty (eds.), *The Irish Journals of Elizabeth Smith, 1840–1850* (Oxford, 1980), pp 80–1

7   *Freeman's Journal*, 22, 28 Oct. 1845; Nation, 25 Oct. 1845

8   *Freeman's Journal*, 29 Oct., 4 Nov. 1845

9   *Nation*, 8 Nov. 1845

10   *Freeman's Journal*, 13 Nov. 1845; *Nation*, 8, 15 Nov. 1845; O'Neill, 'Administration of relief', op. cit., p. 213

11   *Freeman's Journal*, 19, 21 Nov. 1845; *Nation*, 22 Nov. 1845

12   John Smyth to Daniel Murray, 28 Nov. 1845 (Dublin Diocesan Archives); *Freeman's Journal*, 26 Nov. 1845; *Waterford Freeman*, 29 Nov. 1845

13   *Nation*, 6 Dec. 1845; *Tablet*, 9 Dec. 1845

14   *Chronicle and Munster Advertiser*, 10 Dec. 1845

15   *Nation*, 20 Dec. 1845; Maurice R. O'Connell (ed.), *The Correspondence of Daniel O'Connell*, vii (Dublin, n.d.), p. 352

16   Nation, 27 Dec. 1845; Edwards/Williams, *Great Famine*, pp 117, 213; Kevin Whelan, 'Pre and Post-Famine Landscape Change' in Póirtéir (ed.), *Great Irish Famine*, p. 29

17   Routh to Trevelyan, 1 Jan. 1846 (*Correspondence explanatory of the measures adopted by Her Majesty's government for the relief of distress arising from the failure of the potato crop in Ireland*, HC 1846 [735], xxxvii, p. 56); *Freeman's Journal*, 6 Jan. 1846; *Waterford Chronicle*, 2 Jan. 1846

18   *Freeman's Journal*, 11, 13 Jan. 1846

19   *Limerick Reporter* quoted in *Freeman's Journal*, 14 Jan. 1846; *Freeman's Journal*, 17 Jan. 1846

20   Report submitted by Edward Lucas, Randolph Routh and Edward Twistleton, 21 Jan. 1846, RLFC3/1/408 (Relief Commission papers, National Archives, Dublin); Christine Kinealy, *This Great Calamity* (Dublin, 1994), p. 43

21   Kinealy, *Great Calamity*, pp 39–40; O'Neill, 'Administration of relief', op. cit., p. 213

22   *Nation*, 10 Feb. 1846

23   *Nation*, 14 Feb. 1846; *Downpatrick Recorder*, 7 Feb. 1846

24   *Nation*, 21 Feb. 1846

25   Kinealy, *Great Calamity*, p. 41; RLFC3/1/629

26   *Freeman's Journal*, 3 March 1846

27   *Hansard*, 3rd series, lxxxiv, cols 987–8; *Nation*, 14 Mar. 1846; Woodham-Smith, *Great Hunger*, pp 71–2

28   *Nation*, 17 Mar. 1846; *Journals of Elizabeth Smith*, p. 93

29   *Illustrated London News*, 4 Apr. 1846; Kinealy, *Great Calamity*, p. 48

30   Luke Fowler, Freshford, Co Kilkenny, 23 Mar. 1846, RLFC3/1/899; Noble Seward, Caherconlish, Co Limerick, 24 Mar. 1846, RLFC3/1/900; Richard Pennefather, Dublin Castle, 17 Mar. 1846, RLFC3/1/815

31 Sub-Inspector R.B. Fletcher, Listowel, Co Kerry, 28 Mar. 1846, RLFC3/1/1088; *Freeman's Journal*, 10 Apr. 1846

32 *Hansard*, lxxxv, 703–10; John Smith, Clifden, 21 Mar. 1846, RLFC3/1/854; *Coleraine Chronicle*, 2 May 1846; *Journals of Elizabeth Smith*, p. 95

33 *Nation*, 27 Apr. 1846; Woodham-Smith, *Great Hunger*, pp 75–7

34 George Shaw, Annaduff Rectory, Co Leitrim, 20 Mar. 1846, RLFC3/1/823; D. Flanagan, Robertstown, Co Kildare, 20 Mar. 1846, RLFC3/1/840; Noel Kissane, *The Irish Famine: A Documentary History* (National Library of Ireland, 1995), p. 35

35 George Wyndham, Petworth, 6 Apr. 1846, RLFC3/1/1255; Thomas Brereton, Portumna, 16 Apr. 1846, RLFC3/1/1536; *Freeman's Journal*, 7 May 1846

36 Elias Thackeray, 20 Apr. 1846, RLFC3/1/1622; John Cullinan, 17 Apr. 1846, RLFC3/1/1579; Patrick Hayden, 17 Apr. 1846, RLFC3/1/1540; John French, 23 Apr. 1846, RLFC3/1/1733

37 *Nation*, 16 May 1846; Kinealy, *Great Calamity*, pp 49–50

38 *Nation*, 23–30 May 1846; *Journals of Elizabeth Smith*, p. 96; Woodham-Smith, *Great Hunger*, pp 79–84

39 *Freeman's Journal*, 2 June 1846; *Castlebar Telegraph*, 27 May 1846; list of subscribers to Corofin relief committee, 20 June 1846, RLFC3/1/3470

40 *Freeman's Journal*, 9 June 1846; RLFC3/1/2324; Ignatius Murphy, *A Starving People: Life and Death in West Clare, 1845–1851* (Irish Academic Press, 1996), p. 23

41 Abstract return of number employed on roads, 20 June 1846, RLFC3/1/3542. John Smith, 16 June 1846, RLFC3/1/3380; Fr Roche, 17 June 1846, RLFC3/1/3381; Tim Robinson, 'Connemara after the Famine' in *History Ireland* (Summer, 1996). When Thomas Martin died of Famine fever in 1847 his estate was sold to the Assurance Society of London (Peter Somerville-Large, *The Irish Country House: A Social History*, London, 1995, p. 286)

42 James Donnelly, 'Famine and government response, 1845–6' in W.E. Vaughan (ed.), *A New History of Ireland*, v (Oxford, 1989), pp 279–84

43 Michael McDermott, 5 June 1846, RLFC3/1/2977; enclosures from Office of Public Works about Roundstone, RLFC3/1/2883

44 William McClelland, 3 June 1846, RLFC3/1/2858; John Aylward, 16 June 1846, RLFC3/1/3351; Kinealy, *Great Calamity*, pp 50–1; Woodham-Smith, *Great Hunger*, p. 89

45 Ballaghaderreen relief committee, RLFC3/1/4398

46 Blight reported, RLFC3/1/3909

47 W.B. Cooke, 31 July 1846, RLFC3/1/4938; Woodham-Smith, *Great Hunger*, p. 90

48 Mathew to Trevelyan, 7 Aug. 1846 (*Correspondence relating to relief of distress*, HC 1847 [761], li); Thomas Cuthbert, JP, Kinsale, 4 Aug. 1846: 'Crop completely destroyed . . . people actually starving', RLFC3/1/5121

49 *Nation*, 15 Aug. 1846; Kinealy, *Great Calamity*, p. 52

50 Kinealy, *Great Calamity*, pp 72–5; Peter Gray, 'Potatoes and Providence' in Jim Kemmy (ed.), *Old Limerick Journal* (Winter, 1995), pp 84–91

51 George Hudson, Kildare Street Club, 23 July, 1846, RLFC3/1/4646; Stephen J. Campbell, *The Great Irish Famine* (Famine Museum, Strokestown, 1994), p. 47

52 Woodham-Smith, *Great Hunger*, pp 112–5; Mark Tierney, 'The Great Famine in Murroe' in *Old Limerick Journal* (Winter, 1995), pp 75–83

53 Thomas O'Carroll's diary, 13, 15 Sept., 6 Dec. 1846 (copy in Glenstal Abbey, Murroe, Co Limerick)

54   John Smith, RLFC3/1/4693; Jonas Studdert, RLFC3/1/4965; Offaly police report, RLFC3/1/3880; J.J. Heard, RLFC3/1/5499
55   *Nation*, 26 Sept. 1846
56   *Vindicator*, 3 Oct. 1846; extract from report of Sub-Inspector George Pinchin, Skibbereen, RLFC3/1/5028
57   John Killen (ed.), *The Famine Decade: Contemporary Accounts, 1841–1851* (Belfast, 1995), pp 68–70
58   *Nation*, 16–19 Oct. 1846; Kinealy, *Great Calamity*, pp 91–93; Woodham-Smith, *Great Hunger*, pp 114–5
59   *Vindicator*, 24 Oct. 1846; G.M. Massey, RLFC3/1/5595
60   Woodham-Smith, *Great Hunger*, pp 116–9
61   Kissane, *Documentary History* (NLI), p. 51; Woodham-Smith, *Great Hunger*, p. 122
62   Kerr, *Catholic Church and Famine*, pp 14–6; Donnelly, 'Administration of relief' in *New History of Ireland*, v, pp 27–8
63   *Nation*, 21 Nov. 1846; *Vindicator*, Belfast, 31 Oct. 1846; Woodham-Smith, *Great Hunger*, pp 127–9
64   *Nation*, 28 Nov. 1846;
65   *Nation*, 5 Dec. 1846; Woodham-Smith, *Great Hunger*, p. 140
66   *Transactions of the Central Relief Committee of the Society of Friends during the Famine* (Dublin, 1996 edn.), Joseph Crosfield's report, pp 145–7; Woodham-Smith, *Great Hunger*, pp 157–9
67   *Vindicator*, 23 Dec. 1846; *Transactions of Society of Friends*, pp 148–51
68   Michael MacMahon, *A History of the Parish of Rath* (Ennis, 1979), p. 69; Brian A. Kennedy, 'Sharman Crawford on Ulster Tenant Right' in *Irish Historical Studies*, xiii (1963), p. 252; Woodham-Smith, *Great Hunger*, pp 153–5
69   *Times*, 24 Dec. 1846; Woodham-Smith, *Great Hunger*, pp 162–5
70   *Transactions of Society of Friends*, pp 153–4; *Northern Whig*, 22 Dec. 1846
71   *Nation*, 16 Jan. 1847; Irish University Press/BPP Famine series, vol 1, Castlebar Union, 16 Jan., 23 Jan., 16 Feb. 1847; vol 2, Westport Union, 4 Aug. 1847
72   David Fitzpatrick, 'Famine, entitlements and seduction: Captain Edmond Wynne in Ireland, 1846–1851' in *English Historical Review*, cx (1995), p. 602–3; Mainchín Seoighe, 'The Famine in Limerick' in *Knockfierna Remembers* (Cnoc Firinne Heritage and Folklore Group, 1997), p. 19
73   Kinealy, *Great Calamity*, pp 97–101; Kerr, *Catholic Church and Famine*, pp 17–18; Woodham-Smith, *Great Hunger*, p. 171
74   *Hansard*, lxxxix, 943–5; Oliver MacDonagh, *The Emancipist: Daniel O'Connell, 1830–47* (London, 1989), p. 313
75   Canon John O'Rourke, *The Great Irish Famine* (Dublin, 1989 edn.), p. 185; Woodham-Smith, *Reason Why*, pp 120–5
76   Kerr, *Catholic Church and Famine*, pp 19–20; Louis Hymam, *The Jews in Ireland*, pp 120–1
77   Kinealy, *Great Calamity*, pp 120–8; Donnelly, 'Production, prices and exports' in *New History of Ireland*, v, p. 289
78   *Achill Missionary Herald*, 24 Feb. 1847
79   *Nation*, 13 Mar. 1847; Edwards/Williams (eds.), *Great Famine*, p. 289
80   *Transactions of Society of Friends*, pp 160–4; Cowman/Brady (eds.), *The Famine in Waterford*, pp 160–3; Kinealy, *Great Calamity*, p. 163
81   *Nation*, 13, 27 Mar. 1847; Kerr, *Catholic Church and Famine*, pp 25–35

82 *Nation*, 27 Mar. 1847; *Transactions of Society of Friends*, pp 163, 168
83 *Nation*, 13 Mar. 1847
84 *Nation*, 17 Apr. 1847; Timothy J. Sarbaugh, '"Charity Begins at Home": The United States Government and Irish Famine relief, 1845–49' in *History Ireland* (Summer, 1996)
85 *Nation*, 24 Apr. 1847; *Tablet*, 30 Jan. 1847; Andres Eiriksson, 'Food supply and food riots' in Ó Gráda (ed.), *Famine 150*, pp 84–7; Kinealy, *Great Calamity*, p. 121
86 Kinealy, ibid., p. 105; Laurence Geary, 'What people died of during the Famine' in *Famine 150*, p. 98; Kerr, *Catholic Church and Famine*, p. 20
87 *Tablet*, 8 May 1847
88 Reprinted in *Tablet*, 1 May 1847
89 *Nation*, 22 May 1847; David Fitzpatrick, 'Flight from Famine' in Póirtéir (ed.), *Great Irish Famine*, pp 174–8; Kinealy, *Great Calamity*, p. 102
90 *Tablet*, 22 May 1847
91 Kissane, *Documentary History*, pp 162–3
92 *Nation*, 12 June 1847; *Tablet*, 29 May 1847; Kinealy, *Great Calamity*, p. 129; Kerr, *Catholic Church and Famine*, pp 32, 37
93 Fitzpatrick, 'Emigration' in *New History of Ireland*, v, p. 582; Woodham-Smith, *Great Hunger*, pp 220–2, 230–7
94 Kinealy, *Great Calamity*, pp 183–4, *Death-Dealing Famine*, p. 123; Oliver MacDonagh, 'Irish emigration . . .' in Edwards/Williams (eds.), *Great Famine*, p. 336
95 Woodham-Smith, *Great Hunger*, pp 222, 239–40; Michael Quigley, 'Grosse Isle: Canada's Island Famine memorial' in *History Ireland* (Summer, 1997)

    Captain Robert Forbes of the *Jamestown*, who brought a shipload of food to Cork, saw enough in a five-minute walkabout with Fr Theobald Mathew to horrify him.

    The words of Emma Lazarus were not inscribed on the Statue of Liberty until 1886:

> Give me your tired, your poor,
> Your huddled masses yearning to breathe free,
> The wretched refuse of your teeming shore,
> Send these, the homeless, tempest-tost to me.
> I lift my lamp beside the golden door.

96 Kinealy, *Great Calamity*, pp 149–51; Kerr, *Nation of Beggars*, p. 41; *Transactions of Society of Friends*, p. 307
97 Quigley, 'Grosse Isle' in *History Ireland*; Kerr, *Catholic Church and Famine*, pp 43–50
98 *Nation*, 24 July 1847; Kinealy, *Death-Dealing Famine*, p. 104
99 *Nation*, 31 July 1847; Campbell, *Great Irish Famine*, p. 41;
100 Kerr, *Catholic Church and Famine*, p 46–9
101 *Nation*, 17 July 1847; *Transactions of Society of Friends*, p. 300
102 Ibid., pp 311, 315
103 Ibid., pp 314, 316; Kinealy, *Death-Dealing Famine*, p. 105; Kerr, *Nation of Beggars*, pp 61–2
104 Robert James Scally, *The End of Hidden Ireland: Rebellion, Famine and Emigration* (New York, 1995), pp 5–6, 170–72, 200–2
105 Ibid., pp 199–200, 204–6; Woodham-Smith, *Great Hunger*, p. 278
106 Scally, *End of Hidden Ireland*, pp 207–16; Woodham-Smith, *Great Hunger*, pp 279–83
107 Kinealy, *Great Calamity*, pp 177–8, 182, *Death-Dealing Famine*, p. 125; Woodham-Smith, *Great Hunger*, p. 315

108 Kinealy, *Great Calamity*, pp 165, 183, *Death-Dealing Famine*, p. 112; Kerr, *Nation of Beggars*, p. 74; Woodham-Smith, *Great Hunger*, pp 306–7
109 Kinealy, *Great Calamity*, pp 186–96; Woodham-Smith, *Great Hunger*, pp 316–7
110 *Nation*, 23 Oct. 1847; Kevin Whelan, 'Cultural effects of the Famine' in *Comhdháil an Chraoibhín* (Roscommon, 1997), p. 50; Kinealy, *Death-Dealing Famine*, p. 109
111 Kerr, *Nation of Beggars*, pp 21, 22, 81–3
112 Ibid., pp 83–7; *Nation*, 25 Sept. 1847
113 Scally, *End of Hidden Ireland*, pp 219–27. In Boston during 1841–5, it was estimated that 61.5 per cent of Irish immigrants died under the age of five (Woodham-Smith, *Great Hunger*, p. 252). Later when prime minister, Palmerston was observed dining on two plates of turtle soup, a dish of cod with oyster sauce, a paté, two entrées, a plate of mutton, a slice of ham and a portion of pheasant (Roy Jenkins, *Gladstone*, London, 1995, p. 260)
114 Kerr, *Nation of Beggars*, pp 92–4, 120, *Catholic Church and Famine*, pp 57–60; Scally, *End of Hidden Ireland* pp 38–9, 53, 59–60; Campbell, *Great Irish Famine*, p. 48
115 Kerr, *Nation of Beggars*, 95–101, *Catholic Church and Famine*, p. 58; Scally, *End of Hidden Ireland*, pp 94–5
116 Kinealy, *Great Calamity*, 198–200; Kerr, *Nation of Beggars*, p. 104
117 *Nation*, 2, 23, 30 Oct., 6, 27 Nov., 4, 11 Dec. 1847
118 *Nation*, 6, 27 Nov., 11 Dec. 1847; Kerr, *Catholic Church and Famine*, p. 40; Kinealy, *Death-Dealing Famine*, pp 107–10, *Great Calamity*, pp 207–8; Woodham-Smith, *Great Hunger*, pp 309–10; *Transactions of Society of Friends*, pp 205–7
119 *Nation*, 11 Dec. 1847; Kerr, *Nation of Beggars*, pp 62–3, 99; Woodham-Smith, *Great Hunger*, p. 323
120 *Nation*, 23, 30 Oct., 11, 24 Dec. 1847; *Catholic Directory, 1848*; Kerr, *Catholic Church and Famine*, p. 49; Woodham-Smith, *Great Hunger*, p. 278; Michael Quigley, 'Grosse Isle . . . ' in E. Margaret Crawford (ed.), *The Hungry Stream* (Belfast, 1997), p. 36; Frank Neal, 'Black '47: Liverpool and the Irish Famine' in ibid., pp 130–1; Kinealy, *Great Calamity*, p. 202; Woodham-Smith, *Great Hunger*, p. 328

EPILOGUE

1 Cormac Ó Gráda, 'Making Irish Famine History Today' in *Ireland's Famine: Commemoration and Awareness* (Famine Commemoration Committee), p. 46; Kinealy, *Death-Dealing Famine*, pp 125, 128, 137
2 IUP/BPP Famine series, vol. 2, p. 156; James Donnelly, 'Landlords and Tenants' in Vaughan (ed.), *A New History of Ireland*, v, p. 337; Kinealy, *Great Calamity*, p. 196
3 *Chronicle and Munster Advertiser*, 12 Feb. 1848
4 Kerby A. Miller, *Emigrants and Exiles: Ireland and the Irish Exodus to North America* (New York ,1985), p. 287
5 Kinealy, *Great Calamity*, p. 220, *Death-Dealing Famine*, pp 125–6; Woodham-Smith, *Great Hunger*, p. 364
6 Fitzpatrick, 'Captain Edmond Wynne in Ireland' in *English Historical Review*, cx (1995), p. 602
7 Kerr, *Nation of Beggars*, p. 138

8   Ibid., pp 44–5, 99

9   Kinealy, *Great Calamity*, p. 219

10 Ibid., p. 213

11 Kinealy, *Death-Dealing Famine*, p. 148

12 Kinealy, *Great Calamity*, pp 314–5

13 Miller, *Emigrants and Exiles*, p. 292

14 Quoted in *Freeman's Journal*, 25 Oct. 1848; Robert Kee, *The Laurel and the Ivy . . . Charles Stewart Parnell and Irish Nationalism* (London, 1993), p. 15

15 *Rossa's Recollections* (New York, 1898), pp 142–3

16 Kerr, *Nation of Beggars*, p. 45

17 Eva Ó Cathaoir, 'The Famine and the Workhouse' in *Comhdháil an Craoibhín* (Roscommon, 1997) pp 71–5

18 Denis G. Marnane, 'The Famine in South Tipperary' in Marcus Bourke (ed.), *Tipperary Historical Journal 1997*, p. 141; Kerr, *Catholic Church and Famine*, p. 89

19 *Nation*, 15 Apr. 1848

20 *Knockfierna Remembers* (Cnoc Firinne Heritage and Folklore Group, 1997)

21 Kinealy, *Great Calamity*, pp 200–1

22 Kinealy, *Death-Dealing Famine*, pp 138–9, 145

23 Kerr, *Catholic Church and Famine*, p. 79

24 Laurence Geary, 'Epidemic Diseases of the Great Famine' in *History Ireland* (Spring, 1996); Kinealy, *Great Calamity*, p. 122, *Death-Dealing Famine*, p. 137

25 Ibid., p. 141, *Great Calamity*, p. 236; Campbell, *Great Irish Famine* (Strokestown), p. 42

26 *Times*, 2 April 1849; Donnelly, 'Landlords and Tenants', op. cit., pp 340–1

27 Kerr, *Catholic Church and Famine*, p. 89

28 Mary E. Daly, 'Farming and the Famine' in Ó Gráda (ed.), *Famine 150*, p. 42

29 Miller, *Emigrants and Exiles*, pp 290–1

30 Laurence Geary, 'Medical Relief and the Great Famine' in Morash/Hayes (eds.), *Fearful Realities*, p. 55

31 Kerr, *Nation of Beggars*, pp 229–30

32 *Nation*, 4 Mar. 1848; Donnelly, 'A Famine in Irish politics', in *New History of Ireland*, v, pp 366–70; Kinealy, *Death-Dealing Famine*, pp 129, 136

33 Brendan Ó Cathaoir, *John Blake Dillon: Young Irelander* (Irish Academic Press, 1990), p. 55; Kerr, *Nation of Beggars*, p. 138

34 Ibid., pp 133–41

35 Ó Cathaoir, *Dillon*, pp 40, 52–3, 62, 68, 73–6

36 Kerr, *Nation of Beggars*, p. 149

37 Ó Cathaoir, *Dillon*, pp 83, 91

38 Ibid., p. 86; Charles Gavan Duffy, *Four Years of Irish History, 1845–1849* (London, 1883), pp 526, 628

39 Kerr, *Nation of Beggars*, pp 162–4

40 Miller, *Emigrants and Exiles*, pp 310–1

41 Thomas Flanagan, 'Literature in English' in *New History of Ireland*, v, p. 508; Ó Cathaoir, *John Mitchel* (Dublin, 1978, pamphlet)

42 Richard Davis (ed.), *'To Solitude Consigned': The Tasmanian Journal of William Smith O'Brien, 1849–1853* (Sydney, 1995), pp 280–1; Kinealy, 'Beyond Revisionism' in *History Ireland* (Winter, 1995)

43 Fitzpatrick, 'Emigration, 1801–70' in *New History of Ireland*, v, p. 582

44 Oliver MacDonagh, 'Irish emigration . . . during the Famine' in *Great Famine*, pp 371–6

45 Joel Mokyr, *Why Ireland Starved: A Quantitative and Analytical History of the Irish Economy* (London, 1983), pp 268–75; Miller, *Emigrants and Exiles*, pp 293–8

46 Frank Neal, *Black '47: Britain and the Famine Irish* (London, 1998), pp 78, 280

47 Andre Charbonneau and Andre Sevigny, *Grosse Isle: A Record of Daily Events* and *A Register of Deceased Persons at Sea and on Grosse Isle in 1847* (Canadian Heritage, Ottawa, 1997)

48 MacDonagh, op. cit., pp 374, 379

49 Donnelly, 'Excess mortality and emigration' in *New History of Ireland*, v, pp 353–6

50 HC 1847–8 [50], xlvii; Eva Ó Cathaoir, 'The Famine and the Workhouse' p. 77

51 Fitzpatrick, 'Flight from Famine' in Póirtéir (ed.), *Great Irish Famine*, p. 175

52 Quoted in Scally, *End of Hidden Ireland*, p. 228

53 Miller, *Emigrants and Exiles*, pp 316–23

54 Scally, *End of Hidden Ireland*, p. 218

55 Enda McDonagh (ed.), *Survival or Salvation? A Second Mayo Book of Theology* (Dublin, 1994), pp 248–9

56 *Irish People*, 21 May 1864

57 Lynch to Cullen, 9 June 1864 (Dublin Diocesan Archives)

58 Lynch to Barnabo, 28 Sept. 1864 (ibid., translation of letter in Latin)

Bibliographical Note

The 1845–6 Relief Commission papers in the National Archives document the widespread destitution in the first year of Famine. This conscientious body developed an almost country-wide intelligence network, receiving hundreds of letters each month.

The *Nation* and *Freeman's Journal*, the Dublin newspapers most concerned about the Famine victims, also published extracts from the provincial press.

The diary of Thomas O'Carroll, curate in Clonoulty, County Tipperary, 1846–52 – Cashel Diocesan Archives – was consulted on xerox supplied by Dom Mark Tierney, Glenstal Abbey.

This synthesis volume relied heavily on the following published works (many other books and articles are cited in the notes):

Kinealy, Christine, *This Great Calamity: The Irish Famine, 1845–52*. Dublin, 1994
—— *A Death-Dealing Famine: The Great Hunger in Ireland*. London and Chicago, 1997
Kerr, Donal A., *'A Nation of Beggars'?: Priests, People and Politics in Famine Ireland, 1846–1852*. Oxford, 1994
—— *The Catholic Church and the Famine*. Dublin, 1996
Edwards, R.D., and Williams, T.D. (eds.), *The Great Famine: Studies in Irish History, 1845–52*. Dublin, 1994 edn.
Woodham-Smith, Cecil, *The Great Hunger*. New York, 1989 edn.
Transactions of the Central Relief Committee of the Society of Friends during the Famine in Ireland in 1846 and 1847. Dublin, 1996 edn.
Kissane, Noel, *The Irish Famine: A Documentary History*. National Library of Ireland, 1995
Killen, John (ed.), *The Famine Decade: Contemporary Accounts, 1841–1851*. Belfast, 1995
Póirtéir, Cathal (ed.), *The Great Irish Famine*. Dublin, 1995
Thomson, D., and McGusty, M. (eds.), *The Irish Journals of Elizabeth Smith, 1840–1850*. Oxford, 1980
Scally, Robert James, *The End of Hidden Ireland: Rebellion, Famine and Emigration*. Oxford University Press, New York, 1995
Morash, Chris, and Hayes, Richard (eds.), *Fearful Realities: New Perspectives on the Famine*. Irish Academic Press, 1996
Ó Gráda, Cormac, *Famine 150: Commemorative Lecture Series*. Teagasc/UCD, 1997

Ireland's Famine: Commemoration and Awareness. Famine Commemoration Committee/European Community Humanitarian Office

O'Rourke, John, *The Great Irish Famine*. Dublin, 1989 edn.

Vaughan, W.E. (ed.), *A New History of Ireland, v: Ireland under the Union, I, 1801–70*. Oxford, 1989

Nowlan, Kevin B., *The Politics of Repeal: a study in the relations between Great Britain and Ireland, 1841–50*. London, 1965

Much valuable research was published in local studies, e.g.:

Cowman D. and Brady D. (eds.), *Teacht na bPrátaí Dubha: The Famine in Waterford, 1845–1850*. Dublin, 1995

Ó Conaire, Breandán (ed.), *Comhdháil an Chraoibhín*: Proceedings of the Douglas Hyde Conference, 1995–7. Roscommon County Council

Bourke, Marcus (ed.), *Tipperary Historical Journal*, 1995–8

Campbell, Stephen J., *The Great Irish Famine*. Famine Museum, Strokestown, 1994

O'Gallagher, M. and Dompierre, R.M., *Eyewitness Grosse Isle, 1847*. Quebec 1995

Index